Competitive
Figure Skating

By the same author

Basic Ice Skating Skills

Competitive
Figure Skating

—— A Parent's Guide ——

Robert S. Ogilvie

1817

HARPER & ROW, PUBLISHERS, New York
Cambridge, Philadelphia, San Francisco, London
Mexico City, São Paulo, Singapore, Sydney

Grateful acknowledgment is made for permission to reprint the diagrams of the compulsory figures in chapter 22: they are adapted from the *USFSA Rulebook* with the kind permission of the United States Figure Skating Association.

FIRST EDITION

Designer: Abigail Sturges

Library of Congress Cataloging in Publication Data

Ogilvie, Robert S.
  Competitive figure skating : A parent's guide

  Bibliography: p.
  Includes index.
  1. Skating—Handbooks, manuals, etc. 2. Skating—
United States—Handbooks, manuals, etc. I. Title.
GV850.4.035 1985   796.91   84-48052
ISBN 0-06-015357-1

85 86 87 88 89 10 9 8 7 6 5 4 3 2 1

Contents

Illustrations

Foreword

Many times when I have been acting as a judge or a referee of a figure skating event I have been surprised at the questions asked by skaters or, more often, parents of skaters. So often these questions reveal a lack of knowledge or awareness of things that are fundamental to the sport of figure skating. We tend to expect that people who are spending a great deal of time learning this sport (and spending considerable money in the process) will have acquired a sound understanding of all the customs, rules, and general lore of the world in which figure skating operates. We tend to forget that the rules and guidelines are large in number and tediously detailed in our 350-page rulebook, and much is scattered through guide books for judges, referees, and accountants if, indeed, it is detailed anywhere. Little wonder there are so many gaps in the information skaters and their parents possess.

Up until now the *United States Figure Skating Association Rulebook* has been the chief repository of this information, even if it seems to resist revealing what one wants to locate in it. Robert Ogilvie, a world class competitive skater and for many years a prestigious teaching professional, has recognized this need for more information and more accessible information on figure skating. In this book he starts at the very beginning, with sage advice on what kind of boots and blades are best, what type of instruction is advisable, and how to get started in the sport. Then he orients the reader in the organization of the sport from the international level down to the local rink where several organizations intersect.

The explanation of our test structure is complete and helpful in showing its progressive nature and how it fits into the competitive area. Any skater at whatever level can learn something useful from the chapter on testing, the judging of tests, and how to improve the chances of passing tests. Problems faced by the advanced skater are not neglected. The competitive scene is described and explained, from the local, nonqualifying "fun" competition to the USFSA Regional and Sectional competitions that lead to our National Championships. Beyond that are the many international competitions and finally Olympic and World Championships.

The mystery of how skaters are placed in any competitive event by the judges will no longer be impenetrable to the spectator who reads the chapter "How Championships Are Conducted." The author's clear explanation of this troublesome area will alone justify the purchase of the book for many readers. But there is also guidance for competitors in training, dress, choice of music and its preparation, choosing a trainer—all these important areas are covered with wisdom and the practical suggestions that come from a long experienced teacher who has been immersed in every aspect of the sport. Later chapters explain some of the technical aspects of figure skating for the benefit of the nonskating parent and make helpful suggestions about the role of the parent in guiding the aspiring young figure skater.

The author has a clear sense of organization, and his dry wit enlivens material that in the hands of a less gifted writer and teacher might prove forbidding. Considering the time and money spent in pursuit of excellence in figure skating, no parent can help but be rewarded many times over for time spent with this useful volume. Truly, *Competitive Figure Skating: A Parent's Guide* was needed, and Robert Ogilvie has done a superb job of putting it all together.

BROOKS STEWART

Brooks Stewart is a former Chairman of the Judges Committee of the United States Figure Skating Association, and is now an Honorary Member of the USFSA Board of Directors, having served on it, in various capacities, for twenty-one years.

Preface

If the average parents of a beginner skater are asked what goal they have in mind for their child, the answers may range from a guarded "Well, I'd like him (or her) to be able to skate nicely round the rink," to a thoughtful "Let's see—*when* are the next Olympics?" In the first case the sights are probably set too low, and in the second, one can only admire the euphoric optimism of the answer. To be realistic, the final achievement will almost undoubtedly lie somewhere between the two extremes. But one must know where one is going and set goals accordingly.

This book is aimed primarily at those parents who would like to give their child the opportunity to reach the top of the skating tree, or at least attain as high a level of competence as desire, talent, and budget will allow. You will learn how to start your child on the way to the top, and by "top" I mean the highest pinnacle possible in figure skating, i.e., winning the World Championship or a Gold Medal in the Olympic Winter Games. Whether or not the ultimate goal is reached, the skater may attain other goals along the way that also carry with them high prestige, such as inclusion in the U.S. World Team, or winning a national, sectional, or regional event. Figure skating is a disciplined, challenging sport that develops a young skater's physical ability, mental skill, and concentration. Surprised parents often comment on the improvement in their child's school grades after exposure to test and competitive figure skating.

But figure skating is a highly complex sport, and those already in the field seldom realize how complicated the organization of ice skating appears both to parents and to would-be skaters when they first enter an ice rink. The whole building is a hive of activity and nobody seems to have the time to slow down and give a comprehensible answer to a sensible question. What on earth do the letters USFSA, ISIA, or PSGA stand for? What, or who, is a "scribe"? And above all, how do you get a child started, and where do you go from there?

During our years as figure skating trainers my wife and I have repeatedly tried to explain to bewildered parents this complex and many-sided sport; but the time available has usually been limited to a few moments here and there between lessons and skating sessions; such snippets of information are quite inadequate for giving parents an overall picture of the sport as a whole. It is distressing to see how much time and money is wasted, for example, by the purchase of inadequate equipment, by the wrong kind of instruction, or by a lack of information about the correct path on which to set the youngster. Two or three seasons, vital to the skater's development, may be wasted. It was clear that a book was needed, not so much on how to do it (my other book, *Basic Ice Skating Skills,* takes care of that), but on how to approach the sport and how to get the best out of the facilities and services available. *Competitive Figure Skating: A Parent's Guide* will, I hope, fill the gap.

A great source of information is the *United States Figure Skating Association Rulebook;* but the rulebook now consists of well over three hundred pages printed in rather small type, and since most of it is in the nature of a legal document, it does not make light reading. You will, however, eventually need a copy. What I have tried to do here is to set down such knowledge as may be immediately necessary for you in the first couple of seasons, explain or expand some of the points that may not be immediately clear and, for the sake of clarity, leave out as many as possible of the "ifs," "ands," and "buts." I've also included a number of chapters dealing extensively with other aspects and interesting side lights on the sport that may have bearing on the career of your child. You may wish to skip certain chapters, returning to them later when the information is required—there is no harm in this. When you have absorbed the greater part of this work, however, you will find that new information and further details are much more readily assimilated—almost unconsciously—and you will be in the happy position of being able to talk with other parents with the same sophistication as that of a world champion's mother. You will no longer fear making a fool of yourself when you ask a question—in all likelihood you will know more than the next parent.

By absorbing the information presented here you will discover how to avoid going off on unproductive tangents and utilize your child's training time to the best advantage. In the long run all of this will save you money. There is also advice that will be helpful if you are ever asked by your club to take on such duties as the supervision of practice sessions or the test chairmanship. At a later stage you may even have to take on the job of club president, in which case I am sure that chapters like "Club Harmony" will enable you to approach the task with considerable confidence. At the end of the book you will find a useful list of addresses should you need further information.

In the early stages parents are often confused by the choice of two distinct programs of instruction, tests, and competitions: that offered by the United States Figure Skating Association (USFSA) on the one hand, and by the Ice Skating Institute of America (ISIA) on the other. Since the USFSA is recognized by the U.S. government and the International Skating Union (ISU) as the body officially in charge of the sport in this country, it is from those competitors who excel in USFSA tests and competitions that the team for the World Championships and Olympic Winter Games is chosen. As is implied by the title, this book has been written with those skaters in mind who would like to see how far they can progress up this steep and rugged path. I have, therefore, dealt mainly with the role and activities of the USFSA in the sport, and relatively little with those of the ISIA; but this must not be taken as any slight on this active and valuable organization. There is no reason why a skater should not take part in both the USFSA and the ISIA programs simultaneously, since one complements the other.

I am not a chauvinist—my wife has seen to that—so I hope nobody will be offended by my frequent use of the word *he* as a neutral pronoun. The constant repetition of the phrases "he or she" and "him or her" would be both irritating and cumbersome, even though there are admittedly more girls than boys in the sport. Indeed, most of the moves appearing in the photo illustrations here are demonstrated by young women, and if I had used *she* throughout, a reader might conclude that I consider figure skating exclusively a girl's sport, which it is not. It is a highly athletic sport, and the boys must be encouraged, otherwise where will we find those spectacular jumpers, or partners for our pair and dance teams?

Finally, it is most important that the reader understand that although it is I who sit at the typewriter, this book is the result of a joint effort of me and my wife, Joan. Over the years we have shared the same experiences, taught side by side, and, strangely enough, seem to have reached the same conclusions, not only in our teaching, but in our approach to this strange and complex sport. She has spent hours reading my voluminous copy, helping me to get it down to size, making valuable comments of her own, and, what has been a vital contribution, prodding me to get it finished. There always seems to be a point about three-quarters of the way through a book when the writer gets tired of the whole thing and desperately wants to start something else. At such moments she has stepped in with that firm and unique approach so well known to her students. So, thanks to her, here it is.

Acknowledgments

I should like to extend my sincere appreciation and gratitude to Mr. Brooks Stewart, national judge and referee for the United States Figure Skating Association, for the hours spent in the preliminary editing of this work; for his very helpful suggestions, and for checking certain references to the rules and regulations of the USFSA; also to Mr. Michael Booker, president of the Ice Skating Institute of America, for his help and cooperation in discussing with me at great length the aims and functions of that organization.

I am also deeply grateful to the dedicated group of top-rank skaters who so willingly gave hours of their time in acting as models for the photographs designed to assist the reader in identifying the various free skating moves. The skaters are: Audrey King Weisiger of the Fairfax Ice Arena; Robin Williams, Robin Ward, and Brienne Pratt Fiske of the Ice Club of Baltimore; and Leslie Shackelford of the Washington Figure Skating Club.

Further, I wish to thank the USFSA for permission to reproduce the official illustrations of various skating figures; Frank J. Zamboni & Co., Inc., for photographs of the Zamboni ice resurfacer; and Riedell Shoes, Inc., for the diagram of their Royal figure skating boot.

The photography was made possible by the generous donation of ice time by the Fairfax Ice Arena, Fairfax, Virginia, and the Meadowbrook Ice Rink (now the Northwest Family Sports Center), Baltimore, Maryland.

Competitive
Figure Skating

1
The Many Forms of Figure Skating

What Is Figure Skating?

Originally figure skating, as its name suggests, was the art of tracing intricate designs on the ice, the skating blade leaving a distinct white line on the surface. Over the years this fascinating diversion gave rise to three variations, namely free skating, ice dancing, and pair skating. At the same time, the complicated drawings on the ice became formalized and reduced to a set number of symmetrical designs recognized by skaters throughout the world as the basis for test and competitive skating. These designs were still called *figures,* or sometimes *school figures,* but drawing them on the ice had now become just one aspect of ice skating. Nevertheless, the name *figure skating* was still kept as a generalized term for its three main off-shoots, causing considerable confusion among the general public. Nowadays, the term *figure skating* covers (a) the skating of the figures themselves, (b) free skating, (c) pair skating, and (d) ice dancing. Here is a brief description of each branch; you will find further details in later chapters.

There are forty-one internationally recognized figures (eighty-two if you include starting on the left foot), all based on the two-circle "figure eight" form or the three-circle form. The circles result from the fact that the figure skating blade is slightly rounded from front to back, so that if a skater leans to one side of the blade or the other, he will skate a curve, and when he has developed sufficient control, a symmetrical circle. He may vary the figure by turning on one foot from forward to backward, or vice versa, in a clockwise or counterclockwise direction, these various movements producing different designs on the ice. We shall take a closer look at the figures later.

Although it originally grew out of the figures, free skating has now completely abandoned any connection with making marks on the ice. I am sure that you have all seen at one time or other an ice skating championship or an ice show on television. When you see skaters on TV programs skating solo, you are watching free skating, and you will notice that it consists of jumps with a varying number of turns in the air, spins in all kinds of positions, intricate turns on the ice known as *footwork,* and various arm and body movements taken from ballet and other dance forms such as modern dance and jazz. Free skating is by far the most popular branch among younger figure skaters. In the U.S. free skating is commonly referred to as *freestyle. Free skating* is the more formal and official term, while *freestyle* is the common or colloquial term for the same thing. For example, I might speak of the USFSA Preliminary Free Skating Test because this is its official designation, but if I mention freestyle sessions, I do so because this is the informal term in general use.

For the purpose of competition, exhibitions of free skating are invariably executed to music lasting from one and a half to four and a half minutes, according to the level of competence and the sex of the skater. The skater is allowed free choice of instrumental music and, within certain limits, free choice of the contents to be included (back somersaults, for example, are illegal). He may also lay the movements out on the ice surface in any way he pleases. The total presentation is known as a *program,* hence the phrase, in constant use among skaters, "to skate a program." During a training session you will frequently hear the person in charge of the music ask a skater, "Do you want your program on?" meaning, of course, should he play the skater's music?

Pair skating is basically free skating, executed simultaneously in harmony and unison by two persons of the opposite sex; it has, however, the added attraction that the man is permitted to lift his partner, spin with her, and execute all kinds of movements in a variety of holds. Pair skating, because of its endless possibilities for variation, interplay between partners, and spectacular lifts, is usually considered to be the most exciting of all the branches of figure skating to watch. As with free skating by a single person, pair skating is presented in the form of a program set to music.

Ice dancing is fundamentally a skating version of International Ball-room Dancing and, like ballroom dancing, consists of certain individual dances and exhibition dancing. On the ice these two branches are referred to as the *compulsory* dances and *free dance,* or *free dancing.* For the purpose of competitive skating there are, at the moment of writing, nineteen inter-nationally recognized dances. A further seven, used almost exclusively in North America, bring the total to twenty-six. Most of these dances consist of variations of the waltz, the tango, and the foxtrot, with the addition of a blues, a paso doble, a rhumba and a polka, plus two other dances that do not fall into these categories. Unlike the equivalent ballroom dances, the majority of these compulsory ice dances are skated to a predetermined pattern over the ice surface, a pattern that continues to repeat itself after each half or whole circuit of the rink. Free dance, on the other hand, does not require a repetitive sequence of steps and, as in single and pair skat-ing, is presented in the form of a program to music. The difference between free dance and pair skating is similar to the difference between an exhibition ballroom dance and a pas de deux in ballet. In order to preserve the character of free dance there are strict limitations on lifting, spinning, and separation of partners. For example, in a free dance lift the man may not raise his hands above his waist, spins must not exceed three revolutions, and partners may not separate for a period longer than five seconds or for a distance further than two arm's lengths. At one time this gave free dancing the look of watered-down pair skating, but in recent years free dancing has overcome these restrictions and blossomed into a unique, beautiful, and highly complex art form of its own. It is the free dance event that you see when you watch a championship on television; the compulsory dances, like the figures in single skating, are not consid-ered to have sufficient audience appeal to warrant showing, but in my opinion both the figures and the compulsory dances could be of interest to the public if they were presented in an imaginative way and with a clear explanation of the technical points involved. Some years ago a short portion of the figure section of a championship was aired on television, and the next day I was amazed at the number of viewers among the general public who told me how interested they had been.

A fourth type of figure skating, fast gaining popularity, is that of drill and precision line skating. Those of you who have attended ice shows will have seen the chorus lines of twenty-four or thirty-six girls skating those incredibly accurate and complex interweaving patterns, interspersed with kick lines and usually finishing with a giant wheel. Well, groups of amateurs are beginning to form all over the country to do the same thing. It is great fun, and not only youngsters but adults also are forming teams. The difference between a drill team and a precision team is simply one of degree, the drill team executing the more elementary movements, while the precision team is made up of higher-level skaters executing complex footwork as well as very advanced maneuvers. The U.S. and Canada now have a firmly established competition structure for this form of skating.

Figure Skating: Art or Sport?

The question of whether figure skating is an art or a sport has been argued heatedly and continually for well over a hundred years. About thirty years ago I remember listening to Herbert Clarke, an eminent international figure skating judge and former president of the International Skating Union, state quite categorically that in his opinion skating was a sport. "It's like golf," he said, "the fellow that gets the ball in the hole in the least number of strokes wins." Opinions and skating have, however, changed drastically since then. If you consider art to mean creating or doing things that have form and beauty, and sport to mean carrying out a physical activity according to a set of rules, then modern figure skating is clearly a mixture of the two. It is interesting to note that for test and competition purposes, all branches of figure skating are carried out to music, except the figures themselves. The figures have been reduced to a systematic schedule of unchanging designs that allow for no creativity or latitude in their execution, with the possible exception of an attempt at elegance on the part of the skater. Such attempts are rarely made, as it seems to make little or no difference to the marks awarded by the judges, whose creed, whether right or wrong, is usually, "It's what's on the ice that counts." This is not to decry the figures (see chapter 22), it simply shows that they allow less artistic interpretation, and therefore partake more of the sporting element, than the other branches.

However artistic a free skating program may be, as soon as it is to be used for competitive purposes, the sporting element must enter. In order to score points for content, certain movements—jumps, spins, etc.—are expected by the judges to be included in the program, and the skater must be able to bring them off successfully; he cannot, in the interests of his art, just leave them out. And, of course, some skaters are more artistic than others; but art alone does not win championships, although it may be an integral part. Figure skating is in reality a finely balanced marriage of art and sport, the emphasis on one or the other shifting from skater to skater and from branch to branch.

Which Branch Should My Child Take Up?

In the early stages the question is premature. The first thing for a skater to do is to learn the basics. These basics are the same whatever field is chosen (even hockey and speed skaters find the basics of figure skating a great help as a preliminary to adopting their eventual specializations). A complete mastery of the fundamentals, as taught in most group lessons using one of the official teaching and testing structures (see chapter 3), is essential. These fundamentals should never be taken lightly or skipped through, since their mastery will save an enormous amount of time and money in later seasons.

Once the fundamentals have been learned, two decisions will have to be made: which branch to follow and how seriously to take the sport. The first decision is the easier. Probably 99 percent of all skaters start with single (solo) skating, which consists of the freestyle and (if the skater eventually wishes to compete) the figures. For ice dancing, a grounding in freestyle to develop strength of skating, and in figures to develop control, is still highly advisable; in fact, if competitive skating is the goal, such a grounding is essential. Neither my wife nor I have ever favored pushing young children into competitive dancing before they have developed a certain maturity in their skating (they will probably develop into strong skaters well before they gain the maturity and sophistication necessary to make good ice dancers), but we do believe that the mastery of the first three dances in the schedule helps young skaters develop a sense of timing and flow over the ice. Pair skating is a form of free skating, so the answer here is clear: the skater must first of all be a good freestylist, preferably with a sound basis in the figures as well. Pair skating can be taken up at almost any stage of a skater's active career, but it should be borne in mind that it takes a minimum of three years to weld a pair together so that each partner knows instinctively exactly where the other is and how he or she will react under given circumstances. It is of great help if one of the skaters has previously skated pairs with another partner.

The second decision, how seriously to take the sport, can only be decided on the basis of the talent and personal ambition of the skater (not, it is hoped, the personal ambition of the parent), and the time and money available. The decision will become easier as you read and absorb the contents of this book and watch the progress of your skater, which, I must warn you, may not always follow a smooth learning curve but is more likely to proceed rather erratically by a series of fits and starts. At a later stage, thought should be given to whether or not the child should take tests or compete seriously in two branches at the same time. It can be self-defeating for a child to have to skate figures at six o'clock in the morning and then stay up late to take part in evening or night dance sessions. Local circumstances and the stamina of your child must be the guide.

2
Equipment
for the Beginner

Much of the advice in this chapter has already appeared in my how-to book, *Basic Ice Skating Skills,* which makes good companion reading to this present work. Here, the advice is presented in a somewhat different form, and in a later chapter I have included details on equipment for the advanced skater, difficult to find elsewhere in print. As this present book is devoted entirely to figure skating, everything written here applies, of course, specifically to figure skates.

Renting Equipment

First attempts on the ice are almost invariably made on rental skates, and I have yet to come across a commercial rink that does not have a rental department or *skate hire,* as it is generally known. You are bound to be hesitant about laying out money for a child's own skates until you feel he is definitely interested. Rental equipment does, of course, get a lot of rough use, but provided the boot fits well, it will almost undoubtedly be better than the plastic-soled horrors some well-meaning but misguided relative has given your child for a Christmas present. In fact, if the rental equipment is relatively new, it is usually pretty good, since it will almost certainly have been made by a firm that specializes in skating equipment. Your prime concern should be to get a good fit. Since the skater is trying to balance on a narrow blade, it is essential that the boot fit snugly round the heel and ankle in order to give maximum support. For skating purposes the skater's walking shoe size is almost invariably too large; the required size usually ranges from a half to one and a half sizes smaller than his regular shoe. The toes may come to the end of the boot (although they don't have to), but you must see that they are not uncomfortably cramped.

First try a half size smaller than normal; if there are no half sizes, try a whole size smaller. At first you will have to lace a small child's boots up for him. In order to do this, seat him on a chair or bench in front of you, loosen the laces well, place the boot on his foot, and then give the tongue an upward pull to see that it is not rucked up over his toes. Then, gripping the sides of the boot between your knees, lace the boot firmly and evenly, not too tightly at the toes or at the top of the boot. Figure 1 shows you the area of tightest lacing. While you lace, try to see that the tongue is centered. When properly laced, it should be quite difficult to insert your finger under the laces at the firmest point. To prevent loosening, some skaters cross the laces twice round each other halfway up, just at the finish of the eyelets where the hooks start. All this takes a little practice, but at first you will certainly make a better job of it than your small child. Nevertheless, at the very earliest possible moment a child should be taught to lace his own skates—there may not always be someone around to help him

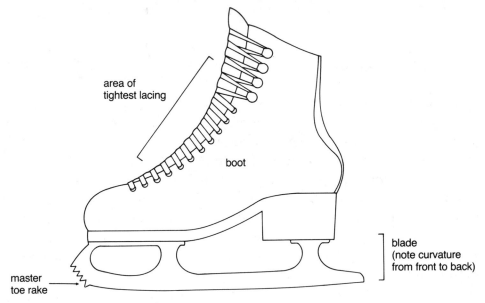

Fig. 1. Good-quality boot and blade, showing general structure and area of tightest lacing.

if they come loose. You should note that a properly fitting boot always has a gap where the boot is laced—if the sides meet over the tongue, the boot is either very old or too large.

Every pair of skates, even those of the same make and size, have a different balance and feel to them. In many rinks each pair of rental skates has its own particular number, so you will find two sets of numerals painted somewhere on the boot, one denoting the size and the other the rental number. If you find a pair that suits your child, take note of the rental number and ask for it next time you come; if you arrive early and are lucky, you might get it, but if the sessions are busy, please don't ask the management to hold them for you, just try to be there in time.

Buying One's Own Equipment

At what stage should a skater have his own skates? The answer is, as soon as possible, provided that the quality is as good as, or better than, the available rental skates. With proper precaution one can be assured of an excellent fit, the setting of the blades on the boot can be adjusted to suit the skater (see "How the Blade Is Positioned on the Boot" later in this chapter), and, because the skater will always be wearing the same pair, he will not have to readjust his balance every time he goes onto the ice. Remember, however, that just because a pair of skates is new, it is not necessarily better than a rental pair.

What You Should Look For in Buying Equipment

Figure 1 shows the construction of a pair of skates, i.e., the boot plus the blade. Many years ago a skate consisted of a metal blade set in a solid piece of wood with leather straps attached so that it could be strapped to an ordinary stout walking boot—a most unsatisfactory arrangement, as you may well imagine. This wooden sole plus the blade were together known as the skate. But later, when special skating boots and separate blades were manufactured and it became the practice to screw the blades directly and permanently onto the boot, the word *skate* came to mean the whole thing—that is, the boot plus the blade. In England, however, the word *skate* still means just the blade (including sole and heel plate), a point worth remembering if you ever read brochures of British blade manufacturers, who, incidentally, supply the bulk of the better blades for the United States market.

You will see that the cutting edge of the blade has a slight curve from front to back and that there are little jagged spikes at the front, known as *toe picks* or *toe rakes*. These are there for a purpose, and in most equipment bought for the beginner level they are usually sufficiently high off the ice not to cause any problem. Their purpose is for spinning and to assist the landing and takeoff during certain jumps. Although ideally the toe rakes should never be used for propelling the skater across the ice (the unforgivable fault of "toe pushing"), they do help the beginner to stabilize the blade at the end of a thrust, as any skater who has transferred from figure to hockey skates (which have no toe rakes) and has fallen flat on his face through their absence, will confirm. So don't have the toe rakes taken off —the skater must learn where they are, when they may and may not be used, and learn to thrust properly. If you, the parent, are also learning to skate and have expensive equipment, in which the toe rakes tend to be placed rather low to the ice surface, you *might* consider having the lowest toe rake carefully blunted, but just a very little at first: when they are gone they are gone, and cannot be replaced. If the foot is returned properly after the stroke (this is explained in detail in *Basic Ice Skating Skills*), there should be no problem.

You will need a blade made of good steel that can take proper sharpening. If you look at Figure 2, you will see that the blade has a groove running down its length. This groove is known to skaters as the *hollow,* and is highly important because it helps to create a better cutting angle to the edge of the blade and therefore a better grip on the ice. Sharpening or grinding a blade (*sharpening* is the more common term) consists largely of restoring this hollow, which has been flattened by use, causing the blade to slip sideways. Some blades are made of metal of such inferior quality that they are almost impossible to sharpen. A couple of passes of this type of blade across a grinding wheel causes the surface of the wheel to clog up with fragments of molten metal, resulting in a violent vibration and chattering of the blade against the wheel—a most horrible effect that can cause damage both to the grinding machine and the nerves of the operator. Many skate sharpeners simply will not undertake the grinding of such blades, and, if they do, the result is usually highly unsatisfactory.

As for the boot, you are looking for a good, firm leather that will

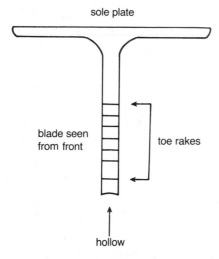

Fig. 2. Blade seen from front, showing position of toe rakes and hollow dividing blade into two edges.

support the ankle well and stand up to hard use. As described earlier, the boot must fit snugly; it should not be possible for the skater to move his heel up and down inside the boot after it has been properly laced. When being fitted, the skater should wear a pair of thin socks or Danskins. Note that the heel of a skating boot is considerably higher than that of the average walking shoe. It is important that the sole and heel should be of leather. Many of the cheaper boots have black plastic soles and heels; the drawback here is that the blade is usually attached to a plastic sole by rivets, making it quite impossible to change the position of the blade on the boot should it prove necessary.

Matched and Unmatched Sets

Normally the beginner skater buys his skates with the blade already attached to the boot. This is usually done at the factory, the combination being known as a *matched set.* The more advanced skater, however, invariably buys his boots and blades separately and then has the blades attached to the boots by an expert. There are several reasons for buying boots and blades separately, the most important being that (a) in advanced figure skating different types of blades are preferred for the various branches and (b) most good skaters develop strong preferences for one well-known boot or blade over another. At the beginner level the equipment does not have to be so specialized (or so expensive), and a reasonably priced matched set will be quite satisfactory provided the boots and blades have been made by firms specializing in the field. In this respect it is important to realize that not every bootmaker has the know-how to build an ice skating boot, nor can the average hardware manufacturer necessarily turn out a scientifically designed blade.

At first glance even a beginner's matched set is not likely to strike you as exactly inexpensive, but you will find the price really quite reasonable when you consider the job it has to do. To repeat what I have already said: the leather must be of a high quality that will support the ankle and not break down after a month's use; the blade must be constructed of steel that is sufficiently hard to run well on the ice and permit proper sharpening; the blade must be set correctly on the boot; and both boot and blade must have been designed and constructed by experts working in a highly specialized field. Cheap junk—and there is a lot of it around—has none of these qualities, and if you buy it, you will waste a considerable amount of money in the long run, because your child will find it very difficult, if not impossible, to perform many of the movements required in his lessons. So what you save on the skates you will end up paying on extra lessons that will be a complete waste of time and money until the equipment is improved.

How the Blade Is Positioned on the Boot

Positioning and attaching a blade to a boot is called *mounting,* or *setting,* a blade, an operation that has to be carried out with considerable care. Few newcomers to the sport realize that the blade is not placed down the center line of the boot. For the average skater the front of the blade should be aligned between the base of the big toe and the second toe. If you look at figure 3A, you will see that this type of setting usually coincides with the seam of the boot. I say usually, because this will not be so if the seam is crooked. The back of the blade is positioned *inside* the midline of the boot (figure 3B). Because of the angle at which the leg meets the foot, such an inside setting helps to offset the tendency of the ankle to drop over to the inside, i.e., to pronate. The degree to which the blade is placed to the inside of the midline can vary considerably, and if a child really has problems keeping the ankles erect, we often move the blades to a strong inside setting as shown in figures 4A and 4B. Most skaters can adjust to and feel comfortable on varying degrees of inside setting, but if the blade is set either dead center or over to the *outside* of the midline, trouble almost

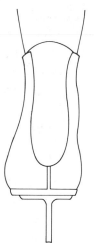

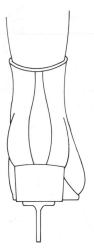

Fig. 3A
Normal setting of blade
seen from front

Fig. 3B
Normal setting of blade
seen from back

invariably arises. In such a case the skater will find that when he has progressed to making curves, he cannot lean over onto the outside edge of the blade. You can see now why it is highly advisable to avoid plastic soles. It is, of course, possible to cut the rivets holding the blade to the boot with a hacksaw, but if you cannot screw the blade back on again, this is no help. In the case of leather soles some distributors nowadays wisely put only three screws in the sole plate of the blade and two in the heel plate. Thus, if the blade has to be moved, other screw holes can be made and it may not be necessary to plug the original ones. Surprisingly

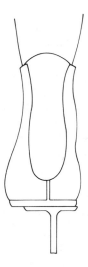

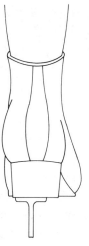

Fig. 4A
Exaggerated inside setting
seen from front (may help
persistent dropping of
ankles)

Fig. 4B
Exaggerated inside setting
seen from back

enough, it is not normally necessary to use all the screw holes available in order to hold the blade firmly to the boot, but it is important to see that what screws are used are kept tight. In new skates particularly, check the screws every few days, otherwise water will leak in under the screws and cause problems. Also, with use, the blade tends to embed itself a little into the sole, and this can cause the screws to loosen.

Custom-made Boots

At this early stage I really think that a *good* matched set will give you all the service you want. There are, of course, exceptional cases: if your child has a really difficult foot to fit (an exceptionally narrow heel, for example), or if he or she is very large, a more expensive boot will provide the better fit or the extra support needed. But as soon as the skater has learned the elements and is starting to tackle jumps and spins seriously, then custom equipment is usually essential unless he is lucky enough to fit exactly into a less expensive stock boot. If you are going to skate yourself (and I am presumably now talking to an adult), then you should buy the best equipment your finances will bear. You will get many seasons' use out of it; you have obviously decided that skating is going to be your sport; and you will feel that you are learning with every possible advantage. If your resources are unlimited, there is no earthly reason why you should not buy your child the most expensive equipment right from the start—but that must be for you to decide. As this part of the book is devoted to the beginner stage, I have left the discussion of many of the subtleties of equipment to a later chapter, "Equipment for the Advanced Skater." I do not want to confuse those of you new to the sport with too many niceties that do not really apply right now.

Buying for Growth

The temptation to buy a boot a little too large in order to allow for growth is very great. Don't do it. It will hold the skater back in his progress. There is the very natural feeling that the child will grow out of his boots quickly, and that you will very soon have to lay out all that money again, but there are ways round this. Once you have made the initial outlay, there are nearly always other parents around who will be happy to snap up a pair. In fact, in the early stages you might consider a used pair. Used skates are often available from members of the local figure skating club, and because youngsters do grow out of their boots quickly, such equipment is often still in excellent condition. In these days of rapid inflation it is unwise to quote prices, but I can tell you I have often seen first class equipment previously used by a competitive skater being sold off for under a quarter its original cost. So check the local club's bulletin board or make inquiries of some of the members.

When you finally decide that your child's feet are really getting too big for his boots, there are a couple of emergency measures you can take until the new pair comes through. See if the boot has a loose flat insole and, if it does, take it out. This can make a considerable improvement. Even if the sole of the boot is now a little rough, skaters never seem to notice much difference. As an alternative, or in addition, you can have the boot stretched up to the equivalent of about half a size. Ask the skate shop whether they have a stretcher; if not, go to the local boot repairer and explain how you want the boot stretched, and where. It is around the toes that the trouble usually lies, so explain if this is the area in which you want the boot stretched and whether you want it stretched for length, breadth, or both. Don't expect it to be done while you wait. If a boot is to be stretched effectively, it should stay on the stretcher for about three days.

Making Sure the Price Is Right

The question at the back of everybody's mind is, How do I know I'm paying the right price? The solution to this problem is, if there is a pro shop attached to the rink at which you skate, buy there! But, you may ask, shouldn't I shop around? Might I not be able to get the same thing cheaper down the road? You have every right to ask such questions, but I stick to my original statement. Aha! you will say—pros obviously receive commissions on rink sales and it is in their interest to make such statements. In this case nothing could be further from the truth: I have never received any commission from any pro shop located in any rink at which I have taught. Maybe I should have, but I haven't. What *is* in my interest is that students come to me wearing equipment that enables me to teach them efficiently. Schroeder, in the comic strip *Peanuts,* does manage to extract magnificent Beethoven out of his toy piano, but we are not all Schroeders, and the chances are very slim of getting to the Olympics on a pair of toy skates.

The Rink Pro Shop

I have headed this section "The Rink Pro Shop," but I much prefer to use the older term *skate shop* to distinguish it from other types of pro shops located away from rinks that sell all kinds of sporting equipment and a few cheap skates as a sideline. Of course, skate shops sell more than just skates, they sell all the auxiliary equipment that the skater is likely to need, but the whole point is that the skate shop is a specialist type of operation, so that is what I shall continue to call it.

You will be concerned with three questions: Are you getting the right type of equipment? Is it fitted right? Is the price right? Unlike the general sporting goods or department store, the rink skate shop sells nothing but ice skates and auxiliary skating equipment; it is, therefore, the specialist in the field. The assistants spend the greatest part of their time fitting skates, and thereby become highly proficient in this skill.

Although the skate shop usually stocks equipment in a wide range of prices, the lower-priced matched sets will do an efficient job of allowing the beginner to learn the essentials and get the most out of his early lessons. There is, however, a price level below which you cannot go and still get a skate that will do a reasonable job, and no reputable skate shop would risk its reputation handling cheap junk. Without trying to sound like a TV commercial, I must point out that the skate shop dare not give you a bad deal: when you leave the skate shop, that is not the last they are going to see of you. Most probably you or your child will be skating at their rink at least once a week, and if the equipment they have sold you is faulty, they are going to hear from you; and if there is something really wrong, they have to do something about it to preserve their good reputation.

And what would happen to the rink group lesson programs if the equipment was not adequate? Most professional instructors are not employees of the rink, but they do (or should) try to work in close harmony with the management. Although they may not openly criticize a badly fitted pair of skates, they will in all probability have a quiet word in private with the skate shop, and thus protect your interests. Don't forget, you are a valued customer both of the rink and the skate shop, and you will be treated as such.

There are only a handful of manufacturers specializing in boots, blades, and matched sets, and their prices are very standardized. The markup added by the skate shop is competitive, particularly in view of the fact that there may be other rinks with skate shops in the area, and the rink wants the skater to continue with the sport and become a regular customer. It is in the interest of the rink, therefore, to give the skater a good deal financially. Some years ago a supplier marketed a matched set with two slightly different types of blade, one a little cheaper than the other—the boot was the same in both cases. The boot with the slightly cheaper and inevitably inferior blade was supplied to sporting goods and department stores, while the boot with the more expensive, better blade (at the time in short supply) was reserved for rink skate shops. A young adult student of mine, working on the assumption, I suppose, that anything bought at a large department store must automatically be sold at a lower price than anywhere else, saw a pair of this manufacturer's matched sets in such a store and snapped them up. When she showed them to me, not only was the fit unsatisfactory, but she had the cheaper blade and had paid $3 more than the going price for the better set at the rink skate shop. Caveat emptor!

Quite apart from other considerations, many skate shops have trade-in schemes, provided, of course, that the equipment was bought from them in the first place. So inquire locally.

But what if the rink does not have a skate shop? This is occasionally the case, particularly with rinks owned by schools or universities. In these circumstances there is very often a local source of supply run by some enterprising dealer (frequently working from his home) who has set up his own specialized skate shop and can be trusted to provide excellent service. If you do have to deal with some store located away from the rink that deals in generalized sporting equipment, they may, given the local circumstances, stock a better type of equipment than is normally available in such stores. In this case, even if it is only for your own peace of mind, it might be a good idea for you to make friends with someone at the rink who does seem to know about equipment, and persuade that person to accompany you when you go to buy. No store should resent this—they may even welcome it—and there is always the chance that you may get hold of some nonspecialist salesclerk; if neither of you knows what you are talking about, disaster may well result.

Before leaving the subject of the skate shop, here is one last word of advice. Fitting skates has to be done very carefully, and usually involves trying on many different sizes. Most busy skate shops, therefore, set up an appointment schedule, often at half-hourly intervals. In order to get the best possible attention, it is vital that you arrive on time. Even so, you may have to wait a few minutes. Someone before you may have been late, and the assistant cannot just push them out of the shop once he has started to fit them. I am reminded of a most extraordinary incident (absolutely true—I was a witness) that occurred at a rink where my wife and I were once teaching. The skate shop was frantically busy one Saturday morning and the staff was desperately trying to keep to its appointment schedule. Some woman, who had completely missed her appointment (by something like an hour), was asked in a very polite manner if she would come back at some more convenient time. The next thing we knew, she had gone into the most frightful tantrum, flinging herself onto her hands and knees, beating the skate shop carpet with her fists, and screaming that she *would* be attended to. The staff, finding the commotion somewhat distracting, sent for the rink manager, a young man new to the business, who had already formed the opinion that figure skaters had an unbalanced streak somewhere in their makeup. Even so, the situation caught him a little unprepared and some time was spent trying to decide whether to call the police or the local hospital. Fortunately he was young, good-looking, and possessed of a charming manner. We last saw her being led gently away to the office, where a pacification process took place and a new appointment was made. The moral is, moderation in all things, even if the service *is* a little slow.

Miscellaneous Advice

At the beginner stage the skater can wear almost anything provided that it is warm and does not hamper movement. Forget long scarves or long flaring jeans that nearly touch the ice surface and are ragged at the ends. This latter type of clothing is so dangerous that it should be barred from use on all ice surfaces, quite apart from its unaesthetic appearance, which is totally inappropriate to figure skating. And no chewing gum, please, either on the ice or near it. Some children spit it out just before they step onto the ice, with the result that another skater gets it stuck on the bottom of his blade, steps onto the ice, and takes an almighty fall. Never let any child go near the ice surface with gum in his mouth—an unexpected fall can cause choking. Apart from any other consideration, skating is an elegant sport, and should be approached in an elegant manner.

Always use skate guards (blade protectors) when walking to and from the ice surface, but keep your eye on them as they have a habit of disappearing. Many rinks install excellent rubber matting, but do make your child aware that he must never step on any metal or concrete with unprotected blades. If the cutting edge is turned over, the blade will skid and this will mean an unnecessary sharpening job.

Sharpening

Earlier in this chapter I referred very briefly to sharpening, an operation that not only sharpens the edges of the blade but restores the hollow running down its length. Sharpening, particularly for the advanced skater, is a highly complex subject and is dealt with quite extensively in chapter 11. At the moment, there is no need to bother with all the technicalities, but you must understand it is very important that a skater's blades (a) should not be allowed to get too blunt, and (b) should be sharpened correctly. It is not generally realized that a beginner will often drop his ankles over to the inside not because of insufficient support in the boots, but because the blades are so blunt that this is the only way he can get a grip on the ice. A young child will do this quite unconsciously, so the true cause of the trouble is seldom apparent to the parent. This tendency to drop the ankles to the inside can soon become a habit, and may even distort the boot so much that it is difficult under any circumstances for the skater to bring his ankles upright. Sharpening the blade may not effect an overnight cure, but it will at least give the child a chance. The same result may occur when the edge feels sharp, but the hollow is too flat; this will make the blade tend to skid. An adult skater can usually tell when his blades need sharpening by the way they behave on the ice, but a young child may not be able to do this. You must have considerable practice and a knowledge of correct hollows before you can accurately judge whether another person's blades need sharpening. Make friends with some of the more advanced skaters and ask to feel their blades after they have just been sharpened. You will soon learn at least to suspect when your child's blades need attention. The theory of the degree of hollow is very complicated, but if you ask the sharpener for a hollow into which a fifty-cent piece will just fit, you will not go too far wrong. One last tip: never try to assess the sharpness of a blade with a wet finger or thumb: if you do so, the blade will always feel duller than it actually is. Dry your hand and the blade first.

3
Instruction
for the Beginner

Bad Habits Cost You Money

Poor techniques are devastatingly easy to acquire in skating and, once acquired, require long and painstaking work on the part of a good instructor to correct. When you first introduce your child to the ice, you may have no thoughts of his going on to competitive skating; you may, however, change your mind later on and curse yourself for not having given him a better basic training. If a child is to go on to higher things, proper supervision at the start is vital. A sound technical basis must be laid while he is still young and malleable; you simply cannot afford to waste time backtracking to correct faults that should never have been allowed to develop in the first place. The danger is that there are certain types of faults that are almost impossible to completely eradicate, and although the skater may develop into a first-rate performer, he may never be quite as good as he might have been. Having scared you with this ominous prospect, let me tell you that in the very early stages the average rink or club instructional program—particularly if it is one sponsored by an official skating organization—should, if properly administered, be sufficient to keep the skater on the right track. Private lessons should also be considered, even at this early stage, so I shall try to give you a clear picture of what you may expect from both group and private instruction.

Group Instruction

Nearly all rinks offer some type of group instruction, sometimes referred to as class lessons to distinguish them from private lessons. Group instruction is relatively cheap. In this inflationary period I hesitate to quote actual prices, particularly as they vary somewhat from rink to rink; but on average a half-hour group lesson will cost you about one-third that of a private lesson from a good professional instructor. Group lessons are commonly sold in courses of ten half-hour classes held once a week. The entrance fee to the rink is invariably included in the price of the class, but, with few exceptions, the cost of renting skates is not. In some rinks the price of the course will include a certain number of free practice periods, either immediately after the lesson or at some other session during the week. Colleges, girl scout groups, YMCA groups, and others may be able to make advantageous deals with the rink, and you might get a cheaper rate through such organizations, but these may only be a good buy if they are taught by the regular rink instructors using one of the accepted official programs (these programs will be outlined later in this chapter).

Some rinks that sell a large proportion of their ice to private clubs (usually affiliated with the United States Figure Skating Association) may not offer group instruction, but in such cases classes are usually provided by the club during its own private time. These programs, too, can be very good. Practices of clubs vary, some including the classes in the membership fee, others making a separate charge. Attractive though it may seem to have free group lessons, there is the drawback that attendance at such classes is not nearly so regular as when the parents are paying out hard cash that may be unrecoverable when a class is missed. This sporadic attendance is very disrupting to a class because the teacher feels he must backtrack to bring skaters up to date with what they have missed, thereby diluting the quality of instruction for the more regular students. Theoretically, of course, the teacher should go ruthlessly on with the set plan, but this is not easy when on a given week he finds he has a group of skaters almost entirely different from the group he had the previous week. To paraphrase a well-known American principle: If you don't pay much, don't expect much.

One of the great advantages of group lessons—provided they are well organized—is that the skater is part of a structured program, learning a logically ordered series of movements in graded classes, each class working toward a certain goal, the attainment of which is awarded by colorful badges, which make a fine display and give an exhilarating lift to the skater's ego when displayed on his jacket.

Nevertheless, a class is a class and must be accepted as such. It is blatantly unfair to expect a teacher to stop teaching the rest of the class in order to give individual instruction to any one particular child. If you want private lessons, they are available, but don't expect private lessons at group lesson rates. And the fact that in a class a child is not given individual attention may, in the very early stages, be a blessing in disguise. I have often watched a group of about sixteen young children between the ages of six and eight who had never been on the ice before, stand clinging to the barrier while the teacher encourages them to take a few steps forward on their own. It is quite obvious that she has not the time to go all down the line cajoling each little skater to do his best. They may all hold back from taking the plunge, until suddenly one bold spirit takes half a dozen quick steps forward, sits down, and bursts into delighted laughter. After a moment's startled surprise, the others follow suit and in no time find themselves at the other side of the rink—all except one, and he or she stands immobile by the barrier, thumb in mouth, looking wistfully after the others. It is then quite in order for the teacher to come quickly back to this little child, offer a few words of encouragement, and coax the child to move a few steps forward. Under the circumstances none of the parents of the rest of the children in the group should have cause for complaint that their own child is not getting the same individual attention. Nine times out of ten the child will still not move, so with an encouraging "You just watch the others, dear," the teacher goes back and leads the rest of the class, stumbling and laughing, several times back and forth across the ice. Then suddenly, after having watched the rest of the class for five minutes or so, the child takes off from the barrier, joins the rest of the class, and the battle is won. He has figured out that he is going to get no more individual attention, and so he decides to join the group. While all this is going on, the parent, quite naturally, is suffering agonies; but this is the advantage of a class: the skater must shape up to the average. Had this child been given private lessons at the start, he might still, at such an early stage, have been unable to go by himself, even with the attention of a very gifted teacher.

It is, I regret to say, extremely difficult for a parent to hold himself emotionally aloof while watching his child being taught to skate. Parents fall roughly into three categories: those (only a very few, thank heaven) who feel that their child—because of some supposed incompetence or bias on the part of the teacher—is not getting his, or her, rights, and tends to make complaints to the management; those who, disgusted with their child's incompetence or inattention, overreact emotionally and berate the child; and those who, possessing a calm and philosophic outlook, see all that is going on and realize that, like adults, children cannot always be perfect, even if they are our own. I sincerely hope you belong to this last group. Why do so many rinks bar parents from the rink area while classes are in progress, and insist that they stay behind the glass doors of the warming room? Mainly because an instructor cannot function efficiently with parents hanging over the barrier calling out every minute or so, "Listen to what the man says!" or threatening the child with dire punishment at every transgression. I remember one instance that even now fills me with horror when I look back on it. During a class for very young skaters a little girl came off the ice in tears. Before the teacher was able to get to her and give some words of comfort, the mother burst through the glass doors shouting, "Get back on that ice right now, or you don't get any dessert for a week!" Quite unforgivable and scarcely the way to instill a love of the sport into a child—it is because of these few that most rinks decide to bar the ice area to all parents during class lessons. It's very sad, but that's the way it is.

What the Skater Learns in Classes

Most well-conducted classes follow a predetermined schedule aimed at teaching the elements that are basic to all the various branches of figure skating described earlier. Because of the variety of movements taught and the agility on skates that they produce, these classes can be very helpful even to a skater who later intends to take up hockey or speed skating; but never send a child to basic figure skating classes in hockey skates; to do so is a waste of time and money. Other things being equal, it is my experience that a skater who has learned basic figure skating skills can adapt to hockey skates better and more quickly than a hockey skater can adapt to figure skates. If you do have a child whose only interest is hockey, he should join what are known as *power skating* classes, which concentrate on developing those skills specific to the game.

There are several systems (see below) of teaching the elements of figure skating, but fortunately they are all in fairly close accord in regard to what these elements are and, what is very important, the order in which they should be taught. I shall not attempt to list all the various movements here, but I can give you a general outline. The skater is taught to *stroke* correctly, that is, how to thrust with the blade and use his knees and body in such a way as to produce a reasonably smooth movement across the ice; he is taught how to stop and how to get up from a fall; taught backward skating, forward and back *crossovers,* curves on one foot (known as *edges*), turns from forward to backward, basic spins, simple jumps, and many other movements designed to lay a good technical foundation on which he can later build. All this cannot be covered in a ten-week course. To give an estimate of how much can be learned in a specific time is extremely difficult. To begin with, there are so many variables, such as natural talent, time spent practicing, quality of equipment (unbelievably important!), and efficiency of the instruction; but what makes any forecast of a skater's progress so tricky is that he must learn a kind of balance that's not really natural to the human body. In most other activities a fair approximation can be made of the more elementary movements without falling flat on one's face. One rarely sees the floor of a ballet studio littered with bodies, but this is a relatively common sight on an ice rink. So progress depends on balance, and balance depends on practice—lots of it. Remember, however intelligent your child may be, he cannot learn to skate by brain power alone.

Tiny Tots Classes

By *tiny tots* we usually mean five years old and under. Such classes are basically play situations, so don't worry if your child does not seem to be learning a lot. What the child *is* learning is the fundamental balance that I mentioned earlier, a balance that will stay with him for the rest of his life; most important, he is learning to be unafraid of the ice. He will soon be skating happily round the rink in his own way, possibly learning to stop and steer himself round other skaters, that is, if he is looking where he is going. If you get skaters below the age of six doing more than this, you are lucky, but some little ones, mostly girls, do occasionally achieve a higher level. There seems to be a big jump in the learning ability between the ages of five and six, again mostly among the girls. So don't be too disheartened if your son does not seem to make much progress before he is seven or eight; even at that age all most of them want to do is to rush madly round the rink and expend a lot of energy. In doing so they can, of course, create disciplinary problems in a class, so don't be surprised if you see them sent off the ice occasionally, not just to allow them to calm down, but to permit the teacher to retain, or regain, her sanity.

Never push a young child too much psychologically at the start; if he bursts into tears during a class, you should undoubtedly take him off, as it is foolish to insist that he stay on the ice howling his head off. He may well be thoroughly scared by the slipperiness of the surface or annoyed at his inability to control his own feet. If this occurs during the first or possibly second lesson and he is adamant in his refusal to return, most rinks will make a refund. Try him again next season, the main thing being not to insist, or he may develop a strong dislike of the sport. After all, at that age it doesn't really matter whether he starts this year or next; but when he does start, it is important that he does so with a will. Of course, when faced with the prospect of being taken home, he may well decide that that is not what he wants either, and you may find him back on the ice in no time at all. So accept tiny tots classes for what they are; at this stage these little children are only just learning to get their balance, and it is unlikely that they will develop faults that cannot be corrected at a later stage. And do have sympathy with the instructors: they have quite a difficult job on their hands.

In all honesty I must own that I have never felt overenthusiastic about tiny tots classes, but this is doubtless a personal bias. These classes can and do serve a very useful purpose, and with a suitable teacher, the children will get lots of fun out of them. Perhaps my mild aversion to these classes stems from the fact that I have never felt that I was particularly good at teaching small children below the age of six. I always made every effort to be kind, but my whole aspect is rather formidable, and although the class would not necessarily burst into tears as I skated onto the ice, my very appearance tended to cow them into an awed silence. This does have certain advantages, but after having given the class a cheerful smile and suggested that they all try to take a few little walking steps forward, it is discouraging to see them all remain perfectly immobile, grasping the barrier ever more tightly with little fingers that it would take a crowbar to pry loose. Perhaps if I had appeared in a Santa Claus outfit, I might have had more success, but my devotion to class instruction never quite extended as far as that. I am, however, extremely good with adults and unruly teenagers, probably helped by my army experience.

Incentives

Most systems require skaters to perform certain movements adequately before going on to the next level. For this purpose badges, usually paid for separately, are awarded. The required skills are not arbitrarily selected but form a logical sequence. A skater should, for example, be able to skate backward on one foot before he tries to make a turn from forward to backward on one foot. Blundering upward through a succession of classes on the principle of "Here I come, ready or not" accomplishes nothing and is very damaging to a skater's techniques; this is how the bad habits start. Just as damaging is the encouragement in the child of the belief that success in skating does not require practice. It is doing a child a gross disfavor to pass him in a movement needed in a following class if he just cannot do it. So be patient; the management and the instructor want him to pass just as much as you do, but if the skater is missing an essential, he just lays up trouble and frustration for himself at a later stage. Another problem arises when the skater can just fulfill the requirements, but only just. The judge sees the underlying lack of control; there isn't a movement in the whole test that looks strong; but according to the book the skater is performing the movement, albeit with the barest minimum of skill necessary: It is a borderline case. Stirred by the tragic expression on the face of the parent watching the drama, or simply because he likes a quiet life, the judge crosses his fingers and gives the skater a passing mark. Then the same thing happens in the next class, until eventually the skater is really in difficulties and rapidly falling behind his fellows. The best thing to do in such a case is to arrange for the child to have a few private lessons in which the instructor can backtrack and concentrate on the skater's own individual problems. So please try to resist the temptation to argue with the teachers or judges if they appear to be unduly severe; remember that the prime function of a good system is the dispensing of good instruction, not just colorful badges.

I do not think that tiny tots should be pressured into striving for badges. While developing the basic balance, fun should in itself be sufficient incentive.

The USFSA and ISIA Systems for Beginners

When you enter a rink's warming room or lobby, it is highly probable that you will see a board giving details of group lessons for beginners. The chances are that the rink will be using one of two systems: the Basic Test

Program of the United States Figure Skating Association (USFSA), or the Alpha-Beta-Gamma-Delta tests contained in the Recreational Program of the Ice Skating Institute of America (ISIA). You will read more about these organizations in chapter 4, "How the Sport Is Organized." Both these bodies have ongoing programs for the more advanced skater, but the tests mentioned here apply to what is generally regarded as the beginner level. The awards for passing these tests are multi-colored triangular badges in the case of the USFSA, and colored rectangular badges for the ISIA. For many years there were no tests at the beginner level; you may be interested, therefore, to know how they came into being.

Until the middle fifties the only structured system for skaters wishing to take tests was administered and sponsored by the USFSA. But the standard of even the lowest test was so high that the beginner had to spend a couple of seasons learning all the fundamentals before he could attempt it. There was nothing immediately obtainable for the genuine beginner. Because incentive is so important in learning, rinks and clubs had to fill this gap by setting up their own tests and awards so that the skater had something to work for as soon as he could let go of the barrier. These individual test structures had various names, such as *star tests,* or *ribbon tests,* and inevitably no two systems were exactly alike. They were, however, surprisingly alike in overall content if not in terminology and organization, because most professional teachers found that they were in approximate agreement as to what movements should be taught to a beginner and the order in which they should teach them. The trouble arose when a skater moved from one part of the country to another. When I was teaching in Baltimore, for example, a skater would come to me from some rink, let us say, on the West Coast. When I asked how far advanced he was, he might tell me that he had got his "yellow ribbon," the top beginner's badge awarded in his home rink. This would mean nothing to me, and after having watched him skate I might decide that his prized yellow ribbon was only equivalent to the third star of the local club. Confusion reigned over the whole country. Then in the late 'fifties the ISIA, composed almost exclusively of rink owners and managers, created order out of chaos by introducing tests for beginners. Originally these were known as the Alpha-Beta-Gamma tests, but subsequently a Pre-Alpha and Delta were added. In 1968 the USFSA also brought out a system of tests for beginners, known as the Basic Test Program, which filled the gap in its own structure. As nearly every rink in the country was either a member of the ISIA or had a USFSA club using its premises, one or other of the two systems rapidly replaced local programs. Most ice skating facilities open to the public adopted the ISIA program, while clubs affiliated with the USFSA used their own Basic Test Program.

Which system you use will probably depend on which is in use at your local rink or club; some rinks actually offer both. The results achieved depend more on the quality of the teachers and the organization of the program than on the test structure itself. All else being equal, both systems do an excellent job. To be quite frank, I have to tread warily when speaking of these two programs. Since I designed the USFSA Basic Test Program myself, I would be scarcely human if I did not have certain personal preferences. On the other hand, the ISIA Recreational Skater Program (which contains the Alpha-Beta-Gamma-Delta tests) was designed by an old friend of mine, Mr. Ron Priestley, former president of the ISIA, who, by a most extraordinary coincidence, went to the same school as I did, in London, England. You must not, however, picture the two of us sitting together on a bench in second grade compounding a diabolical plot to take over skating in the United States. Quite the reverse —neither of us had the slightest idea of what the other was doing when the programs were in the making. I can only think that in this case great minds, while not exactly thinking alike, thought very similarly.

Should you wish to put your child into both systems, or switch from one to the other, neither the USFSA nor the ISIA has any regulations to say that you may not do so, although the tests themselves are not interchangeable. In any event there is no reason why a skater should not wear both sets of badges on his jacket simultaneously, if he can find room for them.

An important point to note is that the tests in the USFSA beginner program are independent of that organization's more advanced series of tests. That is to say, it is not necessary to have passed all the USFSA Basic Tests before starting up the ladder of the association's official tests, which qualify the skater to take part in competitions leading to the national level. In fact, to take part in the USFSA Basic Test Program a skater does not even have to be a member of the USFSA. The rules of the ISIA are somewhat different. To take part in the ISIA Alpha-Beta-Gamma-Delta beginner program the skater must be registered with the ISIA; but this is no problem, the rink program organizers will take care of it for you. To continue taking ISIA tests in any of the more specific branches of figure skating the skater must have passed the Delta test. The ISIA also holds tests in hockey and speed skating, but for these the passing of the beginner tests is not necessary. Nevertheless I am of the firm opinion that any skater who intends to take up either of these two forms of skating will benefit greatly if he is able to execute the basic moves on figure skates that are taught by the USFSA or ISIA beginner programs. When properly taught and judged, these programs teach agility and basic stroking, both of which are sometimes pointedly lacking in skaters who go directly onto hockey or speed skates.

Other Systems

When the USFSA and the ISIA introduced their programs for beginners, there were, as I have pointed out, a number of independent programs already in existence, and many of the clubs and rinks using them saw no immediate advantage in changing to other systems. The local skaters were used to them, the badges were colorful, and the systems productive. For the most part these other systems were as good as those produced by the USFSA and the ISIA; they were just not sufficiently uniform or nationally recognized. But as the new national systems offered clubs and rinks a "package deal" that included standards and badges valid throughout the United States, together with advice on how to run the programs, these gradually replaced the purely local systems. Nevertheless, there are still a few of the other systems around; so if your club or rink happens to be using one of them, don't hesitate to put your child into the program. If he has to move to another rink and has obviously received good instruction, he will probably be permitted to take as many of the national tests as he is able to in one sitting—if that is the appropriate phrase—so it will make no appreciable difference in the long run.

So that takes care of your immediate problems. When your child leaves the beginner stage, however, you will be faced with certain decisions which become more pertinent as the skater progresses. These will be discussed later.

Private Instruction

Unlike many other arts or sports, more advanced figure skating does not lend itself to group instruction. For the lower levels class lessons are adequate, but because of the physical complexity of skating, the size of the surface on which it must be practiced, and the highly individual peculiarities that every skater rapidly develops, private instruction is a must for any skater who, having left the elementary stage behind, wishes to make the fastest progress possible. Whereas group instruction has to be aimed at the general level of the class, private instruction can be directed toward the specific needs of the individual. When dealing with a private student a teacher can concentrate on the skater's weaker points, on the one hand, and on the other can push ahead with movements for which the skater has a natural aptitude.

The private student is a much more definite entity in the mind of the teacher than the skater who is one of a large group, and thus the parent of a child taking private lessons will be privy to much more specific information from the teacher about his child's progress than could otherwise be expected. When a group instructor comes off the ice after a grueling two or three hours, during which time he may have dealt with a hundred or more children, and is standing with a dazed look on his face, waist deep in excited, noisy youngsters, he should not be expected to answer right off the bat such questions as, "How is Lisa doing?" By this time Lisa, if he can remember what she looked like, may be no more than a vague blur in his mind. But a private student, to whom he gives individual attention perhaps several times a week, stands out vividly in his mind. All good teachers, provided they are not about to step onto the ice to give a lesson, will be willing to discuss a private student's problems and progress provided the length of the discussion is kept within reasonable bounds. Good manners apply, and every attempt should be made to confine such discussions to the rink premises. Many instructors have schedules that start at six in the morning and spread out irregularly throughout the day, so when they arrive home they like to unhook. Evening calls, therefore, should be limited to emergencies such as unavoidable lesson cancellations.

Choosing a Private Instructor

The general practice in the skating world is to use the terms *teacher, instructor, trainer, coach,* and *pro* interchangeably to mean anyone who imparts professional instruction, although *coach* and *trainer* are usually associated with the higher levels of the sport. These last two terms often carry with them the connotation of not merely instructing but preparing an athlete physically and mentally for competition; but nowadays most good skating instructors, through attendance at conventions and seminars and through personal experience, possess considerable practical, though not necessarily formal, knowledge of biomechanics and psychology, so the use of the terms *coach* and *trainer* is usually justified. The most nearly official expression is *professional instructor,* colloquially shortened to *pro,* and this is the term most commonly used. As I have constantly to refer to such a person throughout this book, perhaps two or three times in the same sentence, you will find that I use all these terms, sometimes according to context, but very often in the interest of what is known to writers as "elegant variation."

At every rink and private club you will find, almost without exception, professional teachers available for private instruction. Most rinks and clubs have arrangements with a certain number of pros to teach for them during the season. These pros are not normally direct employees of the rink or club, but the arrangements are such that they are designated as the official, or "staff," pros in return for making their services available, sometimes exclusively, to the organization. As part of the arrangement it is usual for the management to give the official pros exclusive rights to teach those skaters who normally attend the rink. Occasionally an outside pro is allowed to use the facilities if he brings his own students, but he may not, or certainly should not, teach or solicit students who are regular skaters at that rink, or who are already students of one of the official pros.

The choice of an instructor for private lessons at the lower level should not present too much of a problem. In many instances a skater who has been taking class lessons will elect to take private lessons from the same teacher who has been conducting the class; but this is not always possible, as many rinks with a heavy class load have to bring in outside teachers not on the regular staff, and such teachers may not have the privilege of giving private lessons at that rink. The box office should be able to supply you with a list of the official rink professionals and their qualifications, but it is not normally the rink's policy to recommend one instructor over another. The question is whether to go for a high-level and usually more expensive instructor, or a junior instructor whose lessons are more economically priced. The question may be decided for you by the fact that the high-level pro may be fully booked and unable to take on any more students. If, however, his services are available and he is experienced in teaching beginners, and if you can afford his fee, then his instructional abilities and long-term view should be well worth the money. But under most circumstances you will find the junior pro very satisfactory for the early stages. Certain facts that should be taken into consideration when choosing a pro for a more advanced skater are discussed in chapter 19, "Higher-Level Instruction."

As in all professions, there are good and bad at all levels, and in the final analysis a teacher's best qualifications are a good reputation and his ability to produce successful results. Before making a definite decision, you should come into the rink at different times and observe the instructors in action. Then, if you have a particular teacher in mind, ask the opinion of some parent whose child is a pupil of that instructor. Be wary, however, of parents' opinions of other instructors: in many rinks rivalries exist, and human nature being what it is, opinions are not always unbiased.

I want to emphasize the point that to teach a beginner a pro must be experienced in teaching beginners. Certain advanced techniques, particularly in the figures, are not applicable to the less advanced levels, or may at least have to be modified. The order in which the early movements are learned is also highly important. Young champions who have just turned pro and have little or no teaching experience behind them may find it difficult to remember the stages they went through or the methods they used to first learn the basic elements. As most advanced skaters have highly individualistic styles and often purely personal techniques, teaching by demonstration is not—with the exception of balletic or other dance movements—always successful. Teaching beginners is an art in itself and one that requires constant thought and practice.

Taking Lessons
Length of Lessons

The length of a lesson depends a lot on how the pro lays out his schedule. A half hour (or twenty-five minutes in training sessions lasting fifty minutes) is pretty standard all over the U.S., particularly at the more advanced level. In very busy rinks or club sessions, however, fifteen- or twenty-minute lessons are increasingly common according to the way in which the pro organizes his schedule. For a very young child with a short attention span, a fifteen-minute lesson may be as much as the child, or the pro, can stand. But for most bright youngsters fifteen minutes is really very short, as each lesson may have to start with a few minutes spent in orientation and review of material learned in the previous lesson. The more advanced skater should certainly be able and prepared to take half an hour. For some even this seems short. I have had adult pupils, perhaps used to group skiing classes lasting an hour or so, express surprise at the relative brevity of skating classes. The longer lessons in skiing make sense because so much time is spent getting from point to point, replacing skis that have come off, and rejoining the rest of the group after a fall. But a skating instructor can impart a lot of concentrated information to a private student in half an hour, and anything longer than that can be counterproductive.

Arrangement and Payment for Lessons

Group lessons are taken in courses—possibly ten classes over a period of ten weeks—and paid for in advance. Policies differ from rink to rink, but in many cases, if a class is missed, no makeup lessons are given unless the class is canceled owing to some catastrophic circumstance. Most rinks, very wisely, adopt the firm policy of never canceling classes, whatever the weather, provided it is possible to drive a car into the parking lot. They feel that if the pro has turned up and one sole student has struggled through snow and ice in quest of a lesson, then that class must be held. It does stop a lot of argument and misunderstanding. Even if the pro gets lost in the blizzard, there is almost invariably somebody sufficiently qualified at the rink to step in temporarily, even if it has to be the manager himself.

Arrangements and payments for private lessons are relatively informal. In most rinks and clubs it is the normal procedure to book private lessons directly with the instructor for a specific time on a specific day and then continue that lesson or lessons at the same time throughout the season or until further notice. You should, however, make your desires clear when you book the first lesson. Normally there are no discounts given on a series of private lessons, even when booked for the whole season. In a few rinks payment is made through the box office, but more often—and invariably in private clubs—payment is made directly to the instructor. When booking the first lesson, you should ask the instructor how he likes to be paid. Casual lessons are usually paid for on the spot before or after the lesson, either in cash or by check. If you are a regular student taking more than one lesson a week, payment might be made after the last lesson of the week. Some instructors bill monthly or every two weeks, but it should be borne in mind that there is no obligation on the part of the instructor to bill; he does not have a secretary, so you should fall in with whatever method he uses.

Cancellations

In the case of group lessons paid for in advance it is not normally necessary to inform the rink that your child will miss a class: attendance records are almost invariably kept, whether the rink has a makeup policy or not. If, however, you or your child cannot make a private lesson, timely cancellation is of the utmost importance. Under normal circumstances an instructor has the right to require twenty-four hours notice of cancellation, in which case you will not be charged. Shorter notices are, of course, occasionally unavoidable, but however short the notice, the cancellation should be made. This will at least give the instructor a fighting chance to fill the time with somebody else who has been waiting for a lesson or wants an extra lesson, or enable him to switch lessons with some other skater. If he can do so, you will not be charged. For this reason you should not object if your lesson time is occasionally changed on short notice—provided you have not made a special journey. Nearly everybody has to cancel at some time or other, and by going along with the instructor's policy you too may benefit at some time in the future when you cannot make a lesson.

At short notice it is sometimes difficult to get hold of the instructor by phone, particularly as he will not welcome being pulled off the ice in the middle of a lesson. You should take note not only of the rink phone number, but of all the numbers of public call boxes in the building, as the person in the manager's office or box office may be so busy that the message could be delayed. If you phone to a call box, it will usually be answered by someone who knows most of the regular skaters and you should be able to get a message through immediately to the instructor on the ice.

If an instructor is suddenly taken ill, he will, or should, make every attempt to inform his pupils, but if he has a large number of lessons scheduled during the day, he may not be able to get around to all of them by phone and may have to leave a message with the rink. The incidence of cancellation among pros is, however, relatively small because they lose so much money staying in bed. This principle used to be summed up in show business contracts as "no play-no pay."

Practice Between Lessons

You cannot learn to skate just by taking lessons, you must have practice time between—that's the key to the whole thing. Quite apart from learning the movements, there is the question of balance. Balance on ice skates deteriorates very rapidly, particularly in beginners. Even top-rank skaters know how it affects their jumping and spinning when they have been away from the ice for a week or so. If a skater at the lower level skates only once a week, he spends the first hour getting his balance back to where it was at the previous session. In the early stages three times a week works wonders, and even at twice a week a beginner can make some progress. But an hour three times a week gives better results than ninety minutes twice a week; it is, therefore, important that practice times be as evenly spaced as possible.

Punctuality

Punctuality is a must both for the student and the instructor. It is discourteous for the instructor to keep a pupil waiting, and unwise for the pupil to keep an instructor waiting. If a pupil is not on time, the instructor, in order to avoid having to charge for time not given (something that instructors are surprisingly unwilling to do), will immediately try to fill in the lesson with someone else. Once having started a lesson with another student it would be discourteous on the part of the pro to break it off in favor of the latecomer.

4

How the Sport
Is Organized

Introduction to Competitive Skating

Now that you have your child properly equipped and into some type of instructional program, you are probably chafing at the bit and asking yourself, "Now, how do we get to the next Olympics?" The first thing to realize is that all branches of competitive figure skating involve two parallel and interlinking structures, a test structure and a competition structure. Tests are the only means the sponsoring body has of pitting skaters of similar abilities against one another. A skater who thinks he is pretty good cannot simply say to himself, "I think I'll have a go at the World Championship this year." In nearly all countries he must have proved his competence by passing the tests of his national association before the International Skating Union (ISU) will accept his entry. (Be careful not to confuse the initials ISU with those of the ISIA, the Ice Skating Institute of America.) It is quite possible to pursue a skating career just for the satisfaction of passing tests, but if a skater wishes to compete, passing certain tests is mandatory. As it is set up in the U.S. a skater stands little chance (except under the most unusual circumstances) of being selected for the World or Olympic Team unless he has placed among the first three in the National Senior Championships, and to compete in the Senior Championships he must have achieved his USFSA Gold Medal (Eighth Figure plus Senior Free Skating Tests, see "Test Requirements," chapter 12). I must, by the way, remind you not to confuse a gold medal awarded for passing a test with one obtained in a competition. The former is a certification of ability against a theoretically absolute standard, and the

36

latter a recognition of ability in comparison with other skaters of a similarly high level. Of course, a skater does not have to wait until he gets his USFSA Gold Medal before competing. On the way up from the beginner level he graduates through local competitions at various levels, the level depending on how far up the test ladder he has climbed.

If, therefore, you are aiming at the World Championship, or a gold medal at the Olympic Winter Games, you must, as soon as possible, involve your child in the USFSA official test structure, starting with the Preliminary Test, which more or less continues from where the Basic Tests leave off. To do this the skater must become a member of a USFSA club, or an individual member of the USFSA (see "Joining a USFSA Club," chapter 6). This does not mean you should abandon the ISIA; this latter organization has much to offer, and the greater the exposure of the young skater to the public the better. It is simply that the USFSA is the governing body of the sport and sponsors the qualifying championships leading up to the international championships, which are in turn sponsored by the International Skating Union, to which the USFSA is this country's only accredited organization in the field of figure skating.

It should be strongly emphasized that any would-be champion must get started on the USFSA test ladder at the earliest practical age, as it may take two or three years after the skater reaches the higher competitive levels for his potential to be attained and given full recognition. Also, the balance required in most skating movements can only be developed slowly and steadily over a long period; short-term cramming does not seem to work. It can be seen, therefore, that any time lost at the beginning of a skater's career may put him under a severe handicap. Unfortunately, many parents fritter away valuable time before they become conscious of the existence and significance of the USFSA.

If you are involved in an ISIA program, you should consider the advisability of taking an additional membership in the ranks of the USFSA as soon as your child has passed the Delta test. Your skater will still be able to participate in the ongoing tests of the ISIA, but there are slight differences in the tests of the two systems, and the USFSA does not recognize the ISIA tests as qualifying for the official USFSA competitions, although sometimes and under certain circumstances the ISIA will recognize those of the USFSA for entry into ISIA competitions.

Before you start really getting down to the nitty-gritty of serious competition, you can get your child started by arranging for him to take part in some of the many competitions specifically designed for beginners. Nearly all rinks and clubs using either the USFSA Basic Test Program or the ISIA Alpha-Beta-Gamma-Delta tests run such competitions in conjunction with their testing programs. They are great fun for the child and are usually conducted in a more relaxed atmosphere than competitions for more advanced skaters. Normally there is a separate event for each test level, and these events are further subdivided according to age and sex. The structure of these competitions varies so much that it would be pointless to attempt to go into further details here. Your local rink or club will be able to give you all the necessary information on their own particular brand of beginners' competitions.

In later chapters I shall deal in considerably greater depth with the more advanced USFSA test and competition systems, both of which are highly complex. I shall try, however, to restrict myself to those essentials which will enable you to head your skater in the right direction. For further details I shall refer you to the *USFSA Rulebook.*

The systems of the ISIA and the USFSA have many points in common, that of the USFSA being the more rigid and formal in regard to requirements and regulations: The emphasis by the ISIA on the purely recreational side of figure skating has resulted in a more informal approach. For this reason, and because the USFSA route is the one that must be taken on the way to the top—the subject of this book—the USFSA is given the greater coverage here. If you understand the USFSA system, however, you will have little difficulty in understanding that of the ISIA.

The Major Organizations

To help you understand the whole picture, here are short descriptions of the major organizations involved in figure skating and how they relate to one another. Because members of the Professional Skaters Guild of America (PSGA) have a direct and close relationship with parents and skaters, this organization has a section of its own later in the book.

The International Skating Union

In 1892 the leading skating clubs of several countries banded together to establish an amateur body, known as the International Skating Union

(ISU), with the object of setting up rules and regulations for figure and speed skating; it was thus possible to hold international competitions under the auspices of an officially recognized organization. Over the years more and more countries set up their own national organizations to control the sport within their borders, and eventually became members of the ISU—at the latest count the total number of member countries is thirty-three, including China, Korea, and Mongolia.

All national organizations, to a greater or lesser degree, regulate the sport in their own countries in such a way that the rules and requirements for their own national tests and competitions follow closely those of the ISU, thus making it possible to send skaters to international events with some chance of success.

The ISU is the only body officially recognized throughout the world as having the right to sanction amateur international competitions in all branches of figure skating. The most important international events are: the World Championship, the European Championship, the figure skating portion of the Olympic Winter Games, and the fast-growing number of international meets such as the St. Ivel International (London), Skate Canada, the NHK Trophy (Japan), and the Ennia Challenge Cup (Holland), to mention a few. Many of these meets are now taking the name of the commercial company that puts up the money to stage them, but the competitions themselves are still strictly under the control of the ISU. Scandinavia also holds its own championships with entries restricted to skaters from Denmark, Norway, Sweden, and Finland, and there used to be a North American Championship for skaters from the U.S. and Canada, but this has unfortunately been discontinued. There is an annual World Professional Championship, formerly held in Britain, which now takes place regularly in Jaca, Spain, at Easter. It is almost unheard of in the U.S., but is becoming increasingly popular in Europe, where it gets considerable TV coverage. As it is not an amateur event, the ISU has no jurisdiction over this championship (see chapter 15, "Professional Championships").

The United States Figure Skating Association

In the U.S. the official body affiliated with the International Skating Union (ISU) in the field of figure skating is the United States Figure Skating Association (USFSA). Since its scope and activities are dealt with in considerable detail throughout this book, only the briefest summary of its history and responsibilities will be given in this section.

Founded in 1921, the USFSA at the moment of writing consists of 450 member clubs, representing more than forty thousand skaters. Its size increases steadily year by year. Not only is the USFSA a member of the ISU, it is also a member of the U.S. Olympic Committee (USOC) and an allied member of the Amateur Athletic Union (AAU). The ISU, the USOC, and the AAU all recognize the USFSA as the sole body governing amateur figure skating in the U.S., and it is therefore the responsibility of the USFSA to pick the team to represent the U.S. at the World Championship, the Olympic Winter Games, and other international events. The equivalent organization in Canada is the Canadian Figure Skating Association (CFSA), and in the United Kingdom, the National Skating Association of Great Britain (NSA), which also regulates speed and roller skating in that country.

The Ice Skating Institute of America

The ISIA is an association of ice rink owners, operators, suppliers to the industry, and associate members who are affiliated with ice skating in various capacities. One of its major functions is to conduct the Recreational Skater Program designed to service the recreational entry-level skater. To quote the *ISIA Manual,* the recreational skater "wants to enjoy a challenging and exciting activity, but does not want to undertake grueling hard work or long-term practice." Although the program does service the high-level skater, the emphasis is on the recreational skater. The ISIA competitive program is an extension of the test program, but it is a team concept, i.e., skaters become members of a team and these teams compete against each other, in this way differing from the USFSA concept of individual competition (pairs, ice dance couples, and precision teams being regarded as single units). The ISIA concept thus places emphasis on participation rather than on elimination.

The ISIA attempt, very laudably, to conduct their competitions in a relaxed and joyful spirit. Human nature being what it is, this is not the easiest thing to achieve, but they appear to be doing an excellent job and perform a very useful function in introducing hundreds of new skaters painlessly to the sport. Since the ISIA is not a member of the ISU, their competitions are at present confined to the U.S., but they are a powerful organization influencing many ice rinks and are therefore a body to be reckoned with.

There was a time when relations between the ISIA and the USFSA were not as harmonious as they are today, each body suspecting the other of trespassing on its territory. But having the welfare of the sport in mind and realizing that there was nothing to be gained and much to be lost by dissension, the two organizations eventually buried the hatchet and ushered in an era of peaceful cooperation by issuing joint statements of policy, which now appear in every issue of the *USFSA Rulebook*. The full text is quoted below.

USFSA–ISIA Statements of Policy

At their respective Executive Committee meetings in October, 1974, the USFSA and the Ice Skating Institute of America (ISIA) jointly adopted mutual statements of policy for cooperation between the two bodies.

The primary objectives of the two organizations are to normalize their relations and to achieve full cooperation between them in the mutual interest of insuring full participation in skating of each individual recreational skater and figure skater without interference or restriction. In order for these goals to be achieved, it is vital that all Member Clubs of the USFSA implement fully the spirit of cooperation contained in the statements of policy; we are confident the members of the ISIA will do the same.

It is the belief of the USFSA that the adoption of the statements of policy represents a progressive step on the part of both the Association and the ISIA, which will be of great benefit to the thousands of individual skaters whom both organizations serve.

USFSA Statement of Policy

The United States Figure Skating Association (USFSA) recognizes the primary role and interest of the Ice Skating Institute of America (ISIA) in promoting the activity of ice skating for the recreational skater.

Consistent with such recognition, the USFSA agrees to cooperate fully with the ISIA to further that objective. To that end, the USFSA further agrees that the participation of USFSA members in exhibitions and carnivals endorsed by the ISIA shall not be deemed to be a violation of the rules of the USFSA, nor shall it be deemed a violation for USFSA members who are also registered with the ISIA to participate in ISIA tests and competitions, subject only to the limitation that such participation does not result in any direct or indirect financial benefit to the participant.

ISIA Statement of Policy

The Ice Skating Institute of America (ISIA) recognizes that the United States Figure Skating Association (USFSA) has been and is the governing body of the sport of amateur figure skating on ice in the United States and that it is so recognized by the International Skating Union (ISU).

Consistent with such recognition, the ISIA agrees to cooperate fully with the USFSA and its Member Clubs to promote the full participation of the members of the USFSA in the sport of figure skating. To that end, the ISIA further agrees that the participation of skaters registered with the ISIA in activities sponsored by the USFSA shall not be deemed to be a violation of any applicable rules of the ISIA.

USFSA Member Clubs

Early in the nineteenth century, when interest in the sport really began to take hold, the more enthusiastic skaters found it necessary to band together to form clubs. Not only could acquired knowledge be stored and passed on to interested members, but a club could arrange to reserve private ice on a river or lake, where skaters could socialize and experiment with new gyrations without interruption by the common herd. In the U.S., the oldest club is the Philadelphia Skating Club and Humane Society. Originally established in 1849, it derives its present rather bizarre name from its amalgamation in 1861 with the Humane Society, whose purpose was to save the lives of skaters who fell through the ice of the Schuylkill River, where most of the club's activities took place. Members were required to carry with them wooden reels of thin rope, which was thrown to skaters in difficulty. Prospective members should take note that this requirement has now been rescinded.

Now that nearly all serious skating takes place on artificial ice rinks, one of the more important functions of a club is the reservation of private ice time for the exercise of the various branches of figure skating. Not only is the serious student faced with obvious difficulties when he attempts to practice during public sessions, but in a few areas of the country certain rinks, in a praiseworthy effort to protect the public from injury, have limited skating in public sessions to skating forward round and round the rink. Any deviation from this monotonous pattern, even doing the same thing backwards, will be greeted by an indignant whistle from an ice guard. Such measures seem extreme, but I am happy to say that in most cases, during the less crowded public sessions, ice rink managers usually permit the practicing of freestyle as well as ice dancing, provided reasonable caution is exercised. USFSA clubs, apart from renting ice on behalf of their members and programming the session into periods for practicing the various branches of figure skating, also have the responsibility of organizing official USFSA tests; judges, if not available from the local club, frequently have to be brought in from out of town, especially if the test is a high one.

Dues and types of membership vary enormously from club to club according to the amount of ice time rented and the size of the club, which may vary from a membership of fifty or less to five hundred or more. Some of the larger clubs are fortunate enough to own their own rinks, but with the rise in construction costs this is becoming increasingly rare. A full list of USFSA-affiliated clubs is given in the *USFSA Rulebook.*

5

The USFSA
Test Structure

In order to understand more fully many of the terms used in this and the following sections, you may wish to use as a reference chapters 23 and 24, which deal with the recognition of many of the figures and freestyle moves to be found in the USFSA tests.

Separate USFSA tests are held in figures, free skating, pair skating, and ice dancing (subdivided into the compulsory dances and free dance). The tests in each branch cover a similar range of skills, but although they all start with a preliminary test, from then on the number of tests and the method of referring to them differs from branch to branch.

Under each heading I shall give you a brief outline of the total test structure of that branch and then explain in more detail what is required in the corresponding preliminary test, as this is the test which most immediately concerns us here. Contents of the higher tests will be found in the *USFSA Rulebook.*

Surprisingly enough, figures and free skating arose in the distant past as subdivisions of the same basic discipline. For many years free skating had no tests of its own, but was attached to, and part of, tests in the figures, which had seniority over free skating. However, with its advance in techniques and increasing importance in the field, free skating now has its own series of tests. The connection between the figures and free skating still lingers on, as demonstrated by the fact that the National Singles Championship—and any event qualifying for it—still contains both figures and free skating. For this reason, skaters must have passed both the figures and free skating tests at the appropriate level in order to compete; nor can a

44

singles skater call himself a Gold Medalist before he has passed the Eighth Figure Test *and* the Senior Free Skating Test, each of these tests being individually worth a Gold *Bar*.

Figure Tests

Tests in figures consist of a Preliminary Test plus a further eight tests referred to by number: First Test, Second Test, and so on. The Eighth Test is still by tradition known simply as the *Gold,* but as mentioned above the award is now a Gold Bar instead of a Gold Medal. Excepted are skaters who passed their Eighth Tests before the separation of figures and free skating: these skaters are still entitled to call themselves Gold Medalists.

Originally there were only three tests: Bronze, Silver, and Gold, but because tests are constructed from the whole schedule of the ISU figures (plus one peculiar to the U.S., the "waltz eight"), the tests were eventually broken down into smaller bites. In the original Gold Test there were no less than twenty-four figures, and nowadays it would be impossible for any skater to maintain them simultaneously at the standard required for the modern Gold Test.

There is an amusing convention that demonstrates clearly the American spirit of drive, optimism, and desire to get ahead. If you ask a skater his test level, he will invariably tell you the test he hopes eventually to take rather than the actual tests that he has passed. He may, for example, refer to himself as "working on his Fifth Test" or, if he is an ice dancer, as "working on his Pre-Silvers," whereas he will tell you with a touch of condescension that his competitor is a "fourth test skater," or that he has "passed his Bronze."

Incidentally, the practice in some clubs of referring to the Basic Tests for beginners by number instead of by name—calling, for example, the Novice First Class the "third badge"—has frequently led to gross misunderstanding on the part of parents new to the game. If some proud mother tells you her daughter is "working on her Sixth," and you reply with due modesty that your own daughter happens to be on her Eighth (when you really mean the Advanced Second Class Badge), you are committing a gaucherie of the first magnitude, and one which you may find hard to live down.

It should now be quite clear that the USFSA Basic Test Program is completely independent of the "official" USFSA test structure. A skater does not have to have passed any of the USFSA Basic Tests before starting on any of the Preliminary Tests. It is highly advisable, however, that he should know and be efficient in all the movements that are contained in the Basic Tests before he attempts to go further. All these basic movements are carefully explained in my how-to book, *Basic Ice Skating Skills*, which was written as a textbook for the program. If you have any difficulty obtaining it locally, you can always get a copy from the USFSA National Headquarters, which usually has a good stock on hand.

Tests in the official structure, whatever branch, must be taken in order from the bottom up; you cannot, unfortunately, skip those you don't like. All preliminary tests are marked on a pass or fail basis; methods of marking the higher tests will be found under the heading "The Marking System" (chapter 8).

The Preliminary Figure Test

For the Preliminary Figure Test—known in the jargon of the skating world as the *Prelim*—the candidate is required to skate across the width of the rink in half circles, first on forward outside edges, then on forward inside, followed by the back outside and back inside. A minimum of five consecutive edges must be skated on alternate feet. Since the average ice surface is approximately eighty-five feet in width, this means that the size of each half circle normally has a radius of about seven and a half to eight feet. In very narrow rinks the candidate would probably be asked to skate down the length of the rink.

In order to pass the Preliminary Figure Test, the skater must demonstrate that he is capable of skating good, clean, steady curves on one foot, preferably on a flexible knee, and that he can make correct pushes from one edge to the other in the right direction, and from the side of the blade, not the toe.

After having skated the half circles the candidate must then skate three figures: the forward outside eight, the forward inside eight, and the waltz eight—a figure containing forward outside threes (sometimes called *three-turns*), and back edges, difficult at this stage to skate well. The figures are started on the right foot and must be skated three times without pause. Because the majority of rinks use white ice and lighting more suitable to hockey than figure skating, it is difficult for the young, light skater to see his tracings, i.e., the marks he makes on the ice. The USFSA, therefore, now very wisely allows the skater taking a Preliminary Test (but not the higher tests) to mark the center of his figure, i.e., the starting point, by a short line drawn with the heel of the blade. Spectators do not always realize that it is much easier for the onlooker watching from the side to see the marks of the tracing since in most rinks the angle of the light is for him oblique, while for the skater it is vertical.

Judging at this level is usually very lenient. The judges are looking for the qualities required in all figures, but to a comparatively low standard. Circles should be approximately three times the skater's height in diameter, and therefore the same size on each foot. The circles should be placed symmetrically round the long axis of the figure and should touch each other rather like two giant coins placed edge to edge. Because he must skate the figure three times, the skater is now faced with the difficult task of superimposing his tracings, which means that, provided his first circles are correct, he tries to place the subsequent tracings as nearly as possible on top of the preceding ones. The threes in the waltz eight are supposed to be "clean," i.e., directly from one edge to the other, but seldom are at this stage. The two major faults to be avoided are pushing from the toe pick instead of the side of the blade, and "touching down," which means momentarily dropping the free foot onto the ice, usually caused by lack of balance. It is difficult by the printed word alone to give an indication of the precise standard required, but compared with the higher tests the number of failures at the preliminary level is very low; it is generally felt that at this stage encouragement rather than criticism is needed to inspire the young skater to continue with this difficult and often frustrating branch of the sport. (See chapter 22, "The Special Place of Figures.")

Free Skating Tests

In view of the popularity of free skating (or freestyle, as it is commonly called in the U.S.), it is strange that until recent years there were no tests in this branch at all. After a surprisingly long period, free skating was gradually added, rather in the nature of an afterthought, to certain of the figure tests, of which they became a part. If one traces the history of the sport back for a hundred years or so (which I do not propose to do here), it can be seen that the situation was a logical one; but while the figures themselves congealed into a static, though necessary, branch of the sport, the freestyle continued its dynamic growth in scope and popularity, until it has now achieved a clear-cut identity of its own.

The present series of free skating tests consists of six levels: Preliminary, Juvenile, Intermediate, Novice, Junior, and Senior. In the context of these tests the word *Juvenile* has nothing to do with age, but is simply used to denote a particular level of ability. From the Juvenile level up, all free skating tests require routines (programs) to music and must contain certain minimum requirements. The Preliminary Test, however, simply requires the candidate to perform specified, isolated movements without having to link them together.

The Preliminary Free Skating Test

In comparison with other preliminary tests, the Preliminary Free Skating Test is, for the young skater of average athletic ability, by far the easiest. He will be required to perform four specific jumps, namely, a waltz jump, a toe loop, a Salchow, and a half flip or half Lutz; he will also have to perform a spin on one foot and a spin on two feet, each of three revolutions.

The whole test is conducted very informally, very often on quite a small portion of the rink. The Judge-in-Charge (referee) simply tells the candidate the movement he has to do, and the candidate goes out and does it. If necessary, he is allowed a second try. With the exception of the half flip (or half Lutz), all the movements—and considerably more—will have been learned in the USFSA Basic Tests, which is by no means the case with the preliminary tests in the other branches, all of which take the skater to a new and higher level. I think it probable that the illogically low requirements of the present Preliminary Free Skating Test will be revised upward before very long, so keep yourself informed.

Pair Skating Tests

The pair tests consist of Preliminary, Bronze, Silver, and Gold. Testing in this branch is also comparatively new, which is one of the reasons it still retains the classic Bronze, Silver, and Gold format (the original structure of figure and ice dance tests). It would seem logical to suppose that as time goes on, further tests, possibly a Pre-Silver and a Pre-Gold, will be added, as has been done in the case of ice dancing.

The present four-test format means that there are bigger jumps in ability between the tests than in the other branches. Because the majority of skaters do not take up pair skating until they have spent several seasons working at their solo skating, the standard of skating required at the Preliminary Test level is higher than that expected for the other preliminary tests.

At one time a pair could consist of two women or two men skating together, but now the official USFSA tests and competitions require that a woman must skate with a man (or a boy with a girl). Informal competitions, however, sometimes include events for similar pairs, i.e., pairs consisting of skaters of the same sex.

All pair skating tests, including the Preliminary, consist of programs set to music; the routines must contain certain specified minimal elements which demonstrate not only ability in pair movements but also in solo free skating movements, in which the individual skaters must move in harmony and unison with each other, either in "shadow" or "mirror" formation. The lengths of the programs are: two minutes for the Preliminary, three minutes for the Bronze, four for the Silver, and four and a half for the Gold.

In comparison with figure, free skating, and dance tests, the number of pair tests taken is very small, even at the Preliminary Test level. You will see many more dance tests taken than pair tests. On the face of it, this may seem strange since there are certain similarities between the two branches. There are several reasons for this discrepancy. The first, and probably most important, is that, because pair skating is basically free skating with pair lifts and spins added, one has to look for two strong free skaters whose relative size and physical structure is harmonious, the boy of the pair being strong enough to make a good lifter. But good freestylists are usually individualists who enjoy the unhampered freedom of solo skating and frequently, therefore, have to be coerced into forming one of a pair. The situation is made more difficult by the shortage in many clubs of boys or young men. In ice dancing this difficulty is often overcome by a professional, or some long-suffering and good-natured boy, taking girl after girl through the various dances, a situation only possible because the compulsory dances are so set in their format that a little practice together before a test will usually achieve a moderate degree of unison. This is not so in pair skating because every pair devises a different program that needs constant practice. Unlike the compulsory dances, it is of little use practicing the program alone, nor can one of the pair go off and practice it with somebody else when his partner is not there. You cannot at the last moment pick up a partner to take you through a pair test as you can with an ice dance. Fortunately, things are a little easier now that professionals are permitted to partner amateurs in pair tests.

For all the various reasons given above it is unlikely that you will be immediately concerned with your child taking a Preliminary Pair Test, but for the record a description of the test is given here.

The Preliminary Pair Test

The summarized contents of the Preliminary Pair Test are: the couple must skate a two-minute program to music showing that they can move in unison together over the ice both clockwise and counterclockwise, forward and backward; they must also include spirals (arabesques) and pivots in shadow or mirror image sequences, execute one pair spin in hold, one solo spin synchronized with the partner, one solo jump also synchronized, and one simple lift. It is all a little more difficult than it sounds.

Dance Tests

There are seven dance tests consisting purely of compulsory dances, namely, the Preliminary, Bronze, Pre-Silver, Silver, Pre-Gold, Gold, and International. To these have been added a Silver Free Dance (after the Silver) and a Gold Free Dance (after the Gold). A skater only has to take these free dance tests if he wishes to compete at the higher levels. If he is content merely to take tests and not compete, he can earn a Gold Medal by passing just the Gold Dance Test (and, of course, all the other compulsory dance tests leading up to the Gold).

The International Dance Test was introduced fairly recently to include in the USFSA test schedule several new dances (and one old one resuscitated) that the ISU added a few years ago to the international competition structure. This latest test encourages our skaters to practice these dances and prepare themselves for international competition. A Gold Bar is awarded for passing the Gold Free Dance and a similar Gold Bar for the International Dance Test. Each bar bears an appropriate inscription.

Singles skating and pair skating test requirements, on the one hand, and ice dancing test requirements on the other, are handled by two entirely separate committees, which accounts for the differences in approach to the regulation of these branches. After describing the Preliminary Dance Test, I shall explain in simple terms a few of the peculiarities of the dance regulations that are not generally understood and tend to send skaters (and sometimes pros) rushing to the rulebook for clarification.

The Preliminary Dance Test

The Preliminary Dance Test consists of three dances: the Dutch Waltz, Canasta Tango, and Swing Dance, the first two of which only require forward skating, while the Swing Dance requires back as well as forward edges, plus a rather tricky turn from forward to backward known as a *mohawk*. This last dance is considered the hardest of the three.

As with the Preliminary Figure Test, the Preliminary Dance Test is designed to encourage skaters to take up ice dancing. Nevertheless, the number of failures met with in the Preliminary Dance Test is far higher than the number of failures in the Preliminary Figure Test, largely due to the relative difficulty of the Swing Dance, which is often attempted before the back edges are sufficiently strong. The judges are not looking for the great technical ability or the subtleties expected at a higher level, such as expression, carriage, unison, or flow over the ice; a skater should pass if he can demonstrate that he can execute the steps, keep time to the music, has fairly strong edges, and is not entirely devoid of a reasonable posture.

Many skaters work at the Preliminary Dance Test at the same time that they are working for the Preliminary Figure Test, which is an excellent idea. The figure test develops control while the dance test develops smoothness and flow over the ice. Since all the dances in the Preliminary Test have a set pattern or design of required steps in relation to the ice surface, and because each dance is executed to music played at a set tempo, the skater is obliged to cover a certain minimum distance in a certain number of measures, thus improving his speed and general skating ability.

The Piecemeal System

The big difference between dance tests and tests in other branches is that a dance test does not have to be taken all at one time, i.e., the individual dances comprising the test may be split up over several testing sessions at the option of the candidate, whereas in order to pass, for example, a figure test, all the individual figures in that test must be taken and passed at the same testing session. As an example, let us take the Preliminary Dance Test, which consists of three dances. A candidate might try just one or two dances at a testing session or he might try all three; if he passes all three, he obviously passes the whole test, but if he passes, let us say, the Dutch Waltz and Swing Dance and fails the Canasta Tango, he does not fail the whole test but is given credit for the two dances he has passed and is issued a certificate to that effect. Then at some future session, it could be some years later, if he has a try at the Canasta Tango again and passes it, he is now said to have completed the Preliminary Test.

It should be noted that the 27-day rule (see chapter 7), which states that a failed test cannot be retaken until a clear twenty-seven days have elapsed, applies also to individual dances; however, a skater could, before this period was up, try other individual dances which he had not yet attempted, provided they were part of the same test. A candidate is not permitted to try a dance in a higher test before all the dances in the preceding test have been passed.

Soloing

A candidate for a dance test always skates once with a partner, after which he may, or may not, have to skate the dance, or dances, alone; this is known as *soloing* a dance. In the lower tests the purpose of this is to permit the judges to determine whether the candidate is getting too much assistance from his partner in executing the steps or keeping time to the music. In the Preliminary Test, fortunately, a skater never under any circumstances has to solo. But soloing is mandatory in the Silver Test and above, and is sometimes required in the Bronze and Pre-Silver, as is explained in the following section.

Partners

All dance tests may be taken with an amateur or professional partner with no restrictions as to the test level of the partner selected. There is, however, one catch to this: In a Bronze or Pre-Silver test, if the partner is a professional or has completed a test two levels ahead of the test in which he is acting as a partner (e.g., if the partner taking a Bronze candidate through that test has completed his Silver), then the candidate is obliged to skate solo. The most important points to remember at the moment are that a candidate for a Preliminary Test never has to skate solo and may take the test with any amateur or professional whatever his test level.

It is not necessary for a candidate to skate every dance with the same partner, even in the same test; it is quite legitimate to skate every dance in a test with a different partner, but with the limited number of partners around, this does not often happen. A situation can arise, however, when the candidate is required to reskate a dance with some partner appointed by the judges themselves. This frequently happens when the judges consider the partner inadequate in some respect; they may suspect, for example, that he (or she) is causing the candidate to skate out of time with the music. Because such a reskate has to be made immediately, it is only possible if some willing person has his skates on and is unwise enough to be standing around in the neighborhood. At one time, when the restrictions on partners were much more rigid than they are today, this rule led to a certain amount of innocent chicanery. A weak skater might deliberately choose a partner who could barely stumble round the dance, with the result that the judges would look round desperately for another partner. Of course, if by chance the candidate's gold medalist friend happened to have his skates on at the time and just happened to be standing near the entrance to the ice surface, the candidate might easily be asked to dance with a superb skater whose test level would otherwise have excluded him from acting as an official partner.

6
Becoming a Member
of the USFSA

To take an official USFSA test an amateur skater must be a member of a USFSA Member Club, or an Individual Member of the USFSA. It is also possible to qualify by being a student or a member of the faculty or administration of an association that is itself an Associate Member of the USFSA, or by being a member of an association that is a member of the International Skating Union, such as the National Skating Association of Great Britain or the Canadian Figure Skating Association, i.e., any of the thirty-three bodies associated with the ISU. The vast majority of test candidates, however, qualify by virtue of being a member of a local USFSA club. Let me once more remind you that it is not necessary to be a club member, or even to be registered with the USFSA, in order to take the USFSA Basic Tests.

Joining a USFSA Club

If there is no USFSA club using your rink, you will have to ask around or obtain a *USFSA Rulebook* (see chapter 29), which lists every Member Club including the name and address of the secretary to whom you should apply. The annual dues, which go to pay for ice rental and the many other various expenses, differ considerably from club to club, as do the sizes of the clubs themselves, the larger ones usually having the most ice time at their disposal. At first sight club dues may appear high, but they may not seem so bad after a look at the economics of the situation. The cost of renting ice may well average $80 an hour (probably much higher by the time you get this book into your hands), so that a club with a relatively modest schedule of ten hours per week will be paying in the neighborhood of $20,800 per six-month season. Divide this by a membership of possibly 150 and you have a little over $138 per person, and this is before taking into consideration sound equipment, dance tapes, payment to professionals for group lessons, secretarial expenses, and a host of other miscellaneous costs. Fortunately, most clubs offer family memberships in addition to membership for single skaters. The family memberships often show considerable saving if more than one of your family wishes to skate.

All clubs designate a certain rink as their principal skating headquarters, but this does not mean that members may only skate at that rink: you may skate where you like and may be a member of several clubs at once if you wish. You will, however, be required to designate one club, and one club only, as your home club for the period from October first to October first of the following year. For test purposes a skater comes under the jurisdiction of his home club and he must always represent his home club when he competes. It is the home club that has the responsibility of issuing the skater a registration card showing his date of membership and official USFSA number. Should you join some other club, or clubs, it is important to let them know that you already have a home club or you may be registered twice, which is quite unnecessary. Not only does the USFSA refuse to refund dues paid in error for multiple registrations, but there could be great hassle and confusion when your child takes a test. The charge for registration with the USFSA is usually included in the club dues. At the time of writing, the annual registration fee for the first member of the family is $10, entitling him to a registration card and a subscription to *Skating* magazine. Subsequent members of the family, if they are all living at the same permanent address, pay only $3 each, for which they will receive a registration card but no magazine subscription.

There is no objection to a skater changing his designated home club, but he may not do so in the middle of the season; like it or not, therefore, he is stuck with that club until the following October first. If he wishes to change his home club, he will have to file the change on a form supplied by the USFSA national headquarters.

Individual Membership

Circumstances may occur under which it is impractical to become a member of a USFSA club, despite the fact that you wish your child to take part in USFSA activities; there may, for example, be no club in the neighbor-hood, or you may find that the local club meets at times when you cannot attend; you should then apply to the USFSA national headquarters for individual membership. Registration fees are considerably higher than when applying through a club: for the first member of the family you will pay (at the time of writing) $30 annually and $18 for each subsequent family member. The $30 fee includes a registration card, a subscription to *Skating* magazine, and a copy of the current *USFSA Rulebook.* The $18 fee includes only the registration card. Should you subsequently join a USFSA club, your individual membership ceases (you are not permitted to be an individual member and a member of a club at the same time), but as you are already registered, you will not have to pay again; you will not, however, obtain a refund of the balance.

There are obvious disadvantages to individual membership: You are deprived of club activities and much of the social side of skating, and you will have to pay for your own ice time, which, if there is no club in the neighborhood, may be difficult to obtain. Fortunately many rinks, even where a club is active, offer patch and free skating time to the public outside regular club hours. In competitions, individual members are usu-ally listed under the city of their permanent residence in place of a home club.

7

Arranging
to Take a Test

Now that your child is a member in good standing with a USFSA club, or an individual member, and is registered with the USFSA, you will need to know the details of arranging for an official USFSA test. Every club has a test chairman whose job it is to organize the testing sessions, which includes scheduling the ice time, arranging for judges, checking on the eligibility of candidates, and taking care of a host of other details.

Some time before tests are scheduled it is the usual practice for a club to put up a list on which the prospective candidate must enter his name, the test he wishes to take, and his USFSA registration number, which appears on his registration card. Too often this card has been left at home or lost, and the candidate fails to fill in the number before the list is taken down. This number is very important because the USFSA keeps a computer record of tests and test results that is entered according to each member's registration number.

So you must see that the registration card is never lost. You will also be required to pay a test fee, varying according to circumstances, part of which goes to the USFSA and part to help defray judges' travel expenses and other incidental costs.

Individual members should make direct contact with the test chairman of any local club; any professional who teaches for a USFSA club should be able to give you all the necessary information.

A skater is not bound to take his tests at his home club. He may be temporarily out of town or he may have had to switch clubs midway through the season. In such cases the club with which he is currently skating will take care of him. Sometimes, too, a skater might for personal reasons prefer to take a test elsewhere, but in such cases an outside club could only be expected to accommodate him if they have plenty of ice time available. In any event, a skater wishing to take a test at an outside club must present a letter of permission from the test chairman or other authorized representative of his home club.

But one moment, please! Before you do anything regarding tests, there is one big question that must be answered.

Is the Skater Ready?

Tests usually require clean ice and the use of the total ice surface, which means that other club members not taking tests must be deprived of some of their ice time, or ice must be rented at considerable expense outside club hours. Judges, too, are an expensive item. As there may be high tests going on at the same time as low tests, it may be necessary to bring in judges with the requisite qualifications from out of town, in which case they will often help out in judging some of the lower tests. Travel expenses must be paid, and because a test session may go on for many hours and it is generally considered unwise for the session to be conducted by a panel of hungry, irritable judges, refreshment is usually provided, paid for out of the test fees or club funds. All this adds up to the fact that there is great pressure on the test chairman only to accept those candidates who have at least a fifty-fifty chance of success. In consideration, therefore, both of your child and your club, it is imperative to find out whether your child is ready to take the test. Who better to ask than the skater's instructor? A common practice in many clubs is to require the instructor to sign a pupil's test applications before tests may be taken. It is, however, asking a lot of a professional to put his signature to an authorization and thereby, in effect, requiring him to prejudge the test. A more informal and much better arrangement is for the club to make it clear to skaters and parents that they should be guided by the advice of the professional. This is, I believe, the practice in the majority of clubs. But just occasionally there enters into the picture the ambitious parent, totally ignorant of skating standards, who foolishly and selfishly insists that her or his (it is very often a competitive father) child should be "allowed to try," apparently on the presumption that the child's skill will miraculously improve 100 percent on the day. This does not happen. If the skater has never on any single occasion produced the required standard prior to the test, he will not suddenly produce it in front of the judges. Skating a figure or executing a jump is not the same as running a race where a supreme and unique effort might conceivably produce an increase in speed; the predominant skill in figure skating is balance, a skill which is built up gradually and is so delicate that it cannot be forced. What does occasionally happen, however—much to the infuriation of the pro—is that a lazy but talented child, who normally skates below the passing average for the test, manages to put his mind to what he is doing and skates a figure up to the required standard. If this skater is the type who reacts well under pressure, he might just pull it off on the day, but in all fairness to the pro and the club, the skater should have demonstrated a reasonably consistent ability before being allowed to try the test. The whole situation is complicated by the fact that judging panels do differ in their degrees of lenience and severity, but the professional must base his judgment on the hypothetical behavior of an average panel judging to the average standard in that part of the country.

Apart from the considerations discussed above, if a skater is forced to take a test before he is ready and fails, he may be so nervous next time that the chances of passing are still further reduced. This is by no means always the case and obviously depends on the character of the skater, but it is something to be watched for, particularly when a child is passing through a sensitive period; there is nothing so shattering as to watch a skater, alone on a vast sheet of ice in front of a panel of judges, go to pieces through nerves. The best cure for a skater's nerves is the confidence that comes from the knowledge that he is well prepared for the test.

Because they put so much effort into the sport, most skaters really want to try for a test, but on the other hand, if they have been intelligently taught, even the quite young ones usually have a pretty shrewd idea of their own capabilities. Provided there is no undue outside pressure, skater and teacher can usually come to an amicable decision about whether the test should be tried or not. Of course it is possible that a skater who feels unsure of himself will unconsciously hold back in his practice. In this case it may be advisable to set a date in the future for which he should aim, provided it is sufficiently far ahead so that if, despite a genuine effort, he cannot make it in the allotted time, his name can be withdrawn without upsetting the organization of the test session.

The 27-Day Rule

No failed tests, whether in figures, free skating, pair, or dance, may be tried again prior to the twenty-seventh day following the date the test was failed. This rule also applies to individual dances taken as part of a whole test.

The requirements above apply specifically to amateur skaters; professionals may take tests by special arrangement with the USFSA (see the *USFSA Rulebook*).

8
How USFSA Tests
Are Judged

The Judging Panel

For all test purposes a judging panel consists of three judges appointed by the USFSA. This does not necessarily mean that you will see only three people standing on the ice, since there may be up to three trial judges also present. Trial judges are those judges who have not yet been appointed to the official list and are there to gain experience. One of the three official judges is elected Judge-in-Charge and assumes the duties of referee. Theoretically the referee may be a fourth qualified judge not engaged in judging the test, but, because of the shortage of judges, this is very rare.

In figure tests it is necessary to inspect the tracing left on the ice at the completion of each figure; the judges, therefore, stand on the ice close to the figure being skated. During dance and free skating tests the judges stand off the ice in a position where they can see all parts of the ice surface.

In order to pass a test a candidate must be passed by at least two of the three judges; this is known as majority judging. An exception to this rule is discussed below.

The Marking System

With the notable exception of the Preliminaries, all competitions and tests are marked from zero to six in each appropriate division. Six seems a strange number to choose—why not ten? Well, this choice originated in the very early days when judges applied one of six adjectives to a skater's performance, the American version of which is:

0 = not skated
1 = very poor
2 = poor
3 = mediocre
4 = good
5 = very good
6 = perfect and faultless

Judges may also express intermediate opinions by the use of decimals to one place.

The adjectives above are still quoted in official handbooks, but nowadays the marks are not always linked to the classical descriptions, and under certain circumstances and for reasons that are too obscure to go into here, judges mark within ranges (particularly in competitive skating) that are considered appropriate to the particular occasion.

At the Preliminary level, tests are marked on a straight pass or fail basis, no marks being awarded. As your child will, I hope, soon have passed out of this early stage, the principles of marking tests above the Preliminary level are given here.

Marking Figure Tests

The number of figures to be skated varies from test to test. The First Test, which is the next level above the Preliminary, contains, for example, six figures. Whatever the test level, each figure is marked out of six points. This is a composite mark which a judge arrives at by taking two major aspects into consideration; these are, to use the official terms, (1) carriage, flow, and motion, and (2) tracing. The first heading refers to the form (in the sense of *style*) in which the figure is skated, and the second, the accuracy of the marks on the ice. The rulebook requirements and definitions are too lengthy to quote here, so I shall summarize them. *Carriage* means an elegant, upright posture of the whole body and limbs. *Flow* refers to the smoothness of movement over the ice—not too fast or too slow. *Motion* relates to the movements of the body and limbs from one position to another—they must be graceful and even; to quote the rulebook, the skater must avoid "stiffness, or jerky, abrupt, flailing, or angular motions."

With regard to the *tracing,* the judges are looking for good circles, all of the same size, approximately three times the skater's height in diameter (there is some latitude here, since some short skaters like to skate a relatively large circle and vice versa); the circles must be placed symmetrically in relationship to the long and short axes of the figure; the turns must be clean and placed on the correct part of the circle. There is much more, considerably more complicated than I have made it sound here, but this is sufficient to give you the overall picture. After this myriad of considerations has been taken into account, the judge arrives mentally at a composite mark out of six—no mean feat!

In calculating the results of a test there are four sets of numbers to be borne in mind: the maximum number of points obtainable; the minimum mark allowable on any one figure; the passing total required to pass the test; and what is known as the passing average. This last mark is the passing total divided by the total number of figures in the test and serves principally as a guideline for the judges during a test.

In the First Test, since it contains six figures, the maximum points obtainable are obviously 36, the passing total is 16.2, the minimum mark allowable on any one figure is 2.2, and the passing average, 2.7. The real significance of this last mark is that after perhaps the third or fourth figure, the judge can look at his marking sheet, quickly calculate the average the candidate has so far obtained, and thus know whether the candidate up to that point is passing or failing. If the skater is running just below average, and therefore failing, the judge by this time might have it in his mind that the skater may actually be skating a reasonable test and that perhaps he, the judge, may have been a little too strict on the earlier figures (particularly if the last coffee break was several hours previous) and that he should be a little more lenient in the last figures—in order, if possible, to pass the candidate. (In spite of their sometimes rather grim appearance, judges can be quite humane.) The higher the test the more difficult it becomes, not only in the difficulty of executing the actual movements, but in the total mark required to pass. Thus, in the Eighth Figure Test, which contains no less than twelve figures giving a maximum possible total of 72 points, the passing total is 54, and for each figure the minimum mark is 4 and the passing average 4.5.

It sometimes happens that at the end of a test, without having at any one time actually incurred a below-minimum mark, the skater is found to have earned just enough below the average mark to cause a failure. Before leaving the ice, therefore, the Judge-in-Charge always asks the judges individually and privately whether they would like any figure reskated before making their decisions final. In this way a failing test that is close to passing except for one low figure may be pulled out of the fire; but only one figure can be reskated, whether it takes place during or immediately after the test. When a figure is reskated, all previous marks for that figure are canceled and the figure is judged anew by all judges.

Some years ago a test could only be passed if all three judges were unanimous in giving it passing marks. There were objections raised to this, so the principle of majority judging was adopted. Unfortunately this very wise principle is completely negated by another rule stating that if any single judge decides to award a mark below minimum to any one figure, the whole test must fail, whatever the opinion of the other two judges. This means that the majority system only holds good while no single judge marks any figure below the minimum pass level for individual figures in that particular test. In other words, there are two ways in which a figure test can fail: either two of the judging panel (or the whole panel) have each awarded a total of marks below the applicable passing mark for the whole test, or a single judge has marked one particular figure below the minimum mark specified for any one figure in the test.

As soon as a judge awards a mark below the minimum, he must immediately report the fact to the Judge-in-Charge, who must decide whether a reskate of the figure should be allowed (provided the privilege of one reskate has not already been used up), or the test stopped. In the reskate, however, the same thing may happen again if the judge feels that the figure still deserves a mark below the minimum; then the test must automatically fail and be terminated. In all fairness to the judging system, this situation does not often occur, but it is a point that should be understood by skaters and parents alike.

Stopping a Test

Nobody likes to see a test stopped, least of all the skater. Time and time again, just before a figure test, a skater will be heard to say, "Just so long as I don't get pulled" (when a test is stopped, a skater is referred to as being *pulled*). Part of this feeling stems from the fact that to be pulled is so embarrassingly public—the skater is called onto the ice and the reasons explained to him by indicating the errors in the tracings, errors of which he is probably only too well aware. Many skaters, however, particularly those who know themselves to be borderline cases, get a genuine feeling of achievement in completing the whole test, even if the final result is still a failure. If he has completed the test, he can at least go away and learn the results quietly in a corner when the test papers are handed to him. So why stop the test at all? Why not let him continue on until the bitter end and so save unnecessary embarrassment? Painful though it is, there are sound reasons why the test must be terminated in such circumstances. Not only are the majority of test sessions overcrowded, but human nature being what it is, most sessions tend to run behind schedule. This seldom worries the judges, who on the whole tend towards an unhurried method of procedure, but it does worry the test chairman, who may be pacing up and down the side of the rink, biting his nails, and wondering whether they are going to run over time and right into the following public session. If time is wasted unnecessarily, even a small hitch in the proceedings could cause some skater's test to be postponed until a later date—an unthinkable situation. It is, therefore, for the general good that a blanket procedure is followed: if a test is failing hopelessly, it must be stopped. After all, if a candidate fails the parking section of a driving test, he is not permitted to waste the examiner's time by continuing on through all the other parts of the test. It would be useless for him to say, "I've paid my money, I demand to go on!" And so it is in a skating test; the judges donate their time and are willing to stand out on a cold ice surface for many hours. To force them to continue standing there, watching a poor test that has already failed, particularly if there is a long list to follow, would be asking too much. Better to allow them their coffee break, stuff them with doughnuts, and hope that they may see the following tests through rose-colored spectacles. In all probability, skaters in such stopped tests should not have been out there in the first place (see "Is the Skater Ready?" in chapter 7).

Marking Free Skating and Pair Tests

With the exception of the preliminary tests, free skating and pair tests are very similar in structure and marking. Unlike figure tests, which may contain anything up to twelve figures, all awarded separate marks, free skating and pair tests present only one item to judge, i.e., a program to music, which receives two sets of marks, the first for technical merit and the second for composition and style. Since each of these categories is marked out of six possible points, the maximum obtainable is always twelve. Passing totals and minimum marks vary, however, from test to test. As with figure tests, majority marking is used, any one judge holding the power to fail the test by marking either heading under the minimum mark.

The Preliminary Free Skating Test consists of separate moves and is marked on a simple overall pass or fail basis, no individual marks being awarded. Although the Preliminary Pair Test consists of a complete program, it, too, is marked as a simple pass or fail.

Marking Ice Dance Tests

No dance test consists of less than three dances, but because all the dances in a test do not have to be attempted at the same test session, each dance is treated as though it were a test in itself. All compulsory dances above the Preliminary Test level are judged under the two main headings of dance rhythm and execution, each heading being marked out of six. For each dance there is a passing average and a minimum mark, which vary according to the difficulty of the test. (Note that whereas in figure tests the passing average is the average of the individual marks for each figure, in all other tests the average is that of the marks given under the two headings of technical merit, and composition and style—or in the case of compulsory dances, dance rhythm and execution.)

The Preliminary Dance Test, unlike preliminary tests in other branches, is also judged under the two categories of dance rhythm and execution. However many preliminary dances the skater elects to take at one time, each dance will be marked as a pass or fail under each of the two headings. A failure under either heading on an individual judge's card means an automatic failure of the whole dance by that judge, but if the other two judges mark the candidate as having passed under both headings, the candidate passes the dance. Note that because no marks are awarded in any preliminary test, whatever the branch, no judge can veto a test on his own by marking below a minimum mark. Above the preliminary test level, however, dance judges appear to use the veto more frequently than judges in other branches.

As opposed to compulsory dance tests, free dance tests are marked in the same way as free skating and pair tests, i.e., under the two headings of technical merit, and composition and style, each out of six. For further details of what is expected of the skaters under these two headings, the *USFSA Rulebook* should be consulted.

USFSA Judges and Their Qualifications

Contrary to the situation existing in many other sports, judges of the official USFSA tests must be amateurs. (This does not apply to the USFSA Basic Test Program, which may be judged by professionals, often the instructor himself.) In this book the words *amateur* and *professional* are used in their strict senses: A professional is paid for his performance or service, while an amateur is not. In the skating world these two terms have no reference to relative skills.

The Training of a Judge

Judges of the official test structure are appointed by the USFSA, who take great care to ensure that any judge they elect is capable mentally, physically, and temperamentally of doing a good job. No judge may be appointed to the official list until he is eighteen years of age and has served an apprenticeship as a trial judge. During a test a trial judge accompanies the official judges and marks the test as though he were a member of the panel, but his marks do not influence the outcome of the test nor is he permitted to consult with the official judges. His marks are inspected over a long period to measure the degree of agreement with those of the official panels judging the same tests. There may, of course, be divergencies among the panel itself—there often are—but the idea is not only to see whether the judge knows the qualities of a good skater, but to ascertain whether he knows the standard required at that particular test level. There are other requirements, such as attending USFSA-sponsored judging schools and the possession of a temperament suitable for dealing with people. When all these demands have been met, a trial judge may be appointed to the official list, but even then only to the lower levels, however good a skater he may have been during his active career. Even a world champion has to start judging at the bottom.

Categories of Judges

The categories into which judges are divided are numerous, and the regulations governing judges' appointments and functions highly complex. Basically judges fall into the two main categories of (1) those qualified to judge figures, free skating, and pair, and (2) those qualified to judge dance. These groups are further subdivided into the levels at which they may judge, the four levels of the first group being Low Test, Intermediate Test, High Test, and Gold Test. Dance judges are divided into the three levels of Bronze, Silver, and Gold Test. It is very common for judges to hold simultaneous appointments in both main categories, though not necessarily at the same level. For example, a judge might at the same time be a Gold Test Dance judge and a Low Test Figure and Pair judge. Because the free skating has only recently been separated from the figures, judges of figures, free skating, and pair are still officially known simply as Figure and Pair judges, a combination term.

In principle a judge may only officiate at tests which are appropriate to his category (under certain circumstances he may judge one degree above his category provided he is in the minority on the panel); but he may, of course, judge in a lower category. Thus, you may very occasionally find a Gold Test judge on the panel of a Preliminary Test. Should this happen when your own child takes a test, do not be unduly concerned; owing to his vast experience, a Gold Test judge often shows considerably greater leniency at the lower levels than a recently appointed Low Test judge anxious to prove himself.

Test judges may further qualify themselves to be appointed to the ranks of competition judges. This requires a similar system of trial judging during actual competitions. The levels for Figure and Pair judges are Novice, Junior, Senior, and National; and for Dance judges, Bronze, Silver, Gold, and National. The USFSA may also submit names of judges to the ISU for appointment to the ranks of International and World judges.

9
Hints on
Taking Tests

Because a figure test is more complicated and normally lasts longer than any other type of test, and the skater is therefore longest under the scrutiny of the judges, this type of test is dealt with here in considerable detail, but the general principles apply to all test and competitive skating.

The Day of the Test

On the day of the test, or perhaps even a few days before, it is usual for the Test Chairman to post a time schedule on the bulletin board. This schedule gives the time of the candidate's test, and in the case of a figure test, may designate the section of warm-up ice to be used. But do not rely too heavily on the times given, as a vast number of variables and unforeseeable circumstances can make precise scheduling difficult. It is better to be on the spot too early than too late and thus avoid adding to the normal state of panic that goes with taking a test. It is also very important to bear in mind that official USFSA tests are much more formal affairs than beginners' tests in group lesson programs. Failure to arrive, or late arrival, for an official test, except for the most pressing of reasons, is almost unheard of. Remember, too, that there is a test fee to be paid, usually to the Test Chairman on the day of the test; and just in case of emergencies the skater should have his USFSA registration number available. On arrival, the candidate should report to the test chairman, who will tell the candidate shortly before the test is due to start when to go onto the ice for the warm-up.

69

Creating a Good Impression

A skater needs everything going for him in a test. Although a good impression may not actually get the candidate more marks, a bad impression may subconsciously prejudice a judge against a skater to a degree that he may start looking for trouble. For a figure test a girl can use her normal skating dress, provided it is neat and tidy; tights should be without holes, boots freshly cleaned, white laces washed and neatly tucked inside the top of the boot. A boy can use a jumpsuit, or slacks and sweater. The principle to bear in mind is that the skater must show respect for what he is doing. It is the height of folly to arrive for any test wearing ragged jeans and chewing gum. No one nowadays questions a person's right to act in this way, but there is a time and place for everything, and a test session is not one of them.

Good posture also adds its weight towards creating a good impression. It is too often forgotten that a judge is required to mark not only the tracing but also carriage, motion, and flow, as explained in the section on marking figure tests. Carriage is really nothing more than good posture. It is extraordinary that the skating of figures is the only branch of the sport in which skaters think they can get away with the most hideous positions —typically the hunched-up crouch, in which the skater appears to be trying to give the impression of great concentration by getting his nose as close to his skating toe as possible. This is not the place to go into technicalities, but it is sufficient to say that the placement of one tracing on top of another can be carried out effectively without too great a sacrifice of elegance.

Skating a Figure

For the purpose of this description, let us assume that the candidate is required to skate a forward outside eight. The Judge-in-Charge will call the skater from the warm-up patch and, as this will be the first figure of the test, introduce him to the rest of the panel. The skater will then be told the approximate section of the ice to be used. Within certain limits, however, the skater is permitted to choose the actual spot where he wishes to start the figure, i.e., his "center." Natural markings on the ice may legitimately be used as a center, and a skater may sometimes get away with using a painted hockey line as his long axis—it all depends upon the

Judge-in-Charge. The best thing is for the skater to decide for himself where he wants to start and leave it up to the Judge-in-Charge to signal another spot if he objects. There is rarely, if ever, any objection to a candidate skating *toward* a hockey line if he thinks this will help him line up the sides of his figure.

Having decided upon his starting point, the skater should then stand still for a moment and think (or at least give the appearance of thinking). During this period he should plan the figure in his mind. Too often candidates, in a flurry of nerves, rush up to a spot on the ice and start the figure before the judges have even had time to look up from their test sheets. However great an effort may be required, an impression of unhurried poise and confidence should be created. Having thought, the skater should then raise his arms to shoulder level to indicate the long axis of the figure, thus letting the judges know whether they are standing in the right position and are in no danger of being knocked flat on their backs by a flustered skater starting off in a totally unexpected direction. Having completed the figure, the candidate will then be reminded by the Judge-in-Charge of the next figure, and will retire to the warm-up patch while his completed figure is inspected. On his way, however, he should skate to the barrier (remembering never to skate through or over a figure once completed) and, if he can bring himself to do so, take a critical look at his figure to see whether it is symmetrically laid out, and whether the layout can assist him in executing the next figure, which will probably be laid out on the same long axis but with the center moved up a few feet.

Because of the difficulty many young, light children have in seeing their tracings on the ice and the consequent problem of coming back again to the point where they started, the USFSA now permits skaters taking a Preliminary Test to mark the center of their figure with the heel of the blade. The skater may make only one mark, which should be about four inches in length and placed along the short (cross) axis of the figure.

Alternation

When two or three figure tests are to be judged by the same panel, the skaters will sometimes be alternated, that is, two or three skaters will warm up simultaneously and skate the individual figures in rotation, rather than one skater at a time going through the whole test. This system has the advantage of saving time and giving the skaters a longer warm-up period between figures. Although the USFSA discourages the method, it is not illegal. Alternation is seldom attempted with more than three skaters and works best with the lower tests. To be alternated, tests do not necessarily have to be of the same level; for example, a Third, a Fourth, and a Fifth could be alternated. The final decision as to whether tests may be alternated rests with the Judge-in-Charge, but if two or three skaters who wish to alternate get together, they can make their request to the Test Chairman for consideration by the judging panel. Judges vary widely in their attitude towards alternation—some will not have it at any price, while others prefer it, or are indifferent. It has been our experience that the skaters themselves generally prefer alternation; parents, on the other hand, are usually antagonistic towards it as they seem to feel that comparison is made by the judges between one child and another. My wife and I feel that it makes little difference either way and that if the skaters themselves want alternation, every effort should be made to accommodate them. On the other hand, if the judging panel is really set against it, it would be unwise to make a fuss.

Coaching During a Test

Coaching from the barrier during tests is now permitted, provided it is carried out discreetly and only while the skater is warming up. If the skater is fortunate enough to have his instructor present, he should look up periodically in his direction in case there is some necessary advice to be given. During a figure test absolute silence reigns on the ice surface, and it is maddening for a coach to be unable to attract the attention of his student on the warm-up patch without having to resort to hoarse stage whispers, thereby incurring disapproving looks from the judging panel.

Although he usually tries to do so, an instructor cannot always be present during a pupil's test; but even if he is in the rink, it can sometimes happen that two tests are going on simultaneously on two different parts of the ice surface, in which case he tries to give his help where it is most needed. At this stage, however, help is mostly psychological, and skaters differ vastly in their reaction to coaching during a test. In the case of a skater suffering from a bad attack of nerves it often happens that interference or attempts to remedy matters by the coach just makes things worse or, at best, has not the slightest effect; so parents should not be upset by the fact that a coach sometimes stays well away from his pupil while a test is being taken. After all, the skater must learn to be self-reliant, and it is remarkable how many children will not allow their parents anywhere near the building during their tests. In such cases, the skater's wishes should be respected. It also frequently happens that a skater will draw down a mental curtain between himself and a coach trying to give him advice. His pupil looks at him politely, nods understandingly, and then returns to his warm-up patch where, to the exasperation of the coach, he continues to commit the same error as though no word had passed between them. This particularly applies to speed over the ice. Once a skater starts a figure test below his normal speed, even though he may be skating so slowly as to barely make it back to the center, and all the onlookers are clutching each other in apprehension as though watching an unsteady tightrope walker crossing Niagara Falls, a coach can rarely induce him to go faster in subsequent figures, even if the very success of the test is at stake. The reverse can also happen: a skater can start the first figure too fast and be unable to slow down in later figures; but this does less harm—he will at least complete the figure on one foot, although his tracings may become a little rough.

The fact must not be overlooked that coaches themselves tend to get nervous during tests and competitions, and if they are aware of the effect their condition may have on others, they may be wise to restrict their coaching during such periods of tension to absolute emergencies. During the figure section of a recent world championship a world-famous trainer said to me, "As soon as my pupil starts her warm-up, I leave her strictly alone." But there he was half an hour later hanging over the barrier bombarding her with incessant advice which, being a strong-minded, tolerant, and well-bred girl, she accepted gracefully, even though she was obviously finding it highly distracting. She did excellently in the final placements, but I doubt whether she learned much in that last half-hour except, perhaps, to keep her temper.

Taking Free Skating, Pair, and Dance Tests

Everything that has been said regarding making a good impression in a figure test applies equally to free skating, pair, and dance tests. For the boy, proper attire is a sweater and slacks, or a jumpsuit; for the girl, the dress can be a little more ornate than for a figure test. In the case of a pair or dance couple who regularly skate together, costumes which match in color and design can be very effective, but it is important in the case of the boy's costume that it have no trimmings that might catch in his partner's costume when he brings her down from certain lifts. The girl should have practiced in her dress well before the event, so that if any restrictions to movement are discovered, there is time to put them right—there is nothing more devastating to the morale of a girl than to find something wrong with her dress just after she has stepped onto the ice for a test. Nor should any girl skate with a hairdo with which she is unfamiliar, and certainly never with a style that allows her hair to flop over her eyes in the middle of a jump or as she takes her final pose at the end of her program. Bobby pins should be firmly secured, not just for the skater's own sake, but out of consideration for others using the ice. A bobby pin will stop a skate dead, and my wife and I have suffered many falls in ice shows through the carelessness of previous skaters. In fact, on one occasion I fell over the same bobby pin twice when skating in an ice show on a full-size surface, despite the apparently enormous odds against such an occurrence. The danger can be more readily understood when it is realized that skaters tend to make similar patterns over the ice. The very thought that there might be a stray bobby pin on the ice, however large the surface, can be very distracting to a skater.

Most skaters find it beneficial to have skated earlier in the day, even if only for a few minutes. It is not just a question of exercising the muscles: The second time on the ice the skater always seems to have just that little extra balance and security compared with the first time. Before the warm-up on the ice, the skater should limber up with some off-ice exercises. During the warm-up for free skating tests, he should start by simple stroking round the ice, followed by a few simple jumps and spins, perhaps a highlight or two, but it is important not to overdo it (see also chapter 18, "Hints for Competitors"). Above all, if the skater has to wait for another test to go through after his warm-up, he should keep gently moving—he should never sit down.

Basically all the above applies equally to pairs, except that in this case there will also be some stroking together in hold and possibly a lift or two. Dancers usually warm up by stroking round the ice and then running through the dance they are about to take, both with and without a partner. In dance tests there is usually a separate warm-up before each dance.

In the higher dance tests, if the Music Chairman has several records suitable for the same dance, skaters are often given a choice of music. If there are a lot of skaters taking the same dances, particularly at the lower test levels, no choice is normally given, so the skater should have accustomed himself to various melodies (it is remarkable how a change of melody, even when the rhythm and tempo remain the same, tends to confuse many young skaters).

Learning the Result

At the completion of a test the skater should stay for a few minutes in the vicinity of the ice surface without removing his skates, just in case he is required to repeat a figure, or try a dance again with another partner. As soon as the judges are seen either to be coming off the ice or about to continue with the next candidate, the skater may take his skates off and await the result. This is a very trying and nerve-racking period for skaters, parents, and coaches alike.

Clubs differ widely in their methods of conveying the results to candidates. The best method is undoubtedly that in which the Test Chairman collects the candidate's test sheets from the Judge-in-Charge the moment the test is completed, checks the individual sheets for accuracy in arithmetic and whether the result stated (pass or fail) is in accordance with the marks given, and then without further delay hands the three sheets to the waiting candidate who, while all her friends look anxiously over her shoulder, will shuffle the papers around, frantically looking for at least two passes. If these are found, there is a wild scream of joy from the whole group, and the candidate frequently bursts into tears of relief. A trainer rarely has to ask whether a candidate has passed or failed, he just listens.

During dance tests it is not always possible to collect sheets after every dance; not only do judges barely have time to get their marks and comments down before a new couple is in front of them, but some candidates may be taking only one dance while others may be taking two or three. Under these circumstances collecting test sheets before all the dances are finished could cause confusion.

Because of the tension under which young skaters remain until the results of their tests are known, it would seem that (with the possible exception of dance tests) it is cruel and unnecessary to make them wait until all tests are over—which could take several hours—before announcing the results. Quite apart from other considerations, parents are usually present and would like to get home, while the skater, who may have eaten lightly in preparation for the test, is probably ravenously hungry. To make a skater wait unnecessarily, not only for the result, but also for lunch or dinner, is really very inconsiderate.

Attitude Toward the Result

Dealing with success is no great problem, but failure is another matter. Newcomers to the sport, skaters and parents alike, are often surprised at the incidence of failure in tests, particularly in those above the preliminary level. It is, for instance, not uncommon during a mass test session held at the end of a summer skating school for only one candidate out of twenty to pass. There may even be a complete wipeout; this is by no means a regular occurrence, but it can happen. This is undoubtedly caused by skaters having a go, ready or not. Test sessions held during the winter season usually have a higher rate of passes because skaters can be induced to wait until they are better prepared; but even so, the rate rarely reaches 100 percent. The causes are not far to seek: Skating is a sport requiring, in addition to other skills, so refined a balance that performance, particularly when nerves become a factor, tends to be irregular, and perfection rare. In fact, I doubt whether any experienced skater would ever claim to have seen a perfect figure, and a faultless freestyle program or ice dance is distinctly uncommon. Even the most knowledgeable trainer finds it almost impossible to say with absolute confidence that a specific test will pass—a failure is much easier to predict. Judging is difficult, highly complex, and subjective; it is common for one judge to attach a greater or lesser degree of importance to one particular type of error than does his colleague on the same panel. For example, Judge A may place particular weight on the size and shape of circles, Judge B may have a "thing" about neatness of centers, while Judge C may lay particular stress on cleanness of turns. It can easily be seen that a skater facing this type of panel, unless he is good in all three areas, is going to have an uphill struggle to pass. On the other hand, another skater may chance to be in front of a panel of judges all of whom lay most weight on, let us say, clean turns and are more tolerant of other types of fault. If the skater's best point happens to be his turns, but he is rather weak on centers and circles, he definitely has a better chance of passing than if he is skating in front of the first type of panel. The answer is, of course, that skater and trainer must attend to *all* details; but the human factor still remains—on both the judges' part and the skater's. In all this we must be fair: a judging panel exists for the very reason that opinions differ. In any test there inevitably exists, both above and below the passing level, a gray area representing personal opinion.

All this may sound rather negative, but it is not. It simply means that a skater must consider himself fortunate if he passes a test at the first try; even the best of skaters almost invariably fail some tests on the way to the Gold. The encouraging thing is that, provided a skater is genuinely up to the standard required, he will eventually pass—provided he keeps at it— and in the end will be a better skater for his several tries. During a skater's career he fails some tests he should have passed and passes some tests he should have failed; but it all seems to balance out, and eventually he gets as far as he is capable of getting in just about the same time as anybody else with the same talent and opportunities.

The Problem of Nerves

To go up to a skater and say, "Now you mustn't be nervous," is probably one of the most useless and fatuous pieces of advice in the English language. Nerves are undoubtedly a big problem, and I am no stranger to them myself. In fact, when I announced many years ago to my family that I was proposing to enter the competitive field and then go into show work, I gave them the biggest laugh in years. However, an experienced performer told me, "Don't worry about it, after you've done it a few times, it's just like going out to lunch." And so it was. After a shaky start in front of a crowd of about eight thousand semi-savage hockey fans during which I managed to lower my partner gracefully down from a lift onto my own foot—a fact of which neither of us was fully aware until the following step —I can safely say that my nerves decreased with every succeeding performance. The secret is (*a*) to be fully prepared and thoroughly competent in whatever one proposes to do, and (*b*) to have had as much exposure as possible to judges and the skating public. Unofficial rink and club tests as well as local competitions can be of enormous help.

Beware of the skater who shows undue confidence before stepping onto the ice—this could be a good sign, but unless it is the confidence of an experienced performer, it could augur trouble. Some years ago a pupil of mine was waiting to step onto the ice in her first big competition. She was remarkably calm and watched with complete equanimity as the skater before her completed her final spin. While my pupil's name was being announced, we were still discussing casually whether she should have a go at her double Axel. Then, giving me a bright smile, she stepped onto the ice, and went completely to pieces—she couldn't even remember her program. When she was asked what went wrong, all she could say was, "As soon as I got out there, it just hit me—all those people!" Most skaters who make infrequent appearances in front of the public seem to do best when they get their bout of nerves over the day before. So be prepared for some temperament long before it seems to be necessary—it may be a good sign.

The best condition immediately prior to a test or exhibition seems to be one of mild, but controlled, nervous tension; but it would be difficult for anyone except a highly trained adept to put himself consciously into such a specific mental state. A show skater performing two shows a day month after month tends to go through the motions, smiling at the audience, performing excellently, but usually thinking of what he is going to have for dinner after the show, or about a clause in his next contract. But if, just before he goes on, he is told that there is an agent in the audience, or skaters from another show, the adrenaline immediately starts flowing, and he is keyed up to give just that little extra something that makes his performance perfect.

The conclusion is that while some skaters have a natural inborn confidence, most have to develop it through good preparation and exposure to similar situations. I have never used, or counseled anyone to use, sedatives—that must remain a matter between the skater and the family medical adviser. The list of drugs banned by the athletic authorities is so great that almost anything a skater might take just prior to a competition, except perhaps a lightly boiled egg, would seem to be illegal.

10

The Organization
of Practice Sessions

Allocation of Ice Time

Now that you have seen something of what goes into ice skating, it will be obvious that even in the largest arenas figures, free skating, pair, and ice dancing cannot be practiced successfully all at the same time. The skating of figures requires clean ice with no marks on it other than those made by one particular skater, who must, therefore, be allocated a section of ice for his own exclusive use. Although sometimes practiced simultaneously, ice dancing does not mix well with freestyle because ice dances have to be laid out in strictly followed patterns over the ice surface, which makes it difficult for dancers to avoid free skaters practicing jumps or for jumpers to avoid dance couples. Pair skating does not mix well either with free skating or ice dancing since it is almost impossible for a pair to take evasive action once started on a move such as a death spiral or a high lift, quite apart from the fact that the man's vision is often hampered during the lift itself.

In order to accommodate all these different types of figure skating, clubs usually divide their ice time into the following sessions: patch (figures only), freestyle, ice dancing, and occasionally pair skating if there are sufficient pairs to warrant a separate session; but when it is only a question of one or two low-level pairs, they usually practice during the freestyle sessions. Patch and freestyle sessions commonly last one hour, although the patch session, if it follows the freestyle or will be followed by another patch, may be reduced to fifty minutes to allow for resurfacing.

While most patch and freestyle sessions are geared to practicing for tests and competitions, this is not always the case with dance sessions. Ice dancing frequently has a strong lean towards social skating, particularly when a club has a large adult membership who wish to skate for the fun of it and to whom test and competitive skating is secondary. In such cases dance sessions are almost invariably held in the evening and may last up to a couple of hours or more.

Because of the difference in the average age of members between one club and another, and the consequent difference in goals of the individual skaters, clubs tend to lean either towards figures and freestyle on the one hand or towards ice dancing on the other; this tendency may be reflected in the amount of ice time allotted to the different fields. In passing it should be noted that despite the recent complete separation of figure and freestyle tests, figures and freestyle are still grouped together for competitive skating; for some time to come, therefore, figure and freestyle sessions will continue to be offered hand-in-hand. In clubs where ice dancing is the more popular, figure and freestyle skaters may have to augment their practice time at other clubs or at specialized sessions run by the rink outside club hours. In certain clubs, particularly in the rare few that own their own rink and have a highly competitive element, such as the Skating Club of Wilmington, competitive pair skating and ice dancing are often practiced in the early hours of the morning in order to get more space than would be available in the regular freestyle or social dance sessions.

The Patch Session

A patch session is a period—usually an hour or fifty minutes—set aside specifically for the practice of figures. The ice surface is divided into individual sections, each section being known as a *patch;* but the word is also used to denote the idea of the figure session as a whole or may even be used as a verb; for example, a skater might ask, "Which patch do I have?" or "What time's patch tomorrow?" or "Did you patch this morning?"

Size of Patches

The commonest method of apportioning the ice in a regulation-size rink (minimum dimensions, 185 by 85 feet) is first to divide the rink across its

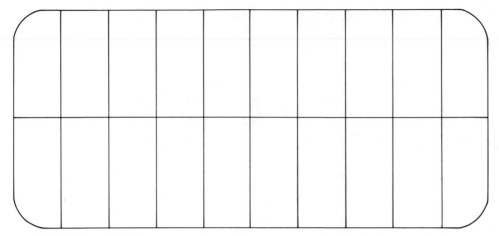

Fig. 5. Division of rink into ten strips, giving twenty patches. The lines are imaginary. Marks on the barrier indicate patch locations. (See also figure 10.)

surface into ten sections of equal width, each section being known as a strip, the boundaries of which are indicated by small marks on both barriers. An imaginary line down the middle of the length of the rink subdivides these strips into twenty patches, one per skater (figure 5). The patches at the top and bottom of the rink are known as the *end patches,* which, because of the curvature of the barrier at the corners, are somewhat smaller than the others. The resurfacing machine—usually referred to as the Zamboni, from the name of the company that manufactures it—makes its turns at the ends of the rink, with the result that the end patches take longer to freeze and tend to be more uneven than the rest of the ice surface; figure skaters, therefore, dislike being put on an end patch. To compensate for this, and in order to give the skaters a little more room, many rinks use each end strip as a single patch, in which case the patch session provides eighteen patches instead of twenty (figure 6). When ten strips are used on a rink measuring 185 by 85 feet, the dimensions of each patch will be 18½ by 42½ feet (except that the end patches will have the corners rounded). This size will comfortably accommodate the width of the average skater's figure, the circles of which, if you remember, are approximately three times the skater's height in diameter. The length of the patch will nearly, but not quite, allow the skater to fit in the length of an average three-circle figure; the answer to this problem is the custom of overlapping (see "Conduct and Etiquette During Patch Sessions" below). Some rinks of 185 by 85 feet try to squeeze twelve strips out of

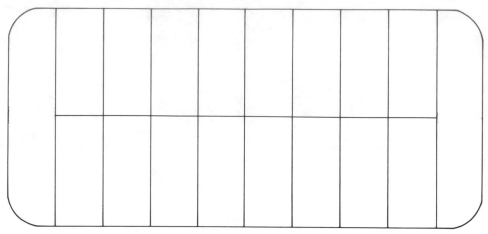

Fig. 6. Division of rink into eighteen patches, each end strip used as one patch to compensate for rounded corners and possibly uneven ice.

their ice surface, but as this works out to a little under 15½ feet in width for each patch, skaters are crowded up against each other, causing them to skate ovals or sub-size circles, much to the detriment of their figure skating. It is difficult to overemphasize the waste of time and therefore money caused by patches that are too narrow. Fortunately, the majority of rinks built in recent years are 200 by 85 feet, out of which eleven strips just over 18 feet in width can comfortably be made, thus providing twenty-two patches (or twenty if the end strips are used as single patches). An

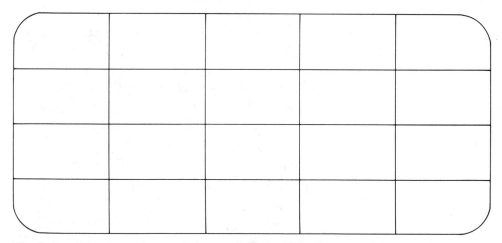

Fig. 7. Possible alternative patch layout, but disadvantages outweigh advantages. Not recommended.

interesting method we saw used some years ago was to divide the rink down its entire length into five sections and then into four sections across its width (figure 7). This gave longer but slightly narrower patches (17 by 46¼ feet). For a time we favored this method but eventually realized that the disadvantages of a narrow patch outweighed the advantages of a longer one because overlapping occurred in either case, so we returned to the conventional system.

Frequency of Patch Sessions

Most clubs and rinks that encourage figure skating hold their patch sessions at regular intervals during the week throughout the season. During the winter, club and rink schedules differ so greatly that it is difficult to give a typical example of when and how many patches might be held during the week. A common practice is to hold patch sessions in the early morning (6 A.M. or even earlier), midday, and early evening, some during club time and some during rink time between hockey matches, public sessions, and group lessons. In those rinks where it is possible to set up a fairly firm schedule for the whole winter season (figure skating programs in multi-purpose arenas are frequently interrupted by hockey games, ice shows, basketball, or other events), patch sessions are usually set up for several weeks or months ahead. If held outside club time, such patches are usually paid for in advance in a series of perhaps six or ten weeks, or even for the whole season.

Assignment of Patches

The problem now arises as to how the ice shall be apportioned among the skaters in as fair a manner as possible. Many years ago in the British rinks (and it was probably the same in the U.S.) there were no specific patch sessions and relatively few private clubs; figures were normally practiced down the center of the rink during the first half hour of public sessions, the public very unselfishly skating round the sides of the rink until the figure period was over. There was no official assignment of patches (or "centers" as they were then called) and the method of obtaining a section of practice ice was crude in the extreme. The serious figure skaters stood at the open entrances to the ice surface—most having already been in line for thirty minutes or more—waiting for the music to begin. At the first

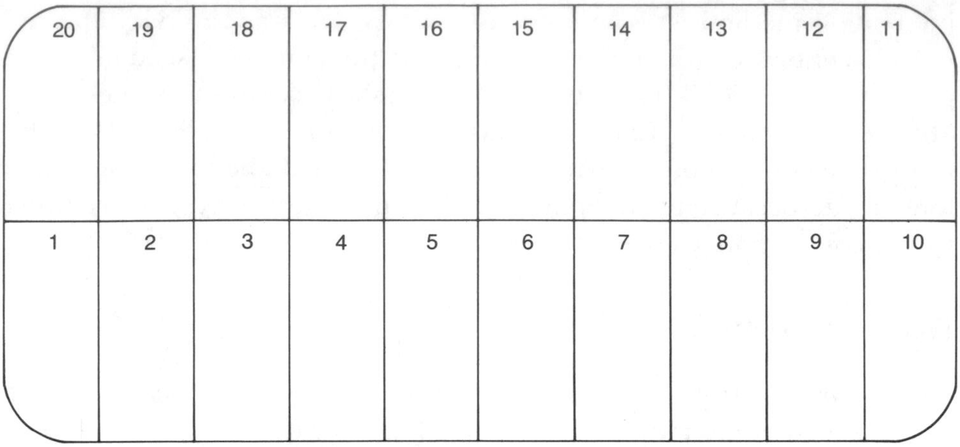

20	19	18	17	16	15	14	13	12	11
1	2	3	4	5	6	7	8	9	10

Fig. 8. Recommended method of numbering patches; easy to remember.

note, something akin to a land rush took place, which at times led to some rather unladylike, or ungentlemanlylike, jostling until territorial rights were established. All that has now changed for the better, but there still remains the problem of the fair allocation of patches. The following remarks are intended for the guidance of clubs and rinks that have not yet decided on a system, and for you as a parent who may one day be roped in to handle this chore.

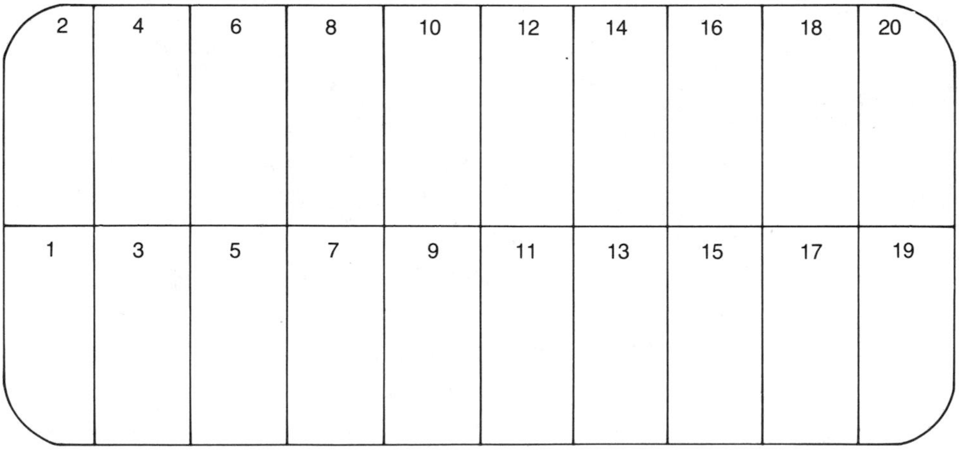

2	4	6	8	10	12	14	16	18	20
1	3	5	7	9	11	13	15	17	19

Fig. 9. A common method of numbering patches, odd numbers on one side, even on the other. Has disadvantages—see text.

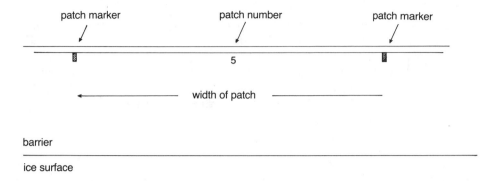

Fig. 10. Method of marking barrier. Number should be legible across the width of the rink.

The first thing to do is to give each patch a number, which, the rink permitting, should be painted on the barrier in line with the middle of the patch concerned. Figures 8 and 9 show two methods of numbering the patches, and figure 10 displays the best method of marking the barrier. Now, taking into consideration the fact that varying ice conditions and lighting make some patches more desirable than others, how are they to be assigned so as to create the least dissatisfaction? Some common methods are as follows:

1. The first come, first served method. Quite good, but has the disadvantage of favoring those skaters who have the most time at their disposal, and needs strict supervision. Can be used occasionally with other methods to discourage tardiness when discipline is slack (see below).
2. Names in a hat method. Time-consuming and needs someone in authority to supervise the draw before every patch session. Also causes dissatisfaction when a skater is consistently unlucky.
3. Assignment of skater to one specific patch for the whole series. Very easy for the organizer, but not really satisfactory as no skater should be permanently condemned to the end patch, and skaters should get used to skating their figures in any part of the rink.
4. Rotation of patches by the dial method. The outer fixed dial has slots for the names of the skaters, while the inner, movable dial has the patch numbers. All right in theory, but the dials are not easy to construct well and are liable to jogging, thus altering the patch distribution. In one rink using this system there was so much judicious jogging that the dial had to be kept in a locked, glass-fronted case, which meant that a responsible

member of the club always had to be on hand to supervise the moving of the dial.

5. Diagram method. Not a method of patch allocation, but a means, usually combined with some rotational system, of showing a skater quickly and clearly the location of his patch. It is simply a diagram of the rink divided into the numbered patches with the skater's name written on his patch space: a separate diagram is required for every patch session. Highly laborious, and in a busy program really needs an office staff with plenty of time on their hands.

6. The rotational chart system. Highly recommended. A detailed description and discussion follows.

Some years ago, during a summer school we were organizing, my wife suddenly rebelled at writing out every day 160 names, distributed over eight patch sheets. In sheer desperation she devised what we now call the rotational chart system. Like many great ideas it is fairly obvious once explained, but at the time we had never seen it used anywhere in the U.S. or Europe. It may seem a little complicated as described here, but it is well worth the trouble and becomes clearer when you actually do it. It brings about the best method of rotation and above all takes care of such complaints as, "I always get the end patch," or "Why does so-and-so always get the best patches?" If you have been put in charge of the job, just take the skater to the chart—he will find its logic and fairness unanswerable. The chart can be set up to cover any period desired—for the purpose of what follows, let us say twelve weeks.

The principle is that, starting from a specific patch, the skater moves steadily round the rink, in a clockwise or counterclockwise direction. The progression is quite automatic and completely fair. Because most clubs hold more than one patch session per week, each usually composed of a totally different mix of skaters, every session must have its own separate chart for the initial week of the twelve-week period. This involves some work, but once it is done, there is little further to do.

The construction of the chart is easiest and works most efficiently if the rink is numbered as in figure 8. Using this method of numbering, figure 11 shows a twelve-week patch chart made out for one particular patch session of the week for a rink divided into twenty patches, all occupied. The skaters' names are listed down one side of the chart and the dates along the top. The numbers within the squares are the patch numbers. Starting with 1, the numbers of the patches for the first Wednesday are written in order down the column, ending, of course, with 20. The second Wednesday starts with the number 2 at the head of the column and finishes with 1, while the third Wednesday starts with the number 3 and finishes with 2, and so on. The skater simply finds his name on the list, looks horizontally across the chart and finds his patch number under the appropriate date. Two weeks in succession the skater gets an end patch, but this is very difficult to avoid if the test chairman is to keep his sanity. If the end strip is used as one patch (giving eighteen patches instead of twenty), this problem does not occur.

If the rink uses a different method of numbering that for some reason cannot be changed, the test chairman must adjust his sequence of patch numbers on the chart so that the uninterrupted progression around the rink is preserved. If, for example, the patches are numbered as in figure 9, then the sequence of numbers in the vertical column becomes 1, 3, 5, 7, 9, 11, 13, 15, 17, 19, 20, 18, 16, 14, 12, 10, 8, 6, 4, 2, then back to 1 again—a difficult sequence to remember when making out the chart and thus subject to error, quite apart from confusing the skaters. You can see what would happen if the sequence of numbers on the chart were to remain 1, 2, 3, and so on: not only would the skater be unable to remember his sequence (which causes a lot of milling round the bulletin board) but, having arrived at 19, he would get four end patches in a row as he jumped from one end of the rink to the other. There is no doubt that the patch numbering system as shown in figure 8, combined with the chart numbering in figure 11, is the simplest and least confusing for all concerned. Note that the system works equally well even when all the patches are not fully occupied. Whatever the system used it helps to put up a plan of the rink showing the numbering system in use and which end of the rink is which, e.g., "Cafeteria End," "North End," "South End," "Music Box."

Obviously this system cannot be used if it is the club's policy to give the choicest patches to skaters working on the higher tests; but we have never felt that this is a fair method, particularly if the patches are being paid for separately from the club dues.

When the end of the twelve-week period—or whatever other period is decided upon—is reached, the next chart starts where the previous one left off. Williams, for example (see figure 11), would start the new period on patch 13 and the remainder of the chart would be adjusted on this basis.

In a heavy training program such as a summer school where a skater is taking several patches a day, it is important to see that his name is spaced

Patch Chart, January 5 through March 23, Wednesday, 6:00 A.M.

	January				February				March			
	5	12	19	26	2	9	16	23	2	9	16	23
Williams	1	2	3	4	5	6	7	8	9	10	11	12
King	2	3	4	5	6	7	8	9	10	11	12	13
Rinehart	3	4	5	6	7	8	9	10	11	12	13	14
Ward	4	5	6	7	8	9	10	11	12	13	14	15
Johnson	5	6	7	8	9	10	11	12	13	14	15	16
Rockford	6	7	8	9	10	11	12	13	14	15	16	17
Grossman	7	8	9	10	11	12	13	14	15	16	17	18
McNulty	8	9	10	11	12	13	14	15	16	17	18	19
Draisey	9	10	11	12	13	14	15	16	17	18	19	20
Fitzpatrick	10	11	12	13	14	15	16	17	18	19	20	1
Pratt	11	12	13	14	15	16	17	18	19	20	1	2
Shackelford	12	13	14	15	16	17	18	19	20	1	2	3
Henderson	13	14	15	16	17	18	19	20	1	2	3	4
Logan	14	15	16	17	18	19	20	1	2	3	4	5
Sims	15	16	17	18	19	20	1	2	3	4	5	6
Lorentzen	16	17	18	19	20	1	2	3	4	5	6	7
Hammer	17	18	19	20	1	2	3	4	5	6	7	8
Burke	18	19	20	1	2	3	4	5	6	7	8	9
Chapman	19	20	1	2	3	4	5	6	7	8	9	10
Brewster	20	1	2	3	4	5	6	7	8	9	10	11

Fig. 11. Sample patch chart for a single weekly session throughout a twelve-week period.

on the various patch lists so that he does not get more than two end patches at the most on any given day.

Now, do you have all that? Is it clear? No, I thought not. Quite frankly, there is nothing more calculated to produce periodic bouts of hysteria than to be put in charge of patches in a busy rink or club. Nevertheless, if by constant practice you master the art of the patch list, you will become a valued member of society and much sought after. But wait, the skaters are barely on the ice yet—there is a lot more to come.

Owing to sickness or other causes it often happens that even in busy rinks or clubs there are patches vacant. If a senior professional is present on the ice, it is usually left to him to make on-the-spot changes if they would benefit any of the skaters present. Empty patches can be used to advantage to remove a skater from a patch where the ice is particularly bad, to separate two high-test skaters working on three-circle figures, or for the use of pros who need some more clean ice for lessons. This must be done as fairly as possible, taking into consideration the fact that the pro in charge may be required to make a snap decision while in the middle of a lesson that is taking all his concentration. To avoid this it is essential that strict punctuality be observed, as a beneficial rearrangement of patches can often be made in the few moments just before the patch starts.

Most rinks where the patches are paid for are very tolerant of the use of empty patches. Occasionally rinks will permit the purchase of strips in order to guarantee the skater the use of two patches end on end (particularly useful when the skater is working on advanced three-circle figures); but if the demand for patches exceeds the supply, this is hardly a fair arrangement and should not really be necessary if skaters are unselfish in their use of overlapping.

Discipline

It cannot be repeated too often or too emphatically that discipline is the key not only to getting ahead of the competition but to providing you as a parent with the greatest return on your money. Skaters using training sessions are almost invariably dedicated to the goal of passing tests or practicing for competitions—they are there to achieve. Admittedly the degree of dedication varies, but this does not alter the fact that no skater should attend these sessions who only wishes to horse around and waste time. If you are fortunate enough to patronize a rink in which all the trainers preserve harmonious relationships and have a common desire to see the local students progress, it is very probable that harmony will exist between individual skaters and that discipline will be good.

Unfortunately there always seem to be a few skaters who neither take well to discipline nor possess a harmonious temperament. The very size of the ice surface makes discipline more difficult to maintain than in the relatively confined space of the ballet studio and is made even more so by the fact that at this level instruction is normally conducted privately rather than in a class. The instructors cannot, therefore, be expected to constantly oversee the conduct of all students using the ice. It has thus been necessary to set down rules of conduct and points of etiquette for the different types of practice sessions. Although many skaters find these rules irksome (particularly those relating to patch), they are the result of long experience of trainers both in this country and overseas. Most intelligent skaters, however, come to accept the logic of these rules, particularly when administered by an authoritative figure who commands respect, realizing that in the long run they get more out of their practice time this way. Parents who first come up against these rules are sometimes surprised at their stringency, but when they have experienced the total anarchy that can prevail where such rules are absent, and come to realize that time wasted is their money wasted—just as though a taxi were ticking it off on the meter—they appreciate the fact that the rules are there for the good of all concerned. The following sections set out the most important principles.

Conduct and Etiquette During Patch Sessions

Since the skating of figures is not the most popular branch of the sport it is unfortunate that it demands such a high level of concentration. The rules of conduct and etiquette during patch sessions are designed to create the right ambience for concentration; to ensure that no valuable time is wasted; to enable those who can and wish to concentrate to do so; to enable the instructors to give their lessons with the least possible interruption; and, finally, to make the best use of the ice surface. The following is not intended to be a set of rules as they would be set up on the bulletin board (such rules should be terse and to the point), but rather an explanation of the reasons behind the rules. If these reasons are explained to the skater, the rules will be much more readily understood.

Skaters must arrive punctually on patch. This does not mean that they should arrive in the rink at 6 A.M. for a 6 A.M. patch; it means that they should be on the ice claiming their patches at 6 A.M. There is quite a lot to do before going onto the ice apart from putting one's skates on. The bathroom may have to be visited; the patch list read, ice scribes extended and made ready for use (an ice scribe is a kind of giant compass). This last-mentioned rule is important, as I have known skaters who fiddle about with their scribes so long that it is ten minutes before they lay down their first figure. If necessary the skater should take with him onto the patch a box of tissues, a sweater, and gloves, so that he does not have to keep going off the ice for them after the patch has started. A skater should always arrive at the rink in time to go onto the ice unhurried and in a calm frame of mind, particularly if he has the first lesson.

Some rinks and clubs have a five-minute rule, which allows the skater to arrive up to five minutes late, but this is worse than useless—you might just as well start the patch five minutes later. It is an excellent idea to make the patch list valid only up to the precise time patch starts; any skater arriving late must then take any patch left open after reallocations have been made. As stated earlier, it is unfair to expect the pro in charge to do this once he has started his lessons. It is of tremendous help if skaters will call up the rink if they are going to be absent so that reassignments can be effected without having to wait for patch to start.

There should be no talking on patch. Skaters who are talking are seldom discussing their figures even though they may be trying to look as though they are. To solve all arguments it is best to have a blanket rule: no talking, except between teacher and student. This also applies to non-skaters and visitors standing round the rink who like to hang over the barrier engaging their friends in small talk.

Skaters should not visit other patches. Borrowing a scribe is often an excuse to waste time—which brings us to a point of etiquette: All skaters should possess their own scribes, as it is most unfair to rely on the generosity of others in this respect, particularly as scribes are very subject to wear and tear. Occasionally, when a skater's scribe is in for repair, borrowing may be justified, but the scribe should be returned immediately after use to its owner, at the original setting to which it was adjusted at the time it was borrowed.

No skater should leave the ice during patch except in dire necessity, in which case permission should be asked from the pro in charge. Given the relatively short duration of patch sessions visits to the bathroom or water fountain should be unnecessary. When a patch session is immediately followed by a freestyle session, skaters are usually allowed to leave the ice five minutes early so that they can change skates, but this decision should be left to the trainer.

Skaters should ask permission before making use of an unclaimed patch as it may have been earmarked by an instructor for a lesson.

At the start of patch it is the custom in some rinks for the skater to draw a straight line with the heel of his blade to mark the sidelines of his patch. Except where it is necessary to prevent very young skaters from straying all over the ice, or where the patches are very narrow, this is not really a good idea; the patch line acts as an artificial aid in estimating the size of a skater's circle, but as he will not be allowed to draw lines in a test or competition, he should learn to make the right size of circle without their assistance. If the skater on the next patch prefers that a patch line should not be drawn, his wishes should be respected.

Overlapping takes place when a skater has to cross the midline of the rink into another skater's patch when he (the overlapper) has moved his figures so much up the long axis that there is no longer room enough on his own patch to fit them in. It is almost impossible to accommodate more than one three-circle figure on a single patch because a three-circle figure rarely occupies less than forty-five feet in length and is usually considerably longer. Although overlapping is strictly speaking only by mutual consent, it is so necessary that no objections are normally raised, provided it is carried out in an unselfish manner. A skater must always remember that once he crosses the midline he is on another skater's patch and that he must give right of way to the owner of that patch. Unless two skaters both want to start three-circle figures right at the beginning of the patch session, overlapping should be delayed as long as possible. Skaters occupying the same strip should begin with their two-circle figures, placing them as near to the barrier of their own patch as is practical.

To summarize the whole situation, each skater should be allowed the use of his own clean ice for as long as possible. It is the height of discourtesy for a skater to start his first figure so far towards the midline that he overlaps immediately; worse still is to start the patch session by scribing out a number of circles right into the opposite skater's patch. In fact, it is better that a skater should confine scribing to his own patch. When a skater overlaps onto a patch on which a lesson is taking place, he should avoid skating between an instructor and his pupil, particularly if they are talking—to do so is just plain rudeness. There are some skaters who are (and regrettably have sometimes been encouraged to be) quite ruthless in their use of the ice and skate as though the whole strip belongs to them, particularly when the other skater is very young and easily intimidated, or too polite to object. It is quite amusing to watch two of these ruthless skaters when they happen to have patches opposite each other. Fortunately these types are rare in most well-run rinks and clubs. It goes without saying that pros should also be careful not to offend against the general principles; a pro should not, for example, spend a long time on his hands and knees examining turns on the patch of a skater who is not having a lesson with him at the time.

There should be no sitting on the barrier. The habit should be discouraged because (a) there is a real danger that a skater out of control could slam into those sharp toe rakes sticking out into the ice area, (b) skaters on the barrier tend to drum their heels on the paintwork, much to the annoyance of the rink manager, and (c) a row of skaters on the barrier makes the practice session look sloppy and undisciplined. Indeed it is sloppy and undisciplined—a practice session is a privileged period that should be devoted to serious training, not lounging about.

No skater should chew gum while on the ice. This may sound somewhat old-fashioned and out of touch, but aesthetic grounds aside, there is at least one very compelling reason: a sudden movement, particularly an unexpected one such as a fall, can cause a piece of gum to be inhaled and produce choking. A lesser but still valid reason is that many persistent chewers become so addicted that they feel they cannot concentrate when they have to temporarily abandon their habit during a test or competition. In fact, gum should be banned entirely from the skating area; it is a sad fact that some chewers have the unprepossessing habit of either sticking their gum on the barrier or simply dropping it on the matting where some other skater can get it on his blade and take an almighty fall as he steps onto the ice.

In a sport such as skating where failure to carry out a movement correctly, particularly a jump, is often embarrassing and painful, the temptation to take out one's feelings on the ice by stamping on it or kicking it is very great. It is a feeling with which I wholly sympathize, but one which must be strictly curbed, especially the habit of kicking the ice. Such habits tend to spread. Kicking the ice is a particularly pernicious practice, and any skater doing so after one warning should be sent off the ice as a disciplinary measure. During the rehearsal of an ice show, I once saw an enraged skater kick the ice with the heel of his blade. Unfortunately, the blade penetrated a pipe and a fountain of brine shot up, raining down over a large area. Everywhere the brine touched, the ice melted. Brine takes hours to remove completely, and just a trace can prevent ice freezing. It was only with difficulty that we put the show on that night. The skater was disciplined with a heavy fine. Should such a thing ever happen when you are present, immediately send someone rushing off at top speed for the man in charge of the ice or the engine room and get the brine pumps turned off; in the meantime try to stanch the flow with whatever materials may be at hand.

Skaters often ask us whether they may be allowed to play music during patch. After having given this a fair trial in the past, our answer is an unqualified "no." It is difficult to find soothing, unobtrusive music that is conducive to concentration. Many youngsters claim that they can concentrate better when listening to rock, but I also know many who have told me that they find it highly distracting—not just rock, but any music played during patch. If music is allowed, it is almost impossible to get 100 percent agreement on what is to be played. So skaters start turning up with their own records or tapes, and during a lesson I find some child, who should be concentrating on her figures, standing at my elbow asking, "May I play so-and-so?" I have probably never heard of it, so I say "Yes, yes," because I am trying to concentrate on a lesson and do not wish to be disturbed. Then suddenly a piece of hard rock bellows out over the rink and I have to stop while it is turned down to a volume at which the walls stop shaking. Perhaps the only thing suitable for patch might be that innocuous background music that is sometimes piped very softly into motels, but all in all patch is better without it. That is certainly the opinion of that great skater, Olympic Gold Medalist John Curry, who wrote in his book that while he had to have music during his freestyle practice, music during patch drove him crazy.

In order that all these points should be more readily accepted, not only should they be explained, but it should also be made clear to the high-test skaters (an occasional one of whom may feel that patch rules are beneath him) that they are expected to set an example to those younger and less advanced.

A Sample Set of Patch Rules

The following suggested set of patch rules is a distillation of the previous section and follows closely patch rules in use by many of the more successful clubs and rinks in the U.S., Canada, and overseas.

1. Skaters will observe strict punctuality (there is no five-minute rule). A skater not actually on his patch at the beginning of the session relinquishes the right to any specific patch.

2. There will be no talking or visiting during patch.
3. Skaters will not leave the ice during the patch period unless otherwise directed by their professional.
4. Skaters will not change patches without first obtaining permission from the professional or club member in charge.
5. Skaters will not draw patch lines.
6. Skaters will not borrow other skaters' scribes.
7. Overlapping must be carried out unselfishly—every skater has right of way on his own patch.
8. There will be no music during patch.
9. Skaters will not sit on the barrier at any time.
10. There will be no eating, drinking, or gum-chewing by students on the ice surface or at rinkside.
11. Onlookers will refrain from interrupting skaters during patch.
12. Skaters are expected to conduct themselves courteously at all times and make every effort to skate unselfishly.
13. Professionals will enforce compliance with these rules and have the right to send any skater off the ice who is uncooperative.

Freestyle, Pair, and Dance Sessions

Conduct of Freestyle Sessions

Freestyle sessions do not present nearly such a range of problems as patch sessions. Most skaters like freestyle, so there is much less difficulty in getting them to practice. It is in fact strange that during a freestyle session very few skaters want to leave the ice or go to the water fountain. The main problem is to conduct the sessions in such a way that moves can be executed and programs run through without interference. I have always been amazed at the ability of well-trained skaters to avoid one another. A really top-rank skater has an instinctive feeling as to where everyone is on the ice and knows not only what others are doing but what they are about to do, and where.

The difficulties arise when strong high-test skaters are mixed with younger, inexperienced beginners. Except in summer schools it is seldom possible to divide the freestyle sessions into grades of ability as there is normally just not sufficient time available. Nevertheless, even mixed sessions can be conducted successfully provided everyone skates unselfishly and there is no unreasonable overcrowding of the ice.

The most important rule is that all skaters must keep their heads up and learn to be aware of what is going on around them. With practice a skater is able to take in the situation on the ice at a glance and judge just where another skater is about to execute a jump or spin. If a skater really thinks about it, he can also learn to judge which are the least crowded areas of the ice—not at that particular instant but in, say, six or seven seconds' time. This latter type of judgment seems to be a special skill; spaces are not usually stationary but tend to move round the rink, a fact that many skaters seem to ignore.

Since two dedicated skaters can often work together on freestyle to their mutual advantage, most trainers do not object to a little talking on the ice provided it is constructive, but skaters should never move round the rink talking or stand around in groups in the middle of the ice. Any talking should be done in the vicinity of the barrier. Before moving away from the barrier or when stepping onto the ice surface, it is absolutely essential that the skater looks to see whether he is about to step into someone's path. Skaters are frequently seen rushing out of the warming room straight onto the ice, heads down, looking at their hands while they pull on their gloves, only to step right in front of a skater getting up speed for a jump. This is quite unforgivable and tantamount to stepping out onto a busy street while reading a book.

A skater who has already started the entry to a jump should be given the right of way. If everyone is playing the game fairly, the frequently heard "Excuuuuuse me!" (which among the more ruthless is intended to convey the meaning "Get out of my way or I'll mow you down!") should not be necessary, and in any event should be discouraged. This warning cry tends to become a habit, to such a degree that I remember one skater who used to give vent to it even when there was no one within a hundred feet of her.

All skaters should get up immediately after a fall—in one action if possible. The only excuse for continuing to sit on the ice is if the skater is so stunned or injured that it is impossible or inadvisable for him to rise without assistance. For a skater to lie or sit on the ice commiserating with himself, trying to elicit sympathy, or simply out of pique, is inexcusable. He is probably sitting in someone's way or causing concern to a watching parent. Skaters should learn to take minor bumps and bruises without undue fuss. If this rule is strictly observed it will then be immediately clear whether a skater is really hurt and enable whoever is in charge to take action accordingly. At one club a skater old enough to know better used to be carried off the ice on an average of twice a week, only to reappear on the ice again five minutes later. There is no room or time for such behavior in a busy and disciplined training session.

When time allows, a separate session or part of a session, during which the ice is cleared, should be set aside for the practice of individual programs to music; when time is short, however, programs may have to be played during the general freestyle while everybody else is skating. Whichever method is used a daily list made out on a roster system showing the order in which skaters may play their music should be placed by the cassette or record player (usually referred to as the *music box*). If all programs cannot be played at that session, a note should be made of the last program played and the list continued from that point at the following session. Programs should be played through once, and skaters should not be permitted to stop and restart their music. In general freestyle sessions, programs or sections of programs may be practiced without music or with music played from a portable tape recorder carried round the rink by the instructor or a friend of the skater. A skater running through a program to music from the official rink music box should be given right of way. During a general freestyle session skaters should not be required to stand by the barrier while programs are being played, but they should be constantly aware of who is officially skating a program and be prepared to give that skater right of way. In nearly all rinks and clubs it is the custom to give preference in the use of the music box to instructors giving lessons.

Conduct of Pair Sessions

As there are comparatively so few pairs, they usually have to practice during the normal freestyle sessions; but as soon as a pair reaches any degree of strength, this arrangement is very unsatisfactory. The choice appears to be one of the following: to set up a separate pair session (often impossible owing to financial or scheduling reasons); to skate at the emptiest freestyle sessions; or to go to a rink that specializes in pairs and can accommodate them (often at night).

During a special pair session rules of conduct and etiquette boil down to common sense, awareness of what the other pairs are doing, and unselfish skating. All skaters should bear in mind that during moves such as lifts and death-spirals there is almost invariably a point where neither skater is able to see where he is going, and even if they could, a pair does not have the ability to make sudden changes of direction. Common sense and observance of the spirit of the rules of conduct already given for freestyle sessions should keep the pair session reasonably safe.

Conduct of Dance Sessions

Dance sessions consist of training sessions, social sessions, or very frequently a mixture of the two. These sessions produce the least problems and are usually well-organized, particularly since all dances, with the exception of the Three-Lobe Waltz, now removed from the test schedule, progress round the rink in a counterclockwise direction, and the majority of skaters are all doing approximately the same thing at the same time.

In American rinks it is the custom for couples to line up one behind the other to start the dance, and to move off at regular intervals. Instructors with pupils are normally permitted to go to the head of the line, and some clubs prefer that skaters dancing solo go to the rear. Skaters who are just learning a dance, or who are very slow, should give preference in the lineup to faster couples. Passing—that is, one couple overtaking and passing another—is normally frowned upon, but may be necessary if one couple is holding everybody up; even so, passing should be done with care.

Clubs usually set out a specific order of dances, but where the majority of couples are training for tests or competitions, the instructors or the couples themselves are occasionally allowed to ask for a specific dance out of order. Skaters practicing some other dance than that being played at the time should give way to couples skating the official dance.

11
Equipment
for the Advanced Skater

In all questions of equipment the advice of the instructor should be sought, not only because he is an excellent source of information, but because his pupil's equipment is one of the tools with which he has to work and he may feel that he is more acquainted or has been more successful with one make or type of equipment than another. It is, however, just as well that you understand the principles on which good equipment is constructed so that you can follow and appreciate his reasoning. The following information will also help you to discuss the matter intelligently with the skate shop if the instructor is not available.

Nowadays, skaters seriously interested in both figures and freestyle invariably have two pairs of boots and blades. The necessity for this usually arises when the skater has reached the level of the First or Second USFSA Figure Test, by which time the standard expected in the figures is such that the qualities required in the figure equipment are quite different from those required for freestyle—one pair will not do for both. The differences lie in the strength of the boot and the design and method of sharpening the blade.

The Boot

The figure boot should be relatively soft so that the skater can feel what the blade is doing and manipulate the ankle more easily; the freestyle boot, on the other hand, should be strong enough to support the ankle when jumping. It is remarkable to what degree boots have increased in strength over the last few years in order to keep pace with the rapidly increasing demands of modern free skating. If you grasp the shaft of a recently made freestyle boot of the heaviest weight and try to move it laterally, it will scarcely budge. The skater has to break it in, so that over a period of perhaps half a dozen practice sessions it eventually molds itself to the foot and develops some mobility—but not a lot. Bootmakers do, however, supply their boots in different weights so that figure skaters, free skaters, and ice dancers (who often use a middle weight) can all be accommodated. The vast majority of free skaters use the heaviest weight, but there is one point that we should like to make here. It is our personal opinion that the small, light child, even if at the stage where the advanced jumps have to be practiced, does not necessarily need boots of this extreme strength. At the beginning of a skater's career he should develop strength in the ankle muscles, and we feel that this development is impeded by excessively strong boots. Certainly the boots should be strong, but the strength should bear some relationship to the skater's weight, development, and skating ability.

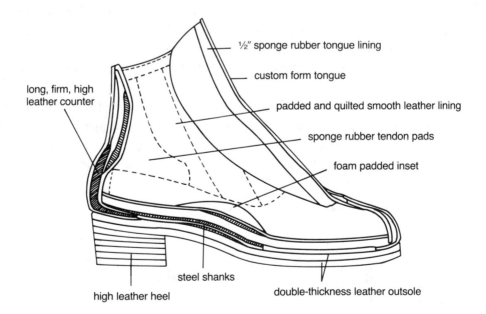

Fig. 12. Typical internal structure of top-level boot for advanced skating.

After considerable use even the finest boot will eventually break down and lose much of its original support; but this does not become a serious problem as quickly as some young skaters (who do not pay the bills) would have one believe. If the skater starts missing a few jumps and blames the boots, the best thing is for parents, skater, and instructor to meet and discuss the matter. In all fairness to the young skater there does come a point at which the boot has weakened sufficiently to affect the accuracy of the landings, but a skater should not need a new pair every couple of months or so. It is impossible to say exactly how long a pair should last as there are so many variables, such as the original quality of the boot, the ankle strength and weight of the skater, and how many hours the boots are used per week—once again, your child's instructor is your best adviser.

The boot used for figures should not be nearly so strong as that used for freestyle. No jumping is involved and the skater needs to be able to feel the edges in and out of turns in order to prevent double lines and other imperfections. My wife and I prefer that our students do not have too high a heel on the figure boot because we feel that an excessively high heel has a detrimental effect on the run of the blade when skating a figure. This view may not, however, be shared by all trainers, so ask before you have any alterations made. A good, regular bootmaker should be quite capable of making the alteration, which consists simply of removing the last layer but one of the heel and then replacing the bottom layer, at the same time doing any necessary plugging of the screw holes.

The possession of two pairs of boots and blades is not as costly as might at first appear. Provided no problems are created by sudden spurts of growth, the skater can usually use the old, weakened pair of freestyle boots for figures and just purchase a new, strong pair for freestyle. From then on, growth permitting, so it continues: the broken-down freestyle boot becomes the figure boot and the old figure boot is sold to some appreciative beginner. You may have to switch blades or buy a new set of freestyle blades, but on balance you save money.

The Blade

Among the many excellent blades on the market slight differences in construction result in some being considered more suitable for figures and others more suitable for freestyle. A surprising number of models, however—and we are speaking now of high-quality blades, not just the least expensive ones—can be used for either, provided that, if they are to be used for figures, some minor modifications are made to the blades after they have left the factory. Highly specialized dance blades are also available, but many dancers use regular freestyle blades.

Unless a blade has been specifically designed for figures at the factory, there are two modifications that may be applied to an all-purpose blade to render it suitable for figures. They are, modification of the master toe rake—the one that is nearest the ice surface and gives so much trouble to beginners— and the way in which the blade is sharpened (see "The Toe Rakes" and "Sharpening" below). An important difference between one model of blade and another often lies in the degree of curvature of the blade from front to back (see figure 1 on page xx). This is known as the profile, radius, or rocker of the blade. Of these three terms, *profile* is the best as the word *radius* could be confused with the radius of the degree of hollow produced by sharpening, and *rocker* is now rather old-fashioned. Some blades have a flatter and some a more rounded profile. Skaters and instructors usually have strong preferences for one or the other according to whether they wish to use the blades for figures or freestyle. It would be outside the scope of this book to go into all the subtleties of curvature and possible effect on the performance of the blade—all types have their enthusiastic adherents, and I advise you once again to consult your pro, as he may be unhappy teaching a skater on a type of blade which he dislikes, or of which he has no experience.

Bad sharpening can sometimes so alter the profile of a blade that it affects its performance on the ice. If the damage is slight the situation can be corrected by a sharpener who specializes in reprofiling; but it is a tricky job, and if the correction requires the removal of a considerable amount of metal, it will probably be better to sell the blades to someone whose needs are not so critical and buy a new pair.

The Toe Rakes

Except for the few special instances of blades constructed specifically for use in figures, most blades come from the factory with toe rakes suitable for freestyle. That is to say, in the freestyle blade the main, or master, toe rake is placed very low to the ice surface (figure 13). In the figure blade this toe rake is placed much higher or is completely absent, as in figure

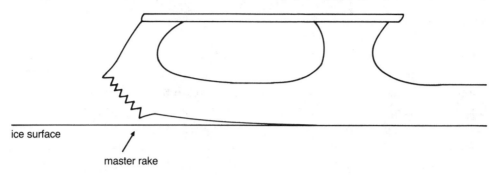

ice surface

master rake

Fig. 13. Front of blade, showing dominant master rake.

14. If the blade is to be used for figures, it is a simple matter for a careful skate sharpener to reduce or remove the master rake if, but only if, the instructor considers it necessary. A common reason for reducing toe rakes is that it lessens the likelihood of toe-pushing, but it should be pointed out that it is quite possible to push correctly even if the toe rakes are left unaltered. Toe-pushing is largely a question of carelessness or poor technique. A more compelling reason for modifying the toe rakes for figures is that in certain models the master rake is so low that it may scrape the ice in forward turns if the skater gets a fraction too far forward on the blade, but whether they should ever be completely removed is open to argument. For reasons which I cannot explore here, my wife and I never do more than slightly reduce them. For freestyle there is no doubt that in modern spinning the low toe rake is very beneficial and should not be tampered with—it will in any event tend to wear down with use.

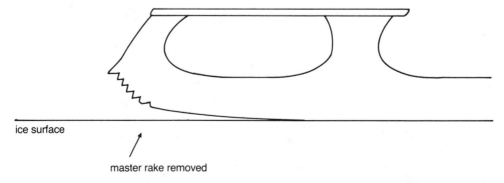

ice surface

master rake removed

Fig. 14. Same blade with master rake removed for figures. Take professional advice— opinions differ widely.

Mounting the Blade

I have already touched on the subject of mounting, i.e., how the blade should be positioned and attached to the boot, in chapter 2, but at that stage I had mainly matched sets in mind in which the blades had already been mounted at the factory. At this more advanced stage it is almost certain that you will have purchased boots and blades separately and will have to find someone to do the mounting for you. This is definitely a job for the expert; not only must the blade be positioned correctly on the boot, but whoever does the work must know how to insert the screws so that there is no tendency for the blade to be bent laterally; this is known as springing or bowing the blade. If this happens, the blades will not run well over the ice and are very difficult to sharpen accurately.

Most specialized skate shops will undertake the mounting of blades and, unless otherwise instructed, will give what is considered to be an average setting (figure 15). Most settings seem strange at first, but unless wildly out of line, the setting should not be changed until the skater has persevered on it for at least half a dozen sessions. Constant changing will

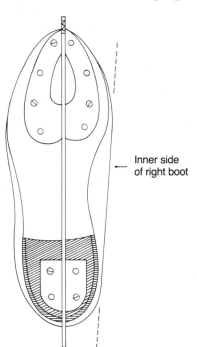

Inner side
of right boot

Fig. 15. Average correct setting as seen from below. Note slight divergent angle of blade to inner side of boot as shown by dotted line. Five trial screws for testing setting of blade.

pepper the sole of the boot with holes, which may need replugging. Provided that the blade is set parallel to the "run of the foot" (something that is almost undefinable and can only be judged by the experienced eye) there is a range within which the setting can be considered correct. Slight differences in setting when going from an old boot to a new one do not seem to be very important, and it is surprising how quickly and easily the body makes the adjustment. The feel of the setting between the figure and the freestyle skates should, of course, be as close as possible.

Just in case the blade does have to be moved at a later date, ask for just three screws in the sole plate and two in the heel (figure 15). This is sufficient to hold the blade, even for simple jumps, but as soon as the skater feels sure of the setting other screws may be added.

To prevent seepage of water into the screw holes, keep all screws tight, otherwise they may rust and loosen. This needs constant attention and every skater should carry a screwdriver in his skate bag. It is amazing how careless skaters can be in this respect; it is not unusual for a skater to arrive on the ice with a blade practically hanging off the boot and ready to detach itself at any moment. If a blade is going to come off, it usually does so at the heel during a toe jump, so pay particular attention to the heel screws.

Length of Blade

The front of the sole plate of the blade should be mounted flush with the front edge of the toe of the boot. Assuming the front of the blade is so mounted, blade manufacturers usually recommend that the end of the heel plate of the blade should lie one-quarter of an inch in from the end of the heel of the boot (figure 16). Here, however, a word of caution is in order. Bootmakers tend to differ one from the other in the way they shape the heels, the majority of which are cut in at a strong angle at the back, as in figure 17, while others are almost vertical, as shown in figure 16. The true length of the blade in relation to the boot is found by dropping a perpendicular line from the projection of the skater's heel and judging the length of the blade from there, as shown by the two long arrows. As can be seen, for practical purposes the length of the blade required depends on the amount it extends past the back of the heel of the skater, not of the bottom of the heel of the boot.

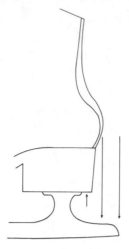

Fig. 16. Normal heel: heel plate finished ¼ inch from end of boot (small arrow). Long arrows show projection of blade past back of boot.

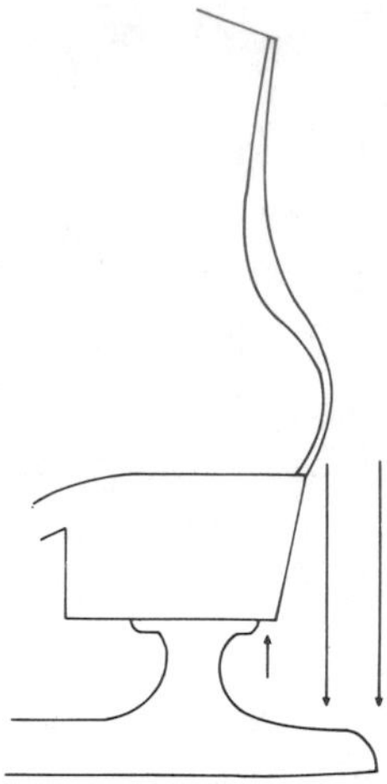

Fig. 17. Tapered heel: heel plate must finish closer to end of boot (small arrow) to obtain same blade projection.

If you have the choice between a blade that is a little too long and one that is a little too short, take the longer. Ice dancers, because of the very close footwork required which may cause them to step on their own heel and take a nasty, unexpected fall, tend to favor short blades, but in freestyle the longer blades give more stability, and in figures they make the back turns easier.

The Hardened Blade

In all good blades the part that actually comes into contact with the ice is separately hardened in the manufacturing process. This extra hardening extends upwards from the cutting edge for one-quarter to three-eighths of an inch. If you look at a good quality blade from the side, you will see a strip of dull metal about an eighth of an inch in depth running along the bottom of the blade from heel to toe. This is not, as is often thought, the extent of the hardening; it is simply where the makers have removed the plating to reduce the chance of it flaking off during use. So do not assume that after this unplated strip is worn away by repeated sharpening, the blade is necessarily down to the softer metal. By this time, however, it is quite possible that the constant resharpening may have distorted the profile of the blade to such an extent that replacement, especially if the blade is used for figures, is necessary.

All other things being equal, a hardened blade will run considerably faster than one that is not hardened. This increased "run of edge" is indispensable in the three-circle and paragraph figures where one and a half or two circles must be skated from a single push. Even in the early figures, such as a simple eight, a skater should not use an unhardened blade as the slowness of its run may cause the skater to develop a jabbing thrust with the toe in order to get more speed—a habit that is difficult to break later on.

Sharpening

The way in which a blade is sharpened is a subject that, when one considers its tremendous importance to the way in which a blade performs, is shrouded in the most amazing fog of ignorance. The main object of the sharpening process is not so much to produce a sharp edge but to restore the hollow (i.e., the groove) which runs down the length of the bottom of the blade, and so produce a cutting edge the angle of which is suitable for the type of skating being practiced. Figure 18A shows a cross section of a blade. The hollow forms part of the circle shown by the dotted line. In this case the circle is relatively small compared with the width of the blade, and the resulting hollow is said to be deep, that is, the effective angle of the cutting edge is quite acute. In figure 18B the hollow is flat, or shallow, the dotted line showing that this hollow is part of a much larger circle; in this case the angle of the cutting edge is relatively oblique.

The difference in performance between a blade having a deep hollow and one having a shallow hollow is very marked. Figure 19A shows how the acute cutting angle of the deep hollow allows the blade to penetrate much more deeply into the ice than the very oblique cutting angle of the shallow hollow. Because of the curvature of the blade from front to back not only does the blade with a deep hollow sink more into the ice, but a greater length of blade is thereby brought into contact with the ice, thus providing the skater with a firmer grip. For this reason the deep hollow is used for freestyle as it allows the skater to take the fast, deep, strong edges so necessary for good jumping. When skating figures, however, the

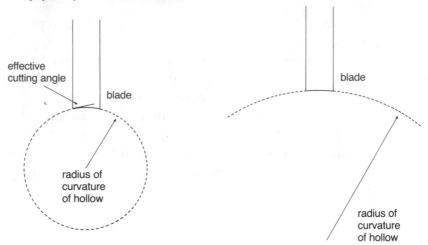

Fig. 18A. Cross section of blade, showing relatively deep hollow for freestyle. The cutting angle is dependent on the depth of the hollow.

Fig. 18B. A flat, or "shallow," hollow for figures. Note large radius of curvature compared with that in figure 18A.

deep hollow is a tremendous disadvantage. The greater penetration of the deeper hollow produces rough, scraped turns, and causes the skater to have to fight the bite of the blade, thus reducing the speed of the blade over the ice—the blade does not "run" well. To make matters worse, because the skater travels relatively slowly in figures, the lean of the body is less and the second edge is likely to come into contact with the ice thereby creating two lines instead of one (figure 19A). These double lines, known as flats, are considered very grave errors in figures and are a constant source of failure in tests. The shallow hollow, on the other hand, because of its reduced penetration, lifts the second edge higher above the ice surface (figure 19B), thus reducing the possibility of flats. (Nevertheless, a skater with poor techniques may still produce flats, whatever the hollow.) The shallow hollow makes possible the desired lighter, less scraped turns, and a more effortless run of the blade over the ice.

Judges do not, and should not be expected to, take into consideration the hollow on which a candidate is skating; it is the skater's responsibility to arrive at a test or competition with suitable equipment. Unfortunately, apart from having grasped the fact that a shallow hollow is needed for figures and a deep one for freestyle, skaters seldom have even the haziest notion of what precise degree of hollow is needed. The terms *deep* and

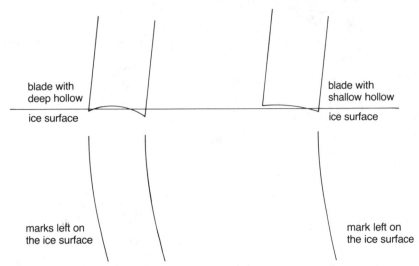

blade with
deep hollow

ice surface

blade with
shallow hollow

ice surface

marks left on
the ice surface

mark left on
the ice surface

Fig. 19A. Because of deep penetration, a deep hollow can cause double lines, or "flats," a bad fault in figures.

Fig. 19B. A shallow hollow does not sink so deep into the ice, thus reducing the possibility of "flats."

shallow are very vague, so the all too frequently heard request "not too deep, please" really doesn't tell the rink skate sharpener very much, with the result that the conception of what is deep and what is shallow varies from sharpener to sharpener all over the country. Many years ago in sheer desperation I decided I would have to sharpen my own pupils' blades, despite the fact that I disliked the job intensely (although not so much as my wife disliked having a dirty sharpening machine in the basement). Over the years we experimented with all types of hollows, so I can pass the following information on with a fair degree of confidence.

Freestyle and General Purpose Hollows

The depth of the freestyle hollow is not nearly so critical as that used for figures and is largely a matter of taste and what the skater gets used to. When dealing with the deeper hollows the most convenient way to determine what hollow a skater has in his blade is to measure it using coins as gauges. Turn the blade upside down and set a series of coins in the groove until you find one that fits exactly, or nearly so (figure 20). For freestyle most of our students like a hollow corresponding to a fifty-cent piece or a quarter, or something in between, but a few like to go down as deep as

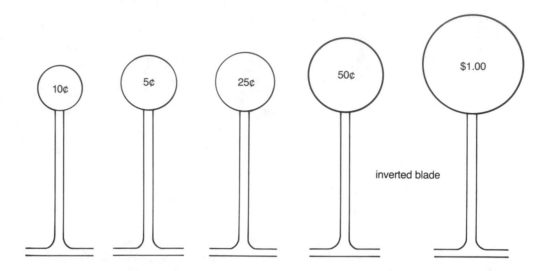

Fig. 20. Coins make good gauges for freestyle and general-purpose hollows.

a nickel, or in very rare cases a dime. The curvature of a fifty-cent piece is a good general purpose hollow, especially for adults who do not do a lot of jumping. At one period I used a hollow corresponding to an old silver dollar for some of my more fragile adults because they felt safer on it, they had no trouble with stopping immediately after sharpening, and it ran well; but the shallower the hollow the more quickly it dulls and needs resharpening, so we seldom use it now except as a "composite" hollow for young skaters who only have one pair of skates for both figures and freestyle. When recommending these hollows I am presupposing an average hardness of ice, a deeper hollow being more suitable for hard ice, and a shallower one for softer ice.

You can see from the above that for freestyle and general purposes it is very much a question of what the skater likes and gets used to, although anything flatter than an old style silver dollar may well give the skater problems if used for freestyle, as he will soon find himself skidding when the first fine sharpness of the edge wears off.

One of the main advantages in being able to measure the hollow with coins (or specially constructed gauges) is that the skater can go to the rink sharpening department with a specific and intelligent request. Nevertheless, in fairness to skate sharpeners, the skater should not be too fussy regarding freestyle and general purpose hollows, as the sharpener may have a series of wheels, or have his wheels trimmed to certain curvatures, which may not produce quite what the skater is used to but will be near enough. The main thing is that the sharpener does a careful job and, once he has produced a hollow to the skater's liking, can produce it again when required.

Figure Hollows

For the skater who really wants to produce the best figures possible, the degree of depth of hollow of the figure blade is much more critical and important than that of the freestyle blade. Unless a sharpener has a good understanding of the subtleties of figures, it is sometimes difficult to convince him of the vitally important part the figure hollow plays in the success of the skater.

Coins are now of no use as gauges, as there are no coins large enough to fit even the deepest figure hollows. The curvature is usually expressed as the radius of the circle of which the hollow is a part. It is essential to make it clear to the sharpener that you are speaking of the radius of this circle and not the diameter. (A sharpener who cross grinds usually thinks of the diameter of the wheel he is using, whereas the sharpener who uses his wheel horizontally thinks of the radius of the arc of the diamond trimmer needed to produce the necessary curvature on his wheel—hence the possible confusion.) The radius of commonly used figure hollows throughout the U.S. ranges between 1⅛ to 1¼ inches (i.e., part of a circle having a diameter of 2¼ to 2½ inches). Despite the flatness of such a hollow we have invariably found that skaters achieve much better results on a hollow that is much shallower. This might be termed an ultra-shallow hollow, as it ranges between 2¾ and 3¾ inches radius—so you would need to have a coin the size of a small dinner plate to measure it. Unfortunately, few modern sharpening machines are constructed to produce such flat curves, so the skater may have to ask his sharpener what is the flattest curve he can get and adapt his skating to that particular hollow or, if this is not flat enough, look round for some sharpener who specializes in this type of ultra-flat hollow (and they are to be found now in slowly increasing numbers as the understanding of this hollow spreads across the U.S.).

With this ultra-flat hollow it is possible to produce beautiful turns, and the skater will be able to extract the maximum speed from the blade.

The blade will feel strange when he first tries it and he will invariably skid at his first few attempts, but he must not let this deter him. The period of acclimatization is surprisingly short and he should be able to adapt himself within the period of a couple of patch sessions. In all our years of using this hollow only one skater ever asked to return to a deeper one; a week later, however, she admitted she had made a mistake and asked to go back to the ultra-flat hollow again. She passed an excellent Sixth Test a couple of weeks later and never complained again. One great advantage of this hollow is that it needs no breaking in, and skaters can go out and skate a test immediately after sharpening. But a few words of warning are in order. The skater must be very careful that he does not walk about off the ice without skate guards, as the ultra-shallow hollow tends to dull very quickly. Keep the blade reasonably sharp—if this type of hollow is allowed to get too dull, the skater unconsciously tends to drop his ankle slightly in order to feel the edge, and he will then have to adjust his technique when the blade is eventually resharpened.

It should be remembered that this chapter gives advice for the advanced skater. A light, moderately talented child should be able to handle the USFSA Preliminary, First, and possibly Second Figure Tests using only one pair of skates for both figures and free, in which case the compromise hollow that I mentioned earlier should be used. Such a hollow could be that of the old silver dollar (approximately ¾-inch radius) or even a little flatter. Such a hollow is not ideal either for the figures or the freestyle, but for many skaters at the lower levels it will serve quite well if kept reasonably sharp.

Bad Sharpening

"I've just had my blades sharpened and they're ruined—I can't do a thing on them!" In all probability they are not ruined at all; the problem may well be that the skater has taken his blades to a sharpener he has never dealt with before and has been unable to tell him exactly what hollow he wants. Many pros and their students passively accept the local sharpener's concept of what constitutes a flat (figure) hollow and a deep (freestyle) hollow. A skater who moves to another area may come up against a sharpener with totally different ideas and must either accustom himself to the different feel of the blades or provide precise information regarding

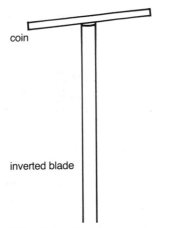

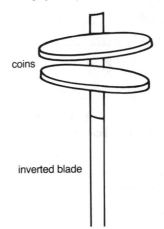

Fig. 21A. Coins balanced on inverted blade shows a bad tilt of the edges caused by poor sharpening.

Fig. 21B. Corkscrew effect caused by even worse sharpening.

the hollow required, preferably backed up by a set of gauges, particularly for the figure hollow.

A blade is not badly sharpened simply because a sharpener has not been able to guess the exact hollow a skater has in mind. However, if the sharpener has any common sense, he will try to determine from the blade what hollow the skater has been using—which may be difficult if the blade is very dull—and then say whether he is able to duplicate it; some of the ultra-flat hollows are outside the range of many machines. Bad sharpening is something else. Bad sharpening is ignorant, careless, irresponsible sharpening. Some of the commonest faults of this type are tilted or corkscrewed edges (figures 21A and B), gross alteration of the profile (the longitudinal curvature of the blade), grinding off a major part of the master toe rake when not specifically instructed to do so, and allowing the blade to become too hot, thus altering the temper of the steel.

If a skate shop offers "precision sharpening," then it must be just that. The operator tacitly undertakes not to commit any of the gross errors mentioned above and is prepared to put in the hollow the skater requires. Having done so, he should be able to reproduce this hollow the next time the skater gives him his blades. More than that one cannot expect given the present state of the art. Precision sharpening takes time and therefore money. When I used to sharpen my own students' skates, four pairs an hour was the maximum I could manage if the job was to be done properly, and even this rate could only be achieved if no problems were met, such as bent blades—which meant removing the heel screws—blades that had previously been improperly sharpened by some ham-fisted operator and therefore needed careful correction, and blades that had been allowed to become excessively blunt. Never resent paying a high price for good sharpening—the best blades are expensive and they *can* be ruined if they get into the wrong hands.

Let me conclude with a personal experience. Whenever my wife and I start to teach in a new area, the first thing I do is to visit the local sharpeners to see how competent they are and whether I can trust them with my students' skates. The quality of work may vary drastically from operator to operator. Quite recently I went into a general sporting goods store that advertised "Skate sharpening $1.00—Precision sharpening $1.50." I was taken into the back of the building where a young man was standing next to a pile of figure and hockey skates about knee high. There must have been about a hundred pairs. It was just before lunchtime and he seemed a little uptight. "I have to finish that lot before we close at five," he said. He appeared very interested that I was a well-known pro willing to give him what advice I could, but I found that what interested him most was not whether I could help him to achieve more accurate sharpening but whether I could assist him in speeding up his production line.

As always, I asked whether I might try his machine, to which he happily agreed. For five minutes I wrestled with the apparatus but the skate holder was so loose that it was impossible to maintain the blade in constant alignment with the wheel; steel filings and stone dust coated everything, particularly the baseboard over which the skate holder was to slide smoothly; and the diamond holder had so much play that accurate trimming of the wheel was impossible. As I struggled with this wreck of modern technology the young man was obviously becoming impatient and said, "You know what? I can do sixty pairs an hour—I get twenty-five cents a pair." Sixty pairs an hour! I couldn't believe my ears. That's a pair a minute—thirty seconds a blade! Even if he could get the blade in and out of the holder in, say, twelve seconds, it would allow him a bare eighteen seconds for sharpening, and this did not allow for time spent brushing the mounting piles of dust off the machine, trimming the wheel occasionally, or even stooping to pick a new pair out of the mound. I could not bring myself to watch him work, but I imagine that to save time each skate as it was finished was thrown over his shoulder into the "done" pile.

"What do you do about the ones that are to be precision ground?" I asked. After all, for $1.50 he had another thirty seconds to spare and I was interested to know how he occupied his time. "Well . . . er . . . you know, we take a bit more care—tie the laces neatly together after they're finished, that sort of thing. . . ." This pleased me—it was something positive and at least ensured that no top rank local skater would leave the shop carrying one figure and one hockey skate. Still seeking a gleam of hope, I asked, "Do you ever change the hollow?" He looked puzzled for a moment. "No," he said, "most of the skates we do here are hockeys anyway."

At that moment the door opened and another half-dozen pairs were thrown onto the mounting pile. "Well, I've gotta get moving," he said. His manner had cooled and he was anxious to be rid of me. Who was this naive person who professed to tell him how to sharpen skates? Anyone who didn't know that the difference between a regular and a precision grind was 50 cents shouldn't be in the business. So I left him, like Sanson, the terrible executioner of the French Revolution, turning to the pile and seizing another victim for his horrible machine. Which all goes to show that you get what you pay for and that you mustn't count the cost when it comes to getting a good sharpening job done on your skates.

Scientifically minded readers who are seriously interested in the subject of skate sharpening should read the excellent series of articles by Sid Broadbent, the first of which was published in the February, 1983, edition of the USFSA magazine, *Skating.* I should also like to draw your attention to the very informative article by P. Joseph DeLio, M.A., in the November, 1981, edition of the same magazine. But since there seems very little consensus on the degree of hollow suitable for figure blades, once again I suggest you accept the advice of your professional. Before leaving the subject of boots and blades we should like to caution parents against unduly pampering young children at the lower test levels in the matter of equipment. A colleague of ours teaching in a southern rink told us the story of one of her little girl pupils, only six years old, who was practicing for her Preliminary Figure Test. When the child was told that she must stop pushing with her toes, she put her hands on her hips, looked up at her teacher and said, "Well, what do y'all expect? I've only got one pair of skates!"

Regarding the choice of blades, years of experiment and observation have enabled the leading blade makers to produce a number of basic designs, nearly all of which can be made to do an admirable job in the field for which they are intended; all that is needed is a competent skater to use them. Skates are like cameras: there comes a point where all the added refinements contribute little to the actual picture; it's the photographer behind the box that counts.

The Ice Scribe

The ice scribe (usually referred to simply as a scribe) is a large, collapsible, telescopic compass used to mark circles on the ice so as to assist the skater in producing circles that are symmetrical and of the right size. The actual marking is carried out by a scratcher, which leaves a white line on the ice, or by a felt-tipped marker, which leaves a black one. As some rinks object to the use of a marker, the scratcher is the more common.

The length of the scribe may be adjusted to draw circles ranging from approximately five to eighteen feet in diameter; the smallest size is used for loop figures. There are several makes on the market, the main choice lying between those having circular and those having rectangular sections —the choice should be based on the experience of skaters using them.

If used correctly, the scribe is a very useful and almost indispensable tool, but if used incorrectly, it is not only a hindrance to learning, but the biggest waster of time, and therefore money, imaginable. In figures, the most important thing a skater has to learn is to create circles as nearly perfect as possible on a clean sheet of ice with no marks to help him. He may be lucky enough in a test or competition to have a few natural markings, or perhaps a hockey line, which may be of some small assistance, but he certainly will not have any circles marked out on the ice for him to follow. Having laid out his circle, the skater's next task is to follow (trace) it the second and third time around. But the skills of creating and tracing circles are quite distinct. If a skater never learns to create a true circle in the first place, his ability to trace a figure already laid on the ice will be quite useless since his original figure will be faulty. Creating a circle from nothing is a far more difficult task than tracing a line—creation demands mental effort, whereas tracing can be practiced while the skater is thinking about what he is going to have for lunch. Hence the overwhelming temptation to use the scribe in the least demanding and most unproductive manner.

It must not, however, be concluded from the above that the scribe has no useful functions and that circles should never be drawn on the ice—quite the reverse. In order of importance, the most constructive uses of the scribe are as follows:

1. To give the skater a mental picture of what a true circle looks like. For this purpose the circle should be scribed out on the ice, viewed from the center, and then skated over so that the skater can view it from all angles. While skating round the figure it is vital that the skater is actively thinking not just of the scribe line but of the shape and size of the circle as well as the distances involved. This is much more a mental exercise than a physical one.
2. Checking what has been done. The skater lays down a figure and checks its symmetry with the scribe without necessarily marking the ice. He then repeats the figure from a new center and checks it again.
3. To get the feeling of the movement of a turn on a true circle. This feeling may be quite different from that of a turn executed on a distorted circle.
4. To learn to trace. Here the skater scribes out the figure and practices getting his subsequent circles as nearly on top of the scribed line as possible. This exercise has some merit, but it would be better if the skater learned to put down a reasonable figure unaided and practiced tracing that.

It is instructive to watch skaters' use of the scribe on patch. Some use the scribe intelligently for one of the reasons listed above, others are scribe addicts who would not dream of attempting any figure without scribing it out first, while a third group scribes out a circle and then ignores it completely. The scribe addict, because he is completely unaware of the psychology of the learning principles involved, may genuinely believe that he is working to the best of his ability; when taught to use the scribe properly, he may suffer agonizing withdrawal symptoms. The third group is just mentally lazy.

Trainers have their own individual ways of getting the best use out of the scribe and require certain pupils to use it one way and others, who may have quite different faults to correct, another. It is therefore important that, before saying anything to a child about the way he is using his scribe, the parent consult the trainer in the matter.

A scribe is not just an important tool; it has also, somewhat regrettably, become a status symbol. Any child going onto patch without one feels its absence far more for psychological than for practical reasons. It has occurred to me that if manufacturers would turn out gold-plated scribes these would outsell the regular ones.

12

USFSA Championships and Competitions

The word *competition* is a general term used to cover all competitive events, while the word *championship* refers to those competitions that carry with them officially recognized titles, ranging from World Champion, or Champion of the United States, down to regional titles such as South Atlantic Champion. It should be noted that the Olympic Winter Games is not classified by the ISU as a championship but as a competition.

USFSA competitions, in order of importance, are as follows:

a. National Championships
b. Sectional Championships ⎫
c. Regional Championships ⎭ Qualifying
d. Juvenile Championships ⎫
e. Open Competitions │
f. Club Competitions ⎬ Nonqualifying
g. Basic Competitions ⎭

A skater whose eventual aim is to compete in the U.S. National Championships and possibly obtain a place on the U.S. World or Olympic Team, must do so via the official USFSA competition structure. But not all USFSA competitions lead directly to the National Championships; those competitions which do lead to the national level are known as *qualifying* and those which do not, as *nonqualifying*.

Qualifying Competitions

The rules governing qualifying competitions are highly complex and are set out at length in the *USFSA Rulebook*. As the aim of this present book is to give parents and skaters an overall picture and working knowledge of how skating is conducted in the U.S., it would be unnecessarily confusing to quote the innumerable rules with their host of finer points. What follows is a general outline, without going into all the ifs, ands, and buts.

Qualifying competitions may be thought of as a pyramid or ladder starting with the local Regional Championships as a base and leading up through the Sectional to the National Championships. To accommodate the hundreds of competitors (nearly two thousand by one estimate) spread out all over the country, the United States is divided into three main areas, which form the sections, each of which is further subdivided into three regions, making nine regions in all. Figure 22 will give you a visual picture.

National, Sectional, and Regional Championships all consist of separate championships in the main branches of figure skating, namely, Men's Singles, Ladies' Singles, Pairs, and Ice Dancing. These championships

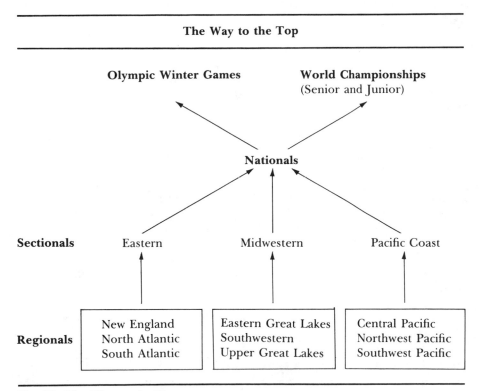

Fig. 22. The Way to the Top.

are therefore normally referred to in the plural, the word *championship* being omitted. Thus the South Atlantic Regional Championships is usually shortened to "South Atlantics."

Which Area Am I In?

Reference to the table below will show which region and section you are in. In principle each state is assigned to one of nine regions, but a part of one state may be in one region and the other part in another.

State	Region	Section
Alabama	Eastern Great Lakes	Midwestern
Alaska	Northwest Pacific	Pacific Coast
Arizona	Southwest Pacific	Pacific Coast
Arkansas	Southwestern	Midwestern
California		
South of Visalia	Southwest Pacific	Pacific Coast
Visalia and north	Central Pacific	Pacific Coast
Colorado	Southwestern	Midwestern
Connecticut	New England	Eastern
Delaware	South Atlantic	Eastern
District of Columbia	South Atlantic	Eastern
Florida	South Atlantic	Eastern
Georgia	South Atlantic	Eastern
Hawaii	Central Pacific	Pacific Coast
Idaho	Northwest Pacific	Pacific Coast
Illinois	Upper Great Lakes	Midwestern
Indiana	Eastern Great Lakes	Midwestern
Iowa	Upper Great Lakes	Midwestern
Kansas (including greater Kansas City area)	Southwestern	Midwestern
Kentucky	Eastern Great Lakes	Midwestern
Louisiana	Southwestern	Midwestern
Maine	New England	Eastern
Maryland	South Atlantic	Eastern
Massachusetts	New England	Eastern
Michigan		
Upper Peninsula	Upper Great Lakes	Midwestern
Lower Peninsula	Eastern Great Lakes	Midwestern

State	Region	Section
Minnesota	Upper Great Lakes	Midwestern
Mississippi	Eastern Great Lakes	Midwestern
Missouri (excluding greater Kansas City area)	Upper Great Lakes	Midwestern
Montana	Northwest Pacific	Pacific Coast
Nebraska	Southwestern	Midwestern
Nevada (excluding Las Vegas)	Central Pacific	Pacific Coast
Las Vegas	Southwest Pacific	Pacific Coast
New Hampshire	New England	Eastern
New Jersey	North Atlantic	Eastern
but Atlantic City, Brick Town, Cherry Hill, Princeton	South Atlantic	Eastern
New Mexico	Southwestern	Midwestern
New York	North Atlantic	Eastern
North Carolina	South Atlantic	Eastern
North Dakota	Upper Great Lakes	Midwestern
Ohio	Eastern Great Lakes	Midwestern
Oklahoma	Southwestern	Midwestern
Oregon	Northwest Pacific	Pacific Coast
Pennsylvania	South Atlantic	Eastern
but Erie	North Atlantic	Eastern
Rhode Island	New England	Eastern
South Carolina	South Atlantic	Eastern
South Dakota	Upper Great Lakes	Midwestern
Tennessee	Eastern Great Lakes	Midwestern
Texas	Southwestern	Midwestern
Utah	Central Pacific	Pacific Coast
Vermont	New England	Eastern
Virginia	South Atlantic	Eastern
Washington	Northwest Pacific	Pacific Coast
West Virginia	South Atlantic	Eastern
Wisconsin	Upper Great Lakes	Midwestern
Wyoming	Northwest Pacific	Pacific Coast

Events in Qualifying Championships

The table below shows the events and categories of ability in Regional, Sectional, and National Championships.

Regionals	Sectionals	Nationals
Senior		
Men's Singles	Men's Singles	Men's Singles
Ladies' Singles	Ladies' Singles	Ladies' Singles
Pairs	Pairs	Pairs
Dance	Dance	Dance
Junior		
Men's Singles	Men's Singles	Men's Singles
Ladies' Singles	Ladies' Singles	Ladies' Singles
Pairs	Pairs	Pairs
Dance	Dance	Dance
Novice		
Men's Singles	Men's Singles	Men's Singles
Ladies' Singles	Ladies' Singles	Ladies' Singles
Pairs	Pairs	
Dance	Dance	
Intermediate		
Men's Singles	Men's Singles	
Ladies' Singles	Ladies' Singles	
Dance		
Juvenile		
Boys' Singles		
Girls' Singles		

Juvenile Boys' and Girls' Singles, and Intermediate Dance have been included in the above because, although they are not qualifying competitions, they are usually part of the Regional Championships.

A winner of any of the above events may style himself a champion; for example, we have the National Junior Pair Champions, the Eastern Senior Men's Champion (a Sectional Championship), the North Atlantic Intermediate Ladies' Champion (a Regional Championship), and so on; but when the meaning is clear from the context, a skater may simply use some phrase such as having "won Regionals" or "placed in Sectionals."

Moving Up

The basic principle of moving up from one level to the next is that every season all skaters start afresh at the bottom of the ladder, the winners of the first four places in each event in Regionals moving up to Sectionals, and the winners of the first four places in the Sectional events moving up to Nationals, provided Nationals has an event in that category. If you look at the list of events at the Sectional and Regional levels, you will see that Intermediate Men's and Ladies' Singles, Novice Pairs, and Novice Dance are only qualifying as far as Sectionals because these events do not take place at the National level. Any singles skater, therefore, who wishes to get to Nationals will have to compete at least at the Novice level. If he has not yet reached that level of proficiency, he may in the meantime still be able to win a Regional or Sectional title and continue to gather competitive experience until his test qualifications (see "Eligibility to Compete" below) allow him to compete at a higher level. There are many exceptions to the principle of moving up as outlined here, particularly in respect to skaters who have already won an event in a previous year, but by the time a skater has come as far as that, he or his parents will probably have their own copy of the rulebook.

The greatest problem in holding Regional Championships is the vast number of entries that may have to be accommodated. When there is a very large number of entries in any one Regional event, such an event is subdivided into elimination rounds. The problem does not arise in Sectionals and Nationals because the entries are automatically reduced by the limitations on the number of skaters moving up from the lower levels.

Normally all events (including elimination rounds) in any one competition are held on consecutive days—four to five days on an average—finishing on a Sunday, but occasionally the competition is spread over two consecutive weekends. Regional Championships do not always take place simultaneously all over the country, nor do Sectionals. The dates of the separate Regionals usually vary between the end of the first week in November and the end of the second week in December. Sectionals follow at some period during the second and third week in January, and Nationals at the end of January or beginning of February. The World Championships are normally held around the middle of March. In Olympic years the Olympic Winter Games precede the World Championships.

Eligibility to Compete

Skaters wishing to compete in any qualifying USFSA competition must first of all be amateurs (see the following section) and citizens of the U.S., or have applied for citizenship, or have convinced the competitions committee that they genuinely intend to become citizens as soon as legally possible. In addition a skater must *(a)* be a member of a club affiliated with the USFSA, or *(b)* be a member of the faculty, administration, or student body at an educational institute that is an associate member of the USFSA, or *(c)* be an individual member of the USFSA.

Any mention of membership implies, of course, membership in good standing. A competitor must represent his designated home club (see "Joining a USFSA Club," chapter 6). An individual member usually competes in the region of his permanent residence.

Amateur Status

Frequently a skater has the opportunity to skate in a rink competition, or to give an exhibition, or to help out in some way with a rink operation. A skater or parent should know the general principles of the amateur status rules so that the skater's future competitive career is not unwittingly jeopardized. The ISU lays down certain basic rules, which the USFSA adopts (as it must), adding at the same time a few rules of its own. ISIA amateur status rules follow the same general principles as those of the USFSA, but skaters and parents should be familiar with the USFSA regulations as they are specifically designed to ensure that skaters are eligible to take part in national or international skating events under the jurisdiction of the ISU. In order to carry this out effectively one of the duties of the USFSA is to oversee the legality of activities such as competitions, exhibitions, and other public skating events. Once the USFSA is satisfied that all is in order, it will, if necessary, issue what is known as a sanction to any skater or skaters taking part in such an event. Sometimes a skater may need an individual sanction, e.g., when he is the only skater involved; at other times all skaters in an event may be covered by a blanket sanction. Very often, however, no sanction is required at all, an important instance being recitals at skating schools (provided certain criteria are met). In some cases all that is necessary is for a skater to have permission in writing from his home club. As the sanction rules are extensive and need careful study, it is always advisable to check with an officer of your home club if your child is asked to give an exhibition, and you are in any doubt.

The following paragraphs contain the most important points you should know about the USFSA amateur status rules. For further knowledge (mastery of which may make you either an object of respect or, more likely, a positive menace in your area) read the twelve pages devoted to amateur status and sanctions contained in the *USFSA Rulebook*.

An *amateur* is one who skates for the pure love of the sport and who has never committed any professional acts as set forth by the USFSA.

A *professional* is one who teaches skating, or uses his personal skill or fame as a skater, or his knowledge of skating, for personal gain (usually financial), either directly or indirectly, or has taken part in a competition open to professionals. Exempted from the first part of this rule are physical education teachers or teachers in schools or colleges who teach skating as a subsidiary part of their duties.

A *reinstated amateur* is a former professional who has stopped committing professional acts and has applied for, and been granted, a partial return of his amateur status. This means that he can do everything an amateur can do with the exception that he can never again compete in a qualifying competition. A couple of dollars for helping someone round the rink, or a nice little cash prize in a competition, and that's it—no Olympic Gold Medal, no World Championship title—ever! Which all seems a little absurd when one thinks of the liberal interpretation put on the international amateur status rules by certain other countries against whom we have to compete. Nevertheless, speaking as a professional myself, I do feel that the division of skaters into the categories of amateur and professional has certain merit, provided the rules are universally applied.

The last category, and one that is quite important to understand, is that of *restricted amateur*. This means an amateur who is temporarily suspended (usually for ninety days to one year) from certain USFSA activities. This can happen if a USFSA member (*a*) takes part in an unsanctioned competition or exhibition which should have received a sanction, (*b*) skates in an amateur carnival or exhibition for which he receives gifts (not cash) exceeding a total value of fifty dollars (at the time of writing), (*c*) allows his name or photograph or his personal appearance to be used for commercial advertising purposes in such a way that his ability as a skater is involved (except in accordance with contracts entered into by the USFSA), or (*d*) is a rink owner, rink manager, or paid employee who is in a position to make decisions regarding the rink operation including allocation of ice time and rules regarding its use. This last is an important rule, as very frequently amateurs are offered financial inducements by a rink to help out off the ice with the organization of group lessons. I would interpret this to be in order provided it did not entail any actual teaching on the ice (which would mean that they would be using their skill as a skater for financial gain, which would constitute an act of professionalism). There are a few gray areas here, but I am sure you can see the underlying principles. Once a skater has stopped doing whatever is causing him to be restricted, or when a specific period of restriction has been imposed and has elapsed, he must apply to the USFSA for reinstatement to unrestricted amateur status; reinstatement is not automatic. While a skater is classed as a restricted amateur, he may not take part in USFSA competitions, act as a judge of USFSA competitions or tests, be an officer or committee member of the USFSA, or act as a delegate of a USFSA member club.

Test Requirements

In order to reduce entries to a manageable number and to ensure that a skater competes at a level approximately commensurate with his skill, the right to participate in any event is determined by the highest USFSA test a skater has passed in that particular branch of skating. The requirements are as set out in the table on the opposite page.

Note that prior to 1977, free skating tests were combined with figure tests; skaters who took tests before that date do not, therefore, have to have passed the free skating tests as given in the table in order to qualify. Also note that *Junior* denotes an ability level and not an age group.

In order to enter a particular event, the required test must have been passed by October first of that year, i.e., the October immediately prior to the competition. *In all the requirements in the table no higher tests may have been passed than those stated.* This date limitation means in effect that if a skater wishes to compete at a certain level, he cannot take any further USFSA tests that season until after the competition. In previous years the cutoff date for passing tests was the day before the competition itself (or very shortly before), but this meant that there was a lot of scrambling through tests at the last moment by skaters who only had a bare level of competence, thus needlessly cluttering up an already almost impossible schedule and putting an extra burden on test judges, many of whom were already committed to giving up a lot of their time to the coming competitions.

In singles competitions, women are not permitted to compete against men. Originally there were no such restrictions, but in 1902, Mrs. Syers of Great Britain applied to compete in the World Championship (hitherto a purely male preserve), and since at the time there were no regulations covering the sex of entrants, she was permitted to do so. She skated so well that she took second place to the great Ulrich Salchow, the existing champion. This was a bit too close, so from that time on women and men were separated, the women being given their own championship. Nowa-

To compete in:	Skaters must have passed the USFSA tests for:
Singles (Ladies and Men)	
Senior	8th Figure and Senior Free Skating.
Junior	6th or 7th Figure and Junior Free Skating.
Novice	4th or 5th Figure and Novice Free Skating.
Intermediate	3rd Figure and Intermediate Free Skating.
Juvenile	2nd Figure and Juvenile Free Skating; must not have reached the age of thirteen by the first day of the competition.
Pairs	
Senior	Gold Pair by both partners.
Junior	Silver Pair by both partners.
Novice	Bronze Pair by both partners.
Ice Dancing	
Senior	Gold Dance and Gold or Silver Free Dance by both partners.
Junior	Two pre-Gold dances by both partners; neither partner may have passed more than three Gold dances.
Novice	One Silver dance by both partners; neither partner may have passed more than one pre-Gold dance.
Intermediate	Bronze Dance by both partners; neither may have passed any Silver dance.

days it is quite likely that in the figures the women would beat the men in a large number of cases, but on the other hand, the men, owing to their most unfair advantage in physical strength, have a certain edge in jumping in the free skating.

Although USFSA and ISIA tests cover approximately the same range of skating movements, they do not exactly correspond. For this reason an ISIA test cannot be used to qualify for entry into USFSA competitions. There is nothing, however, in the policy of either body that would prevent a skater from taking part simultaneously in USFSA and ISIA tests and competitions, provided he fulfills the requirements of the respective associations (see "USFSA-ISIA Statements of Policy," chapter 4).

Contents of Events

Singles. A singles (solo) event at the Senior and Junior levels consists of (*a*) compulsory figures, (*b*) a short program consisting of specified free skating moves, and (*c*) a well-balanced free skating program of unspecified moves. Although the prime object of the short program is to enable the skater to show his mastery of prescribed freestyle elements, it is, like the free skating program, skated to music. The singles short program must not, however, exceed two minutes. The skater is allowed to insert linking footwork between moves, which, although not marked as such, adds to the general presentation of the program. The short program is always referred to by that name, whereas the free skating program is known informally as the "long program." At freestyle practice sessions you will often hear the person in charge of the music ask a skater, "Which do you want —the long or the short?"

The Novice, Intermediate, and Juvenile (a nonqualifying event) levels consist of compulsory figures and free skating only, the short program being omitted. I include the Juvenile category here because it is the only nonqualifying competition for which the precise structure is laid down in the *USFSA Rulebook.*

Pairs. Pair skating is the least complex of all branches in regard to its competition and test structure. First, there are only three levels of competition, namely, Senior, Junior, and Novice; and second, the Senior and

Junior events consist only of a short program of compulsory pair moves, and a long program of pair free skating. In other words, from a test and competitive point of view, pair skating is very much like singles skating without the figures. The Novice event omits the short program and therefore consists only of a long program, which limits the participation of a Novice pair in any competition to a mere three minutes. It is very likely that eventually a short program will be added to this category.

All this does not mean that pair skating is any less difficult than the other branches. To be a good pair skater it is essential to have a sound knowledge of figures and be a strong and technically accurate free skater, all of which takes many seasons of work quite apart from the pair skating itself.

Ice Dancing. Senior and Junior ice dance competitions consist of (*a*) compulsory dances, (*b*) a free dance program, and (*c*) an original set-pattern dance, known as the OSP for short. The OSP resembles a compulsory dance in that it consists of a set sequence of steps laid out in a specific pattern on the ice, and this pattern repeats itself after one-half or one whole circuit of the rink. An OSP differs from the normal compulsory dance in that it is, as its name suggests, invented specially for the occasion by the couple who skates it; in addition, the OSP is usually somewhat more elaborate than the general run of compulsories. Occasionally an OSP is of such caliber that it is eventually included in the international schedule of compulsory dances, but this is rare. The Novice Dance event consists of compulsory dances plus a free dance program, while the Intermediate requires compulsory dances plus a *variation dance,* i.e., a variation of a specified compulsory dance.

Selection of Compulsory Elements

From the eighty-two figures possible (counting starting on the right and left foot) and the vast number of free skating moves—to which must be added those specific to pair skating, such as lifts and spins, and eighteen internationally recognized ice dances—how do the governing bodies choose which elements shall be used in any particular competition? The answer is that the elements are divided into groups, and one group is selected by lot (or by the ISU Technical Committee) before the start of the competition. If I explain how this is done with the figures in a USFSA competition, you will understand the general principle; and this same principle applies to all short programs and the compulsory dances. As a concrete example, let us consider the Intermediate level.

The figure test requirement for the Intermediate event is the USFSA Third Figure Test, which contains eight figures. From these, five are selected and arranged in four groups as follows (the numbers are those of the ISU official schedule contained in the *USFSA Rulebook*):

Group 1: Nos. 10, 26, 15
Group 2: Nos. 11, 26, 14
Group 3: Nos. 10, 26, 14
Group 4: Nos. 11, 26, 15

The numbers refer to the following figures:

10. Forward outside double three
11. Forward inside double three
14. Forward outside loops
15. Forward inside loops
26. Forward outside change three

Shortly before the competition, the referee, or assistant referee, draws by lot one of the four groups shown above, and also the foot on which the first figure in the event will be started (in official terminology this is known as the starting foot); thus, if the first figure is to be started on the left foot, the second figure will be started on the right, and so on. The result of the draw is not made public until fifteen minutes before the competition is due to start; so that right up to the time of the announcement the skaters will have been kept busy practicing all the figures in all four groups.

Changes are made periodically in the rules and the groupings, but the above description shows how things stand at the time of going to press with this book.

The procedure is somewhat different at the Senior and Junior levels. Because the results of these two events decide who shall be sent to the World Championships, the USFSA arranges the structure of its own National Senior and Junior Championships to match those used by the ISU for the World Senior and Junior Championships. A few years ago the ISU decided upon nine figures for Seniors and another nine for Juniors, divided into three groups of three for each category. Unlike the USFSA Intermediate event just described, each group is unique, and no one figure appears in two or more groups. In the case of Seniors, the ISU selects one year in advance two of the three groups to be practiced; the Juniors must practice all three groups. The final draw is made just before the first practice session of the competition and the starting foot announced fifteen minutes before the actual event. Thus, at the Senior and Junior levels no more than three figures are ever skated. As the USFSA uses the same basic groups of figures for their Seniors and Juniors as the ISU, and the U.S. national events always precede the World Championships and Olympic Winter Games, our skaters are well prepared should they be chosen to represent the United States.

Similar principles of grouping and selection of elements apply to the short programs and compulsory dances. All short programs contain four groups of seven elements, and the ice dancing at the Senior and Junior levels consists of four groups of three dances.

Below the Junior level it is not necessary to think in terms of the World Championships, so the USFSA arranges its competition and accompanying test structure in such a way as to bring out the best in American skaters. USFSA tests and competitions intermesh to form a logical unit. Were this not so, the instructor's task would be very difficult. Only trainers who have taught in countries having an illogical test and competition structure can really appreciate the superiority of the American system, a system that has been—and continues to be—refined and honed over the years.

Nonqualifying Competitions

Apart from the official qualifying events that form the official USFSA competition structure there are a mass of competitions for all categories at all levels that are outside the official ladder but which can be regarded as part of the "way to the top" inasmuch as they supply the vital competitive experience for the dedicated skater.

The most important nonqualifying events are the Juvenile Singles and Intermediate Dance. They are important because they not only form part of the Regional Championships, and can therefore result in an official championship title, but they also give valuable experience in the serious, competitive atmosphere that surrounds an official USFSA event. Every year the overall standard of skating in the U.S. gets a little higher and the sport more popular, so that the number of skaters who wish to enter Juveniles has become in many areas so great that time has not always been available to accommodate them. The USFSA has therefore been obliged to leave it to the discretion of the club sponsoring Regionals as to whether the event should be held at the same time or not.

A nonqualifying competition that is now so long-standing that it has attained a semi-official status is the Mid-Atlantic Championship, which is open to skaters from the mid-Atlantic states; in this respect it is very much like a regional competition.

In addition to the nonqualifying events just mentioned, there are a vast number of local competitions held all over the U.S., sponsored by USFSA clubs, that cater to all levels according to the standards prevailing in the area. Often these competitions are open to competitors outside the sponsoring club (interclub) and at other times just for the members of that particular club (intraclub). The levels may reach as high as senior but will almost certainly include events for juveniles. In fact, the level may reach down to beginners' events going under such names as pre-Juvenile, sub-Juvenile, Preliminary, pre-Preliminary, and so on. The bulk of entries for this type of competition is almost always in the singles events, but often dance is included and occasionally pair. The singles competitions may or may not include figures since the structure of these events is left largely to the sponsoring club, but while there are many competitions for free skating only, there are very rarely any just for figures alone. Although at the moment precision team skating is limited to nonqualifying competitions, the USFSA has drawn up regulations for this type of skating and without doubt it will eventually be incorporated into the regular USFSA competition structure.

The number of these inter-club competitions increases from year to year and many escape mention in the skating press, so that it is impossible to give here an up-to-date or fully comprehensive list. The following is a sample of some of the many available. I offer my apologies to those clubs whose events are not listed here.

Event	Sponsoring Club
Annual Free Skating Competition	Wissahickon SC
Arctic Blades Invitational Championships	Arctic Blades FSC
Columbia FSC Summer Competition	Columbia FSC
Columbus Summer Skating Competition	Columbus FSC
Creve Coeur Competition	Creve Coeur FSC
Elizabeth Sigrist Interclub Competition	Niagara Frontier Assn. of FSCs
Lake Placid Free Skating Competition	SC of Lake Placid
Lansing Summer Invitational	Lansing SC
New England Juvenile Championships	North Shore SC
A Competition in School Figures [!]	Alpine SC
Spokane Free Style Competition	Spokane FSC
State of Ohio Figure Skating Championships	Columbus FSC
Tri-Cities Precision Team Competition	Tri-State Council of FSCs, and Euclid Blade and Edge Club
Wilmington Summer Free Skating Competition	SC of Wilmington
Worcester Open Free Skating Competition	SC of Worcester

At the time of writing there are well over four hundred member clubs in the USFSA, so you can see that the above can only be a minute sampling of the competitions available—which all goes to prove that skating is alive and well in the U.S. Many, but by no means all, of these competitions are listed in the calendar of events section of *Skating* magazine. Parents should keep themselves informed, through their home clubs, about what is taking place in their areas.

13

International Championships and Competitions

All international figure skating championships and competitions for amateurs are sponsored by and held under the rules of the International Skating Union. The classes of competitions are as follows:

A. World Championships
World Junior Championships
European Championships
B. Olympic Winter Games
C. International Senior Competitions
International Junior Competitions

The championships listed under *A* and the Olympic Winter Games all contain the same branches of skating as the U.S. Championships—that is, figures and free skating, pairs, and ice dancing. International competitions may contain all branches or a combination of branches, some competitions being for free skating only, while others may include the figures and ice dancing while omitting the pairs. At the time of writing there is no international competition that does not include free skating as at least one of the events.

All the championships (except the Europeans), the Olympic Winter Games, and most of the international competitions are open to all members of the ISU (in this sense, *ISU member* means a country's officially recognized national skating association having membership in the ISU). Some championships and competitions are limited to certain countries, examples being the European Championships and the former North American Championships in which only U.S. and Canadian skaters were allowed to participate. At one time American skaters were permitted to enter Europeans, but after an American, Dick Button, made a "grand slam" in 1948 by winning the United States, World, Olympic, and European titles, the policy of "Europe for the Europeans" was adopted, and from that time on Americans were barred from participation in the European Championships.

Because member associations may, if they wish, set up competitions in which the skating is limited to certain branches or levels, and the entries sometimes restricted to specific areas, such international competitions are frequently referred to as invitational meets. Here is a list of some of the more prominent events of this type:

Skate America International (U.S., October)
Skate Canada (Canada, October)
St. Ivels Ice International (London, England, September)
Ennia Challenge Cup (The Hague, Netherlands, November)
*Grand Prix International (St. Gervais, France, August)
*Nebelhorn Trophy (Oberstdorf, Germany, August)
Asko Cup of Vienna (Vienna, Austria, September)
Golden Spin of Zagreb (Zagreb, Yugoslavia, November)
Prague Skate (Prague, Czechoslovakia, November)

The costs of staging a competition lasting several days is high, and the sponsors may be lucky to break even. Although held under ISU rules, the ISU will not undertake financial responsibility for these events. It frequently happens, therefore, that a commercial company will put up the money to get the competition going, and what they may lose in cash they make up in publicity. A case in point is the Ennia Challenge Cup, Ennia being a large Dutch insurance company.

How Is a Skater Chosen to Represent His Country?

In any of the events mentioned above a skater must be an amateur as defined by the ISU and a member of a national association which is itself a member of the ISU. All entries must be made through the skater's association (in the United States, the USFSA). The ISU lays down no specific demands as to the skating proficiency of any skater entering an ISU championship or competition—it is left to the various national as-

*These two competitions are together known as the *Coupe des Alpes.*

sociations to ensure that the skaters entered are of a suitably high standard. It is, after all, embarrassing to all concerned when, as once happened, a skater from a country new to the sport arrived at a World Championship and, looking at the draw of the figures posted on the bulletin board, said, "What's a paragraph double three? I've never heard of it." There is no record of the trainer's explanation.

Methods of ascertaining whether a skater is worth entering differ from country to country. What follows is the method used in the U.S. and applies mainly to the Singles; the Pairs and Ice Dance couples are chosen on a similar basis.

World Championships. The responsibility for choosing the U.S. team for the World Championships lies with the USFSA International Committee, who normally select a maximum of three skaters from those who have placed among the first five in the most recent USFSA National Senior Championships; they may also choose any American skater who happens to be the current World Champion, even if he did not compete in Nationals. In addition, the committee may consider any skater who, for acceptable reasons, did not compete in the current Nationals but who placed within the first four of the preceding year. It usually works out, however, that the pecking order is preserved, and the first three skaters placed in the current National Championships are selected. One or more alternates are also nominated in case of accident or illness. Nevertheless, however good the skater may be, he can be excluded from the team for conduct unbecoming a representative of the U.S.

The ISU does specify certain age limitations. To enter an ISU senior championship (and the Olympic Winter Games) skaters must, under the current rules, have reached the age of fourteen by the July 1 preceding the event. They are, however, allowed to enter at the age of twelve if they have placed amongst the first three in the World Junior Championship of that or the preceding year.

In the senior events nothing is said about how advanced in age a skater may be, but certainly in the singles the days of the forty-year-olds are now past, and the "mature" skater usually gravitates towards pairs or dance. But even here the average age is now normally quite low. I have in my collection a group photograph taken some fifty years ago of the men competitors in the World Championship of that time, which I'll forego publishing here. What would strike the average viewer today is the skaters' comparatively advanced age. Appearances and size varied enormously: one had the aspect and mien of a frail and elderly taxidermist, another that of a hulking veteran boxer. Training habits, too, differed from those of today. One world-famous skater appearing in the photograph was never —and I have this on the most impeccable authority—at the top of his skating form until he had downed a large tankard of martini.

World Junior Championships. It was stated earlier that in USFSA competitions the word *junior* bore no relationship to age. This is not the case in international championships or competitions. Under ISU rules, the word *junior* means that the skater shall have reached a minimum of ten years of age and shall not be over sixteen (eighteen for pairs and dance) by the July 1 preceding the event. For the World Junior Championships a maximum of three skaters are selected by the USFSA International Committee. The choice is made from those skaters who are the right age and who have taken part either in the USFSA Junior or Senior National Championships but have not competed in the World Senior Championships or the Olympic Winter Games, or placed amongst the first three in any international competition or invitational meet held under ISU rules. As far as the USFSA is concerned the rules of selection are not hard and fast and have to be bent a little on occasions. Such an occasion arose in 1980 when the World Junior event was scheduled to take place on precisely the same dates as had been fixed for the U.S. Nationals. There was a dark suspicion in certain quarters that this had been done deliberately so that the better American skaters would be kept busy at home attending their own National Championships. (This was, of course, only a suspicion, as no international body would ever dream of acting in so devious a manner.) Nevertheless, the U.S. National Championships by no means exhausted the supply of good American skaters and Miss Rosalyn Sumners was dispatched to win the Ladies' event, which she did with no apparent difficulty.

Olympic Winter Games. Selection of the team for the Olympic Winter Games is the responsibility of the (USFSA) Olympic Figure Skating Committee (OFSC) and proceeds basically along the same lines as those followed by the USFSA International Committee in selecting the team for the World Championships.

International Invitational Competitions. In the case of international competitions, the USFSA International Committee once again makes the selection, but these invitational meets are becoming so numerous that our best skaters cannot get around to them all. The idea seems to be to make as good a showing as possible without completely exhausting the time, energy, and resources of our hard-working competitors and to use these events as tryouts for those skaters who show considerable promise for the future.

How Many Skaters May Represent a Country?

A member country is always allowed to send at least one entry, but never more than three, to each event in an ISU championship, the number of entries above one being determined by how well that country's skaters performed in the preceding year. This can be best explained by considering one event only. Let us assume it is the Ladies' Singles.

We start with a basic allowance of one woman per country, irrespective of the results of the preceding year. But, if one of that country's women placed among the first ten in the previous year, then two may be sent the following year—any two, not necessarily including the one who made the extra entry possible. Furthermore, the ISU rule states that the first three women in any one year are permitted to skate the following year without affecting the quota of their respective countries. This means that a country has the opportunity to enter its maximum of three women if, and only if, it can use a woman who has placed among the first three the previous year. If the woman who placed among the first three is not available to skate the following year, her country is back to its quota of two entries again.

The same general principles apply to the Men's Singles and Ice Dancing, if the couples are considered as individual units. There are one or two regulations about switching partners, but they need not concern us here. As far as the Pairs are concerned, any one pair placing in the first *five* the preceding year may be entered by their country as a third entry. With this exception the rules remain the same as for the other categories.

14

How Competitions
Are Conducted

Conduct of International Competitions

ISU regulations state that for all competitions the ice surface shall be rectangular (other shapes do exist) and measure a maximum of sixty by thirty meters, but not less than fifty-six by twenty-six meters. The vast majority of rinks in the world lie between these sizes; the more recently built rinks in the U.S. conform approximately to the larger size. The rink must also be covered, which simply means that it has to have a roof. This is no great protection from the elements, but except for blizzards it does at least prevent direct precipitation on the ice. In recent years I know of no senior events that have not taken place in arena-type buildings, usually almost totally enclosed; but occasionally the juniors have not been so lucky. Until comparatively recently many competitions and championships were held in open-air rinks with no roofs. This was all very well on a nice, sunny day in, say, Switzerland, but more often the conditions could only be described as hazardous. Many years ago my wife and I, who were pair skating at the time, competed in the European Championships in Prague. The stadium is now enclosed, but at the time it was completely open-air. A spell of unusually warm weather accompanied by high winds had set in, causing thawing of the ice to such an extent that there was some doubt as to whether it would be possible to hold the Ladies' Singles; nevertheless, the competition went ahead. When it came to the pairs, the wind was blowing down the length of the rink with such ferocity that we had to start much higher up the ice surface than we normally did, to allow for compression of the program as we battled up the rink in the teeth of the gale, and elongation as we soared in the opposite direction with the wind behind us, splashing through at least an inch of water as we went. This event was immediately followed by the World Championships in Davos, Switzerland, where the pairs were again unlucky, having to skate in a blinding snowstorm. The snow was falling so heavily that men with enormous shovels had to start clearing the ice surface while the competitors were still skating. One pair gave up after the first minute, complaining that they could not see where they were going. During our own program I remember unwisely lifting my head and trying to smile at the public, only to get two great gobs of snow in the face, one in the mouth and one in the eye—it was really quite a nightmare. By this time, the judges, who were sitting muffled in rugs and blankets at the side of the rink on the ice surface, were just white, immobile mounds, making us wonder at times whether they were still alive.

The whole question of outdoor skating came to a head after one badly organized championship in which the men's event was held at 2 A.M., by which time the ice had become so hard it was difficult to get the blade to penetrate, causing constant skidding, making it very difficult to jump and resulting in skaters falling all over the ice. Since that time two very important rules have come into force: competitions are to be held between the hours of 8 A.M. and 11 P.M., and rinks must be covered. Of course, just putting a roof on does not help all that much, but holding the events in arena-type buildings with walls does allow the ice-man to control the hardness of the ice, unless the refrigeration plant breaks down.

Including practice periods, international competitions usually last five days if all categories are included. The order of the divisions for Singles is compulsory figures, short program, and free skating (long program). The starting order, i.e., the order in which the individual competitors are to skate, is decided for the first event (the compulsory figures) by lot. As soon as the results of the figures are known, the total list of skaters, in the order in which they finished, is divided into groups, usually six to eight skaters per group. If there are three groups, the group of skaters lowest down the list skate first in the next event (the short program), the group in the middle skate second, and the group doing best skate last. The object of this division into groups is so that later skaters do not have to wait around too long after they warm up—each group can have a six-minute warm-up on the ice before skating, as close as possible to the time they actually perform. The starting order within each of these groups is also decided by lot. The order for the free skating (long program) is decided by the results of the figures and short program combined.

Judging International Competitions

Whether it be Singles, Pairs or Ice Dancing, all international competitions, including the Olympic Winter Games, require a panel consisting of no less than seven judges and not more than nine; the number must be an odd one and almost invariably nine judges are used, each from a different country. All judges must be amateurs as defined by the ISU. The following description applies to the Singles event.

On the evening of the previous day the group of three figures to be skated, the starting foot, and the starting order will have been drawn by lot. Fifteen minutes before the start of the figures the first five skaters will take the ice for a warm-up on a section of the ice (usually about one-third) reserved for this purpose. At the end of the warm-up period the judges, wearing stadium boots and carrying clipboards, pencils, the necessary papers, and judging boxes containing marking cards slung round their necks, shuffle onto the ice. Judging is never done in skates, as this would make a lot of unnecessary marks on the clean surface of the ice—rather like scribbling over an artist's drawing paper. Accompanying the judges are the Referee, the Assistant Referee, the Substitute Judge, and not more than two other ISU officials, who often act as observers, presumably to see that fair play is done. All this means that there could be fourteen persons watching the competitor skate his figure —quite a crowd.

The first skater is then called by the Referee from his warm-up patch and, to prevent misunderstandings, told which figure he must skate and the foot to start on. Within certain limits the skater may choose the piece of ice on which he would like to skate; having made his choice he indicates, by raising his outstretched arms, the long axis of his intended figure. This indication has a long tradition, but it is hardly necessary for the large figures nowadays as they are almost invariably skated with the long axis across the width of the rink; when skating loops, however, the skater sometimes elects to have his long axis parallel to the side of the rink. In any case, this indicating the long axis does prevent some absent-minded judge from having to leap out of the way if he happens to be standing in the wrong place. While this is going on, skater number six is allowed to start warming up.

In a deathly hush the skater stands at the starting point of his figure (known as his *center*), planning the figure in his mind (at least, that is what his trainer hopes he is doing). Finally, for better or for worse, he strikes off and the competition is on its way. The figure is skated three times without pause (twice only for the time-consuming paragraph figures), while the judges stand motionless, one of the regulations being that they shall not move around while the figure is being skated. At its completion the skater retires to the barrier for consultation with his trainer and the judges start to walk all over the figure observing its good and bad points. At the same time the Referee places markers where the turns have been made so that the judges can see how symmetrically the figure has been skated. Examination of the turns usually involves a lot of bending down and sometimes even kneeling on the ice. Judging has at times its own hazards and on rare occasions the sepulchral silence is broken by a judge falling over, with the accompanying clatter of clipboard, pencils and judging box. In fact, while examining a bracket, a great friend of mine was unfortunate enough to slip and break a hip. He subsequently made a full recovery, but it did cast something of a pall over the proceedings as he was carried off on a stretcher. It is on occasions like this that the Substitute Judge, who has been judging unofficially until then, is brought in.

The basis of the marking is the same as that used for tests: each figure is marked out of six points, one decimal place being allowed. A judge's box, therefore, contains two sets of cards, one set of black numbers for the whole marks, and the other of red numbers for the decimals. Usually after about 1½ to 2 minutes the judges have seen enough and the Referee, when he sees they are all ready, blows a whistle, at which signal all judges simultaneously hold up their marks, which are noted down by an official off the ice while at the same time the numbers are being read off over the public address system, first in the language of the host country and then again in English. A second blow of the whistle and all marking cards are returned to their boxes.

In the case of the first figure, the Referee, before blowing his whistle, goes down the line of judges asking each privately what his mark was.

After making a couple of calculations, he informs all the judges of the average of the marking, upon which any judge may change his mark before the whistle blows. As will be seen later, this makes no difference to the result, but it ensures that each judge starts within the same range. The same process is followed after the first skater has finished the free skating or short program, and is the cause of the apparently interminable wait that so often puzzles the public.

For the short program and the free skating the same judges form the panel as those for the compulsory figures. In these cases the judges sit off the ice, usually on a dais. Two marks, each out of six, are given for the free skating, the first for technical merit and the second for artistic impression. The marking of the short program is similar but not exactly the same as for the free skating. In the case of the short program the first mark is for the required (compulsory) elements and has to take into account not only their technical merit but also whether the element can be considered to have been performed at all; if not, or if there are errors present, deductions are made. The second mark is for the presentation of the program, which has essentially the same meaning as artistic impression in the free skating.

Pairs and Ice Dancing. The short program and free skating for the Pairs is marked in the same way and under the same headings as the Singles, but the addition of moves such as pair spins and lifts, unique to pair skating, must be taken into account. In ice dancing the three compulsory dances take the place of the compulsory figures and each dance is awarded one mark out of six; the original set-pattern (OSP) dance and the free dance are each given two marks, the OSP under the headings of composition and presentation, and the free dance under technical merit and artistic impression. All these various headings have their subheadings; the interested reader should refer to the *USFSA Rulebook.* It should be noted that composition and style, a term used by the USFSA, means the same thing as artistic impression, the expression used by the ISU.

Judging USFSA Championships and Competitions

Although the USFSA base their method of conducting competitions on those of the ISU, there are a few differences, mainly in the judging.

Unlike the ISU system of using nine judges, the USFSA may use as few as three but usually no more than seven. The more important the competition, however, the more likely it is that a full panel of seven will be used. This does not apply to panel judging which, due to its infrequent use, is not described here.

The system of judging international championships and competitions as described above requires what is known as open marking, i.e., the judges show their marks publicly immediately after each competitor has finished skating. This is also the system in use by the USFSA for the U.S. National Championships and for all Senior events in the Sectional and Regional Championships. All other events, including minor competitions, almost invariably use the modified open system. The way in which this method is applied to the Singles is that the judges write down their marks privately for each compulsory figure. Instead of being shown to the public, the marks, after all competitors have skated, are passed on to the accountant and are eventually placed on the rink bulletin board. At the end of the short program, however, after all competitors have skated, a bevy of girls in skates and matching costumes appear on the ice carrying judging boxes. These girls are know as caddies, and are usually members of the host club. One girl stations herself in front of each judge. As each skater's name is called, every judge informs his caddy of his mark, and the caddy holds up the appropriate cards. The same procedure is followed after the free skating. So there is no public marking at all for the compulsory figures, but what might be termed a delayed system of open marking for the short program and the free skating. The ice dancing and pair events are judged in the same way; no public marking for the compulsory dances and delayed public marking for everything else. This method seems to have evolved by long tradition, and I have never seen it used anywhere except in the USA.

There are two other methods that have been tried and may still be used in nonqualifying competitions: they are the closed (or written) system and the panel system. The latter method seemed to show great promise and was generally popular with the skaters, but for some reason it did not find favor officially, possibly because it needed too many judges. Although mentioned in the rulebook, neither of these two systems is described, but official descriptions may be obtained from the USFSA head office.

Finding the Winner of a Singles Event

As the years go by the calculation of the result of any competition held under ISU or USFSA rules becomes increasingly complex. The first thing to realize is that it is not the skater who gets the highest number of marks who wins. This might be so if there were only one judge, but in ISU or USFSA competitions we are dealing with five, seven, or nine. The problem is to devise a system in which no individual judge is in a position to affect the result any more than he is entitled to do as a single member of the panel. To find such a system is extremely difficult, but progress is being made. Until quite recently the ISU and the USFSA had settled on a system for the Senior and Junior levels that seemed workable, but then the mathematicians decided that this could be improved upon, and the ISU increased the complexity—and, I might add, the confusion of the general skating public—by adding a further stage to the process. To give our own skaters and judges experience with the new system, the USFSA adopted it for the Senior and Junior levels but not for any level below, because none of the lesser levels are involved in international competition. To complicate matters further, competitions in the U.S. below the Junior level have various constructions, e.g., the Novice, Intermediate, and Juvenile levels have no short program, and many of the nonqualifying competitions held under USFSA rules are for free skating only. Fortunately, the methods of judging all these different types of events have certain principles in common, which I shall discuss before going on to more concrete examples.

Underlying Principles

All methods of calculating the results of a competition start with the awarding of the marks for each section of the event in the way described earlier in this book—that is to say, a mark within the range of 0 to 6 is given for each compulsory figure (three in all), for each of the two parts of the short program (required elements and presentation), and for each aspect of the free skating (technical merit, and composition and style). It is after all these marks have been collected from the judges that the complexities begin.

The first principle to be clearly grasped is that the final result is not calculated directly from the marks but from what are known as *ordinals*. An understanding of how these ordinals are used to arrive at the final standings is essential. For the sake of simplicity, and so as not to confuse the issue, let us consider a competition with only one part, e.g., free skating —no figures, no short program. At the end of the competition each judge will, according to his marks, have placed all the competitors in order. The number representing the placement is the ordinal. For example, a skater who has been placed sixth by a particular judge is allotted the ordinal 6. As there will obviously be differences of opinion, the skater may have received an ordinal of 5 from another judge, or perhaps 10 from yet another. The final result is arrived at as follows.

Any particular place is given to that skater who has the majority of ordinals for that place (or their equivalent, as will become clear). For example, if there are five judges and three put the skater first and two put him second, his ordinals are 1, 1, 1, 2, 2. He has the majority of ordinals for first place. The ordinals of the skater who comes second might be 1, 2, 2, 3, 4. In this case his single first place would be included in the majority vote for second place since it is better than a 2. So he now has the equivalent of three 2s, which, if no other skater has more ordinals for that place, puts him second. If two skaters have the same number of equivalent ordinals for a given place, those ordinals are added together and the skater with the lowest total of ordinals or equivalent ordinals for that particular place gets the better position. Let us assume that the first, second, and third places have been decided, and we are calculating for fourth place; skater A has 3, 4, 4, 6, 8, while skater B has 2, 4, 4, 6, 9. Each has the equivalent of three fourth places (A's 3 counts as a 4, and B's 2 also counts as a 4, because third place has already been determined). But A's total of fourth place ordinals is 11 (3 + 4 + 4) and B's only 10 (2 + 4 + 4). So B gets fourth place. If the marks for A had been 3, 4, 4, 6, 8 (as before), but those for B were 3, 4, 4, 6, 9, the equivalent fourth place ordinals (3, 4, 4) would have totaled the same (11). In this case the place would have been decided by totaling all five ordinals, A's total being 25 and B's 26, so A gets fourth place. If, however, the marks had been differently distributed among the judges, and the total of all five ordinals had been equal, then, for the first time, the total of the marks given to each skater by all five judges would have to be used, the skater with the highest marks getting the better place. If the two skaters had received the same number of marks, a tie would have been declared, but it is most unlikely that the situation would get as far as that.

The following table is reproduced here in simplified form from the *USFSA Rulebook*. It represents the results of a competition (or section thereof) arrived at by the methods just described. For simplicity the panel is assumed to be of five judges, but the same principles hold good for any odd number of judges from three upward. See if you can figure out how each placement is arrived at; the only other thing you have to know is that Thompson has more total marks than Miller.

Competitor	Judges					Place
	A	B	C	D	E	
Williams	1	6	4	1	1	1
Gray	10	1	1	2	6	2
Taylor	2	2	2	6	3	3
Young	3	3	5	3	10	4
Thompson	5	7	5	4	4	5
Miller	4	4	5	5	7	6
Hunt	6	5	3	7	5	7
Stapleford	7	8	10	8	11	8
Sadler	8	10	11	9	9	9
Johnson	9	9	12	10	8	10
Berry	12	12	8	11	2	11
Smith	11	11	9	12	12	12

Some pretty strange marking, you may say—judge A's dislike of Gray's skating, and E's favored treatment of Berry, would probably arouse comment, to say the least—but the table is a good illustration of all the possibilities one is likely to meet. The rulebook goes into considerably more detail than is possible here; you will find the appropriate section under Rules for Placement (CR 28.00), and it is really quite easy to understand.

Many years ago, when there was no short program and nearly every event consisted of compulsory figures and free skating, the figures were considered the more important branch and were awarded 60 percent of the total marks possible while the free skating received only 40 percent. Owing to the rise in the standard of the free skating, and to make the event more acceptable to the general public, who rarely watched the figures and could not understand why sometimes quite a weak free skater won the title, the figures and the free skating were made equally important, each receiving 50 percent of the total marks. Then came the short program, and a further change had to be made; now the figures were worth 30 percent, the short program 20 percent, and the free skating remained at 50 percent. In any competition not using a short program, figures and free skating were still of equal worth, and so the situation remains at the time of writing.

It immediately becomes obvious that somewhere along the line mathematical adjustments have to be made so that the two, or three, sections of a competition take on the above proportional values. This principle is common to all the variations of the basic system, except, of course, in competitions that consist of free skating only, or of figures only (some do exist). The method of bringing the various sections of a competition into the correct proportional balance is to multiply or divide the marks or placements by what is known as the free skating factor, or place factor, according to the form the competition takes. Although these two factors are used slightly differently, they have the same aim, so I shall call them the balancing factor. The only way I can adequately explain this is to deal with it as we come to it when I describe the individual methods of computing different events.

One other point that should be mentioned at this stage is the use of a factor (of difficulty) for the figures. This factor is fast dying out but it is still used in the Juvenile and Intermediate events, which is why I have to explain it here. Each figure in the ISU schedule is allotted a number from one to six representing how difficult the ISU considers the figure in relationship to those in the rest of the schedule. As an example, two of the figures used in the Juvenile event are the back inside eight and the back serpentine (see chapter 23, "Recognizing Turns and Figures"), the first having a factor of two and the second a factor of three. Although they are no longer used in tests or higher-level competitions, the factors are still listed in the ISU and USFSA rulebooks right up through the Eighth Test; the back paragraph bracket, for example, is considered extremely difficult, so it has the top factor of six. The idea is that if, in a competition, a skater's marks for the figure are multiplied by the factor, then a skater who performs a difficult figure very well has a greater leverage in the marking over a skater who performs a moderately difficult figure (with a lower factor) also very well. I have no doubt that factors will have completely disappeared from the scene in a few years' time.

Now that you have an understanding of the major principles involved, I shall attempt to show how they are used in the various USFSA singles competitions. There are still some points that you will have to look up in the *USFSA Rulebook,* particularly how ties are resolved when first calculating the ordinals from the raw marks, and you will also have to look up how the computations are made for pair and dance events; however, they follow the same general pattern as discussed here, the dancing being a little more complex inasmuch as the compulsory dances may be skated in two rounds—initial and final.

Juvenile Singles

Here we are dealing with an event having only two sections, compulsory figures and free skating. After an adjustment has been made, each section will eventually count for 50 percent of the total marks. As in all competitions containing compulsory figures, only three figures will be skated. Juvenile Singles is one of the two cases (the other being Intermediate Singles) in which factors of difficulty for the figures are used.

The following are the two groups of figures from which one group will be chosen by lot for the competition. The factors of difficulty are enclosed in parentheses.

Group I Back outside eight (2); forward outside—back inside threes (2); back serpentine (3).

Group II Back inside eight (2); forward inside—back outside threes (2); back serpentine (3).

Each figure is marked out of 6 and then multiplied by the factor of difficulty; thus, whichever group is chosen, the total marks possible for the compulsory figures will be 42 (12 + 12 + 18). Since the free skating is marked under only two headings, the total marks possible for the free skating will be 12; and because the figures and the free skating must each contribute 50 percent of the total marks possible for the whole event, an adjustment must be made. This is accomplished by dividing each skater's marks for the figures by the balancing factor (in this case known in the rulebook as the "free skating factor," which is somewhat misleading).

The balancing factor is arrived at by adding the factors of difficulty together and dividing the result by 2. Whichever group is chosen the sum of the factors of difficulty comes to 7, which makes the balancing factor 3.5. The maximum total marks a skater could be awarded for the figures is 42 which, when divided by 3.5, brings it down to 12—the same as for the free skating. After a skater's individual marks are treated in this way, the result is added to his marks for the free skating (unchanged), and this gives his final total from each judge for the whole event. As explained above, these final marks decide the skater's ordinals from which the final placements are derived.

I should mention at this point that in all competitions the standings are published after each section of the event. Although this may not be necessary when calculating the final result, it does let the public know how the skaters are progressing and thus adds interest to the event.

Intermediate Singles

As in the juvenile event, the Intermediate Singles has no short program, and the final results are calculated on exactly the same principle as Juvenile Singles. The only difference is that the balancing (free skating) factor works out to 4 instead of 3.5. This is because the figures chosen in each group (four groups in this case) all have the same total factor value of 8 (2 + 3 + 3), which I need hardly tell you comes to 4 when divided by 2. (When explaining this system I feel that I have to be very careful not to leave any step out.) As you can see, it doesn't matter how many figures there are in a group or what their difficulty factors are, the result of the computation will always bring the maximum marks for the figures down to 12 when judging on a basis of 6 marks to a figure.

Novice Singles

Once again, there is no short program. The calculations are the same as just described except that no factors of difficulty are used for the figures; which means that the maximum marks for the figures must be 18. The balancing factor must, therefore, be 1.5, provided only three figures are skated, which nowadays is invariably the case.

Senior and Junior Singles

The Senior and Junior events both have short programs. No factors of difficulty are used for the figures, so the maximum total of marks possible is 18 for the compulsory figures, 12 for the short program, and 12 for the free skating. As explained earlier in this chapter, the value of the three sections of the event must be adjusted so that the figures are worth 30 percent, the short program 20 percent, and the free skating 50 percent. Marks are awarded by the judges in the same way as for any other competition, but from then on the methods of balancing the three sections and deciding the final placements are carried out according to the ISU instead of the USFSA system. The method was adopted by the USFSA for the Senior and Junior events and first appeared in the 1981–82 issue of the *USFSA Rulebook*. The ISU system is as follows.

After each of the three sections of the event the skaters are placed in order by each judge according to the marks he has awarded them, just as though each section of the event were a separate competition. On the basis of the placements—not the marks—the balancing takes place. This is done by taking a skater's placement in each of the sections and multiplying it by 0.6 for the figures, 0.4 for the short program, and 1.0 for the free skating, leaving this placement unchanged. Each balanced placement is now known as the *factored place*. From the total of the three factored places the final result is determined as explained previously.

To take a concrete example, let us assume that a skater is second in the figures, sixth in the short program, and third in the free skating. He would then have placements of 2, 6, and 3 respectively. These numbers are now multiplied by the balancing factor (the official term is the *place factor*), the result of which would appear as follows:

	Placement	Factor		Factored Place
Compulsory figures	2	0.6		1.2
Short program	6	0.4		2.4
Free skating	3	1.0		3.0
			Total	6.6

It is from this last total of factored places—in the case of the skater above, 6.6—that the final placements are decided: the skater with the lowest number in the factored places being the winner, and so on down the line.

There has been a lot of criticism of this system, some skaters claiming that they would have had a better place in certain competitions if the old system had been used, but this obviously works both ways. In the old system of calculating an event with three sections, all that is necessary is to divide both the marks for the figures (no factors of difficulty being applied) and the marks for the short program by 2.5, leaving the marks for the free skating untouched. Add these three results together and the total is used to obtain an ordinal for each skater, from which the final placements are decided. This method is still legal in nonqualifying competitions held under USFSA rules.

As for the future, it is highly probable that the judging system will continue to evolve and may even have undergone changes by the time this book gets into your hands; but if you have mastered the general principles of the existing system, you should have no difficulty in understanding very quickly any modifications as they come along. But there will be no overnight world-shattering changes. Enthusiasts new to the field constantly come up with seemingly good but highly impractical ideas—the classic being videotaping all the figures and free skating for later examination—quite oblivious of the technical difficulties and amount of time involved if it were to be done properly. By the time a decision by video had been reached, everybody would have gone home. In any sporting event the results must be known within a reasonable time—the sooner the better—and it is not wise to remove decision making entirely from the public eye. Nevertheless, practical ideas that promise to reduce the effect of bias in judging without involving too many judges would be welcomed, at least by the skaters.

15
Professional Championships

The professional tennis player or golfer makes his money by teaching or playing in tournaments, or both. The professional skater, on the other hand, was for many years restricted to earning his living either by teaching or appearing in ice shows. In those days there was only one rather obscure world professional championship which attracted very few entries because the financial incentives and meager publicity hardly made it worthwhile for a busy professional to set aside from his teaching schedule the necessary training time, or to obtain a temporary release from an ice show engagement. Fortunately the situation gradually changed and continues to do so. Great opportunities are now opening up for top-rank professionals to take part in championships and competitions that not only offer substantial financial rewards and valuable publicity, but at the same time are designed to provide excitement and entertainment for the general public.

Attempts have also been made to organize ongoing series of tournaments across the country, as is done in tennis, but it still remains to be seen whether this approach will succeed. For some time to come the promotion of skating will continue to depend largely on television coverage of existing amateur championships, the annual World Professional Figure Skating Championship for the Avon Cup, the periodic visits of large ice shows to major cities, and the small but superb ice shows staged by such leaders in the field as John Curry and Toller Cranston. The World Professional Ice Skating Championships, not to be confused with the championship for the Avon Cup, is held in Spain. Unfortunately, although it is long established, it does not yet get television coverage outside the

European networks. Nevertheless, the field of professional competition seems to be steadily developing along the right lines and the sport as a whole is benefiting enormously as a result. The direction professional championships are taking and the fact that participating professionals are not shackled by amateur regulations and requirements is encouraging more and more the development of the artistic side of freestyle. To give the amateurs and the amateur system their due, however, it must be remembered that it is they who have succeeded in the last few years in raising the technical and athletic side of freestyle to enormous heights.

The format of professional championships changes slightly from year to year but always in the direction of providing better entertainment for the general public. This chapter describes the three major professional championships in the form in which they exist at the time of writing.

The World Professional Ice Skating Championships

In the foothills of the Pyrenees in the province of Huesca, Spain, lies the ancient city of Jaca (pronounced "Hahca," with a gutteral "H"), now developing into a well-known skiing resort. As part of its winter sports activities the town possesses a very fine ice rink which has for a number of years been the annual venue of the World Professional Ice Skating Championships, or to give them their official Spanish name, Campeonatos del Mundo de Patinaje Artistico Profesional sobre Hielo. A winner of any of the events takes the title of World Professional Champion.

Certain organizational problems caused the 1984 championships to be canceled, but it is greatly to be hoped that they will quickly be reinstated at their previous locale. Since it has had a long history, this championship will undoubtedly continue to be held, if not in Spain, then elsewhere in Europe. I describe it below as it has been conducted in Spain, not only because I was at one time actively involved and could therefore observe it at close quarters, but because it brought to the attention of the skating world a unique system of judging.

The forerunner of the above championship was an open professional championship regularly held in England during the 1930s (and possibly earlier) under the auspices of the National Skating Association of Great Britain, the amateur body corresponding to the USFSA. I cannot be absolutely sure of the exact date it started, as records are difficult to obtain, but I certainly remember watching it as a boy in 1934 and it had been in existence for some years then. After World War II the sponsorship was handed over to the British professional body, the Imperial Professional Association (IPSA), who received a certain amount of assistance in staging the event from the Tom Arnold ice show organization. From that time forward the championship underwent a significant change. The figure portion had been abolished some years previously and now the style of free skating shifted gradually towards a type of performance more suitable to a professional ice show than to competitive skating based on amateur rules. The technical aspect was, however, by no means abandoned, and a high standard of spinning, jumping, and footwork was still required. The difference lay in the increased emphasis on presentation, musical interpretation, showmanship, and costuming, requirements which were to become permanent.

After a time it became increasingly difficult to stage the event in England, and the town of Jaca, seeing a golden opportunity, decided to try their hand at it. In this bold attempt they were supported by the International Professional Skaters Union (IPSU). The whole thing was a stroke of genius on the part of the Spaniards because much of the money that had hitherto gone into publicizing Jaca as a ski resort now went into staging the championship, and because of the wide television coverage, more publicity was generated than ever before. Another wise decision was to hold the championship over a four-day period during Easter when the town was full of skiers, which meant a packed arena at all events. This was also the time of the year when pros found it easiest to take time off from their normal work. In addition, the finances of the organizing committee were now in sufficiently good shape to be able to pay the major part of the competitors' expenses—even those coming from as far away as Australia—and to add substantial cash prizes for the first three places in all events (men's solo, ladies' solo, pair skating, and ice dancing). I have attended this championship several times (once as a judge) and can attest to the fact that it is beautifully and efficiently organized, a state of affairs almost entirely due to the untiring efforts of a dynamic young Spaniard, D. Pablo García Márquez, himself a skater, who spares himself no pains to make the event a success. He is, to my mind, a master of public relations. And here I should like to add one very important comment: As a judge I never once felt under any political pressure to come up with any particular result. As far as I could tell, the judges were left entirely free to mark as they saw fit. Mind you, I cannot say that such freely expressed opinions were always universally popular—but then, they seldom are.

An Unusual Marking System

The method of marking in the Spanish world professional championships represents a significant and interesting departure from the system used by amateur bodies. Instead of one judge being faced with the prodigious task of evaluating the entire contents of a free skating program, each judge is assigned a particular field. For example, the solo free skating is judged under seven separate headings: spins, jumps, steps, music, choreography and originality, artistry, and public impression. A separate judge is allocated to each of the first six categories and he judges only his assigned category and nothing else. Furthermore, each category is judged out of ten instead of six—this in itself is of little significance, but it is a break with tradition and may appear more logical in the eyes of the general public. For the final category, public impression, ten prominent local citizens are chosen to sit in a row alongside the regular judges, and at the end of the skater's program each puts up a mark out of ten indicating how much he enjoyed the performance from the point of view of a nonexpert spectator. The citizens' ten sets of marks are then added together and the total divided by ten, the result thus giving the combined opinions the weight of that of a single judge.

The above system is very malleable and has several great advantages going for it, one being that judges can specialize in particular categories, which could result in an enormous increase in the efficiency of judging panels. Under the professional system the way would be clear to influence general skating trends simply by assigning different factors to the various categories. If, for example, it were felt that skaters were tending to put too much emphasis on triple jumps, a lower factor could be assigned to the marks given for jumping than to the rest of the categories, or an increased factor could be given to the marks for artistry. All sorts of intriguing possibilities open up.

As it stands at the moment I have only one major objection to the professional system, which is that the result is decided by the total number of marks from all judges instead of by ordinals (see "Underlying Principles" in chapter 14), thus giving a judge who is marking consistently higher or lower than his colleagues an undue influence over the final result. Otherwise I feel that the system is an excellent one, and with a few adjustments here and there it could be the answer to many problems now existing in amateur judging.

The World Professional Figure Skating Championship for the Avon Cup

In 1980 the two times winner of the Olympic Winter Games and five times world champion Dick Button conceived the idea of a world professional figure skating championship to be held within the United States; but it was to be a championship with a difference. Instead of following conventional lines it was to consist primarily of a competition between two teams, each consisting of some ten professional skaters who had made their reputations as world and Olympic competitors and as established ice show stars. Participation was to be by invitation only—to quote the official program, "determined on the basis of placement in Olympic, world, and national figure skating championships, by freestyle rankings, the number, type, importance, and date of championship wins and the general ability, inventiveness, and reputation of each skater." At the time of writing, the most recent championship included no less than ten world champions and nine Olympic medalists, two of whom were Gold Medal winners. It can be seen that this championship is, in effect, a championship of champions, thus differing from the regular type of championship in which competitors do not already have to have titles in order to participate.

The format and organization of the World Professional Figure Skating Championship for the Avon Cup is in the very capable hands of Dick Button and his staff at Candid Productions, Inc. The task is not an easy one. Having assembled a galaxy of stars, they must then divide them into two teams, balanced as far as possible in talent, one team being known as the Pro Stars and the other as the All Stars. The names now have little purpose other than to distinguish one team from the other. A typical team is composed of two men and two women solo skaters, two pairs, and one dance couple. Each solo skater, pair, and dance couple is regarded as a single unit known as a *member*. Thus, although there are ten skaters to each team, for the purpose of competition they form only seven members.

During the competition each member must present two programs, the first emphasizing athletic ability, and the second, artistry. There must inevitably be some overlap, but it is under the above two categories that the programs are judged. As in other professional championships, marking is out of ten. The judging panel—selected from former champions and highly knowledgeable experts—must contain a minimum of five judges, but almost invariably seven are used. The marking is open, i.e., the marks are shown to the public immediately after the skaters have performed. The high and low marks are dropped and the remaining marks totaled to give the score for that member's program. The score for each team is the total of the scores of its individual members plus the scores of the group number. In addition to an award for the winning team, awards are also given for the winners of the men's and ladies' solo events, which are decided, of course, by the individual scores.

The group number is an important highlight of the evening. Each team provides eight skaters who perform a combined freestyle program designed by a leading choreographer. The music and choreography are the same for both teams but individual interpretation is permitted. The concept dates back to the 1920s and '30s, when amateur championships were held for teams of four or eight skaters. For many years this type of skating had disappeared from the competitive field and it is interesting to see its resuscitation.

Such is the delicate balance of the relative skills of the two teams that rarely does one beat the other by more than a very small margin. Handsome money prizes are awarded, the winning team taking two-thirds of the total and the second place team one-third.

This championship now seems firmly established and to date has taken place annually at the Capital Center, Landover, Maryland, where it has played to capacity crowds. Bringing together as it does the cream of skating, skimmed from top-rank events that have taken place over a period of several years, this championship is able to present an abundance of talent impossible to bring together in any other way; and because many of the events are presented in the form of professional show numbers, mixing high athletic ability with color, artistry, excitement, and humor, this championship provides a wealth of entertainment, suitable for many hours of subsequent airing on television, at the same time that it promotes the image of the sport by giving coverage at a time of the year when the excitement of the amateur competition season has died away.

An important point to notice is that because of the totally different aims, format, and concept, there is no serious clash of interests between this championship and the World Professional Ice Skating Championships held in Spain; each has its own distinct niche in the skating scene. Finally, probably because the team concept minimizes the one-on-one conflict, and the composition of the teams changes from year to year, the World Professional Figure Skating Championship for the Avon Cup is conducted in a particularly relaxed, sportsmanlike manner. No one goes home crushed by defeat; parents do not hiss at one another, nor does the public go on a rampage because its home team has not won. Peace and calm prevail—a welcome state of affairs nowadays.

The U.S. Professional Figure Skating Championship

In March, 1981, the U.S. Professional Figure Skating Championship was inaugurated in Philadelphia under the auspices and sponsorship of the Professional Skaters Guild of America. This was the first national professional championship ever to be held in the United States. This significant step was taken by the PSGA for several reasons, the most important being the urgent need to set up some system to assist in the selection of who should represent American professionals at the World Professional Ice Skating Championships held in Spain, and to accustom competitors to the circumstances under which they would be required to compete. With this in mind the PSGA adopted almost in its entirety the regulations and marking system set up by the Spaniards.

The U.S. Professional Figure Skating Championship will, I hope, establish itself firmly in the U.S. skating scene, particularly as it offers a forum in which to experiment with new ideas and alternative methods of judging not so readily available to amateur bodies. This type of experimentation is one of the many important ways in which the PSGA can assist the USFSA and the ISU in the advancement of the sport.

The championship is open to all U.S. professionals and American amateur skaters who intend to turn professional. Winners in each of the events take the title of U.S. Professional Champion and receive a permanent championship trophy.

16
Club Harmony

Oh, don't the days seem lank and long
When all goes right and nothing goes wrong,
And isn't your life extremely flat
With nothing whatever to grumble at!
Princess Ida, Gilbert and Sullivan

To the cynic, the phrase "club harmony" may seem a contradiction in terms, but harmonious clubs do exist, clubs that are models of decorum, where everybody gets along well together, and much is accomplished competitively, recreationally, and socially. Nevertheless, putting naïveté aside, it must be admitted that there are clubs that do not fit into this pattern. It may well happen that you as a parent will some day have to serve on a club board—you might even be elected president. It is the object of this chapter, therefore, to pinpoint some of the frequent causes of dissatisfaction and strife, and suggest ways in which they may be avoided, or at least kept within reasonable bounds.

Clubs consist of groups of skaters of different age groups and widely differing interests. No two clubs are exactly alike in their membership structure or amount of ice time available. For the purpose of this chapter we will presume that your club is constructed along average lines, that is, it has a group of enthusiastic youngsters working for figure and freestyle tests and competitions, an older group interested in ice dancing mainly from a social point of view, and a number of families with children who wish to skate for purely social and recreational purposes. You are thus faced with providing four types of skating sessions, namely, patch, freestyle, ice dancing, and family. For the moment we will leave out of consideration such activities as precision team skating and power skating for the boys who may eventually wish to play hockey.

Statement of Aims

The first thing a club should do is to state publicly, preferably in the club's by-laws, what its aims are. In the average club under consideration it might be stated that the policy is to encourage and promote figure skating under the four headings listed above.

Definition and Conduct of Sessions

Having decided which forms of skating the club will encourage, and to what degree (which may change as the club grows), the ice time must be mapped out and a clear definition made of what constitutes the type of skating to be practiced at the designated sessions. Guidelines—if necessary, rules—must be set up so that the best possible use may be made of the time available. Such rules and guidelines have been dealt with in chapter 10, so I shall not repeat them here. At the moment we are concerned with defining the sessions and stating who shall use them. Failure to do so can result in all groups being at one another's throats or giving the board of the club a very hard time. Let me give you an example from real life.

The problem in one particular club revolved around what constituted a freestyle session. The periods were listed as such in the club schedule with no further elaboration. Lacking any definition, interpretations varied widely. The juniors regarded it as a time when they could practice their jumps and spins (a reasonable assumption); the senior members, as a time to practice their threes and mohawks; the parents with young children, as an extra family session; while a few of the craftier members tried to practice a few solo dances when they thought nobody was looking. The session was, of course, the most unharmonious of the whole club's schedule. The junior freestyle skaters complained to the board that the beginners got in their way; the adults found themselves distracted in the practice of their threes and mohawks; the elderly totterers complained of being terrified out of their wits; while the family members went blissfully on their way, unaware that anything was amiss or that they were liable to be knocked through the nearest exit at any moment.

The root of the problem was that nowhere in the club literature was a freestyle session defined, and the attitude of club members was that of Humpty-Dumpty when he said to Alice, "When *I* use a word, it means just what I choose it to mean—neither more nor less." Unfortunately, somewhere in the club by-laws there was a very vague statement to the effect that freestyle sessions were limited to those skaters wearing figure skates who were serious skaters—a ridiculously inadequate statement that could scarcely even be called a definition. The club would have been on firmer ground had it labeled the period *general skating*. As it was, a more exact term would have been *free-for-all skating*.

It is, of course, not always possible for a club with very limited ice time to set aside separate sessions for freestyle, which may have to be practiced during a general skating session. Nevertheless, this can be successful to a degree as long as the standard of freestyle is not too high. It can never be an ideal situation, but if everyone is genuinely unselfish in his use of the ice, quite a lot can be achieved.

Controlling the Sessions

Nowadays the term *guideline* is often used as a euphemism for *rule*, but a distinction should be made. The etiquette that requires a very weak dance couple to allow stronger couples to start ahead of them in the lineup for a dance is a guideline, for who would wish to be saddled with the task of telling an influential member and his partner that they were going to hold everybody up? But the requirement that skaters shall not kick holes in the ice is a rule to be strictly enforced.

Once definitions, rules, and guidelines have been set up, it is essential to carry through. Some means must be found of enforcing the rules and diplomatically mentioning the guidelines to offenders. This means that at all sessions somebody must have the final word. At patch sessions this chore can be handled by the pros (if they are a group that work well together), or by the patch chairman or his delegate. Which brings up a point frequently overlooked: No one should be appointed to take charge of a session unless he, or she, knows and agrees with the rules. Obvious though this may seem, it is not always observed, particularly at patch sessions. Freestyle sessions are best handled by the presence of one or two strong-minded pros on the ice, since everything is happening at lightning speed, and pros are usually much quicker than the average amateur adult in sensing undercurrents of behavior and "who is doing what to whom." Dance sessions are usually best handled by the person in charge of the music, provided that the music box is at ice level. Apart from seeing that the normal rules are observed, the person in charge must prevent youngsters from horsing around during the dances or standing and talking in the fairway after a dance has started. Even family sessions, particularly those attended by a majority of children, need overseeing, more so in many instances than other sessions. There should be at least one strong and determined male on skates to take care of the boys, and a few women, also on skates, to look after the really young ones who have burst into tears for some reason or other and need consolation or escorting off the ice for a rest while they regain their composure. You would be surprised at the pandemonium that can result when fifty to a hundred children of both sexes and varying ages are left unattended in an afternoon family or recreational session. One club of which we have experience was so liberal-minded in regard to such sessions that it could not even bring itself to set a rule stating the direction in which the general mass should skate round the rink. They simply skated all ways and in all directions. Even the basic concept that the ice was to be used for skating seemed to have been abandoned. One popular activity, quite new to me and my wife, was rolling races. Children would lie full length on the ice and see who could roll fastest from one side of the rink to the other. Surprisingly, there were a couple of women on skates in attendance but they limited themselves to picking their way carefully round the ice, stepping over recumbent children and looking neither to the right nor left, except when they occasionally escorted a screaming youngster to the first-aid room. The whole session was what might be termed a recreational riot. Adding to the hazards was the ice surface, which was gaily decorated with chewing gum wrappers and other multicolored debris. When I commented on this ghastly chaos, I was told, "Well, you see, parents in this neighborhood don't like their children to be told what to do."

All of which goes to show that even in recreational sessions a modicum of discipline has its place. As a matter of fact it was eventually decided to try the effect of encouraging the general mass of skaters to move in a counterclockwise direction round the rink so that a place in the center could be kept clear for the more earnest children who wished to practice their skating. But the women in charge, intoxicated by a sudden sense of power, completely misconstrued the spirit of the rule, and it didn't matter what the skater was doing, even when practicing in the center, he had to move counterclockwise. It made no difference whether he was moving in and out of spins, jumping, or practicing simple crossovers, he still had to move in the predetermined direction. It was at this point that I gave up any attempt at advice and quietly withdrew.

Whenever new rules and guidelines are set up or old ones revived, particularly for sessions that have previously been rather loosely run, somebody almost invariably makes a fuss; but if the club has already given the matter careful consideration and made a decision, it must stick to its guns. Vacillation and compromise are fatal, as they simply open the floodgates to the malcontents who wish to manipulate the club to their own advantage. One of the greatest pitfalls is to try to please everyone—it just can't be done. Which brings up another important point. If a member is dissatisfied with a rule or does not agree with the club's policies and threatens to resign, experience seems to show that it is always best to accept his resignation even if the club is strapped for funds. In the majority of cases it is purely a threat and he won't resign anyway. If the rules are changed to suit his demands, others will attempt the same ploy. Very few members ever really want to resign if the ice facilities are good and the sessions well run. A complaining member will often give the impression that a lot of people are backing him—"they" are saying this, "they" are saying that. If one tries to get names in an attempt to track down exactly who has made such statements, "they" vanish like a mirage, or are eventually traced to a member of the complainer's own family. This is not to say that serious splits in a club do not sometimes occur, but this usually involves large cliques who have been battling each other for some time, not over some minor point regarding session rules but over much deeper issues, such as who shall control the club, or what pros shall be allowed to teach during the club ice time. And so we come to the role that pros play in the functioning of a club.

Relations Between Clubs and Pros

The most harmonious clubs are those in which there is a happy balance of interests between club and pro. How is this achieved? First, the club must be able to provide the pros with the possibility of making a reasonable living, in return for which the pros must carry out their duties to the club in a reasonable manner and to the best of their abilities. Second, the pros must be compatible and preserve among themselves good ethical standards of conduct (see "Ethics" in chapter 19). We shall discuss here some of the circumstances that make these aims difficult to achieve.

Because most pros try to preserve friendly relations with their students and club members, share the same ice, and sometimes partner club skaters in ice dancing, the membership at large frequently forgets that the prime object of a pro's being there is to make a living rather than to skate for his own pleasure. Indeed, in the case of most top pros, teaching is their only source of income. Failure to appreciate this will often cause clubs to adopt, quite unwittingly, policies that are bound to set up tensions among members of the teaching staff. This can be made clear by examining the two fundamentally different approaches used when inviting pros to teach for a club. It must be remembered that we are dealing here with figure skating clubs (almost invariably affiliated with the USFSA) and not rinks catering to the general public—although in many cases similar principles hold.

The Closed Rink

The closed rink policy is to offer contracts to a fixed number of pros for the coming season, according to the requirements of the club as a whole (rather than individual members). Under normal circumstances the number of staff would not be increased until new contracts are offered for the following season, and then only if the membership has grown or the structure of the club has changed. In other words, the club must take the plunge and commit itself to the pro for the season and the pro does the same in respect to the club; each side assumes mutual responsibilities.

In order to preserve harmony, the ideal situation is for the club to hire just enough pros for the estimated number of lessons available, obviously no easy task. To preserve an absolutely even balance over the whole season, so that no pro ever has empty lesson slots and no club member ever finds difficulty in getting a lesson, is almost impossible to achieve. What usually happens in the average seasonal club where the majority of skaters are at the lower level (as opposed to the all-year, high-pressure training centers) is that the period from October to December is relatively slack and the pros have free time on their hands; in January and February there is a sudden surge in the demand for lessons and they are fully booked; and then in March and April things become quiet again, although not nearly to the same degree as at the start of the season. The pros most likely to be affected by this type of situation are those who draw most of their students from the group of less serious skaters who may be still tied up at the beginning of the season with other activities. Skaters working on USFSA tests are usually only too anxious to resume their regular lessons as soon as the season starts.

The problem of the midseason surge is that those members who have difficulty in getting lessons complain to the board that another pro is needed. If a pro can be brought in on a temporary basis to take care of the extra demand, things may work out satisfactorily, but such pros can be hard to find; and if they are added to the permanent staff for the following year, it is quite clear that the business for the remainder of the pros will be diluted at the off-peak periods. (See also below, "The Instant Lesson.")

Leaving aside the difficult question of temporary seasonal surges, a club is certainly justified in enlarging its permanent staff if the membership is growing steadily or the structure of the club changes. A rising standard of skating may warrant adding another high-test pro to the staff; or an increased interest in ice dancing may mean the engagement of a dance specialist who is capable of taking dancers through tests. As far as possible, however, the engagement of extra staff should be done on a seasonal basis even if the agreement to maintain a closed rink policy is only implicit in the original contract. This chapter is, after all, dedicated to suggesting how harmony may be preserved, and not how far each side can go if it sets its mind to it. Nevertheless, if in the middle of the season a permanent member of the staff leaves for some reason or other and a replacement has to be brought in, or the situation desperately requires an addition to the staff—not because of seasonal surges or the urging of one or two individuals, but possibly because the club, acting in good faith, may have genuinely misjudged the needs of the membership—then it is advisable that the board should discuss the matter with the pros to see whether a solution satisfactory to all can be worked out. If the club simply goes out and hires another pro right in the middle of the season without a word to the permanent staff, a tense situation may be created. Quite apart from the fact that it may contravene some implicit agreement, the club may bring in someone who is anathema to the rest of the staff, known to his colleagues (although not necessarily to the board) as being completely without ethical principles. Then you really have trouble.

The Open Rink

The second approach with regard to pros is for the club to adopt an open rink policy, which means that they grant permission for almost any pro to come in and use the club ice time for teaching purposes, usually at the request of a member or members who want lessons from that particular pro. The open rink policy is more often found in public rinks (as opposed to clubs), particularly those with large group lesson programs, that find difficulty in getting instructors to teach classes. Pros are often granted the privilege of coming to public sessions and picking up what lessons they can, provided they teach the group lessons (for which they are, of course, paid). Sometimes, too, rinks allow pros to bring private students to public sessions for teaching purposes provided that both student and pro pay the session fee. There are many different types of arrangements. Inasmuch as a club has different aims from those of a public rink, the open rink policy has certain disadvantages when applied to USFSA clubs. This is not a criticism of the way in which some rinks work—they have enormous overheads that must be covered and the way they make their money is entirely their own business.

A club with a closed permanent staff protects the interests of its pros, which means that the pros in return must protect the interests of the club. In an open rink, however, if there are only enough lessons to keep, for example, four pros busy, but sixteen pros have teaching privileges, no one is going to make a living unless he can make up his income elsewhere, possibly at other clubs in the neighborhood. Under such conditions loyalties may be split and a very impersonal situation created between the pros and the clubs. The impersonality of the open rink or club frequently shows itself in patch sessions, in which it may be difficult to maintain discipline if many of the skaters are taught by different pros, some of whom may not be present at every session. The student of pro A resents being reprimanded by pro B, with the result that pros eventually close their minds to what is happening on the ice unless it concerns their own students. On the other hand, the members of a closed permanent staff usually have an agreement among themselves that if there is only one pro on patch, all students come under his jurisdiction.

Although closed and open rink policies do not normally mix, a combination of the two is usual in most summer schools. A club having some forty test and competitive skaters during the winter decides to run a summer school that, because of the extra time available, can cope with 120 skaters or more. In this case most of the permanent staff will stay for the summer school with their students, but to attract sufficient skaters to make the school pay, outside pros are invited to teach, usually provided they have a following, i.e., they can bring students to the school. The arrangement works well, everyone enjoys the change in routine and a good time is had by all, except perhaps by the harassed and hard-working summer school chairman.

A difficult situation arises when a club has too little ice time relative to the size of its membership. No single pro can rely on the club time for his total income, even if fully booked, while at the same time there must be a sufficient number of pros on the staff to create the necessary number of lesson slots. The situation is considerably eased if the rink where the club is located offers patch and freestyle periods outside club time and permits club pros to teach during these times. As far as possible members should be encouraged to take lessons during the public sessions, thus relieving the congestion in the club sessions. This kind of situation can work very well if the club and rink are on good terms. On the whole, good relations between clubs and rink managers exist in most rinks, but just occasionally they clash. I well remember one arena manager who persisted in referring to the local figure skaters as "fidget skaters." What might have helped would have been for the club to have set up a small liaison committee of two or three of their most diplomatic members, who would meet on a regular basis with the rink management to discuss problems. There are many ways in which clubs and rinks can assist each other if only both sides will sit down and clarify their respective aims.

The Split Club

Having read the above, you will now be in a position to understand one of the most difficult situations a club can face. Scenarios differ, but the following is typical. A club starts out with a closed rink policy and all is going excellently until one day friction develops between a pro and his student or the student's parents. A test, possibly more than one, may have been failed; student and pro may be psychologically incompatible; there may have been a misunderstanding of something somebody said—never mind the cause, the situation is there. The parents think a change of pro would be beneficial (the pro may be thinking exactly the same thing)—that's fine, skaters are perfectly entitled to take lessons from anyone they choose. Unfortunately in this case there seems to be no one on the permanent staff who meets the requirements, so the parents and skater go off to another rink in the area where there is a pro who seems suitable.

Now this second pro, to put it pleasantly, is one of the go-getter kind, and he sees an opportunity. He's not doing too well at his own rink and his new student's club seems to offer interesting possibilities. The seed of an idea is planted, and very soon the parents, who have never liked the long drive to the new rink, are suggesting that it would be very nice if he could give the lessons at their child's home club. They are sure no one would object; in fact they have the feeling that quite a number of other students would like to take some lessons from him. They will have a word with the president. At first the president does not think the idea a good one, particularly as it is right in the middle of the season, so the parents muster their forces. They persuade some of their friends to agree that if teaching privileges can be arranged, they will definitely have their children take lessons from the new pro. The student's original teacher, hearing that strange rumors are being spread about her teaching and that she might even be replaced, gathers together her own loyal group, who are determined to support her. Certain members of both groups happen to be on the board. A meeting is called that results in one of the biggest rows in the club's history. The "bad guys" have the loudest voices and the board caves in weakly. The new pro comes in, relieves the permanent staff of a number of its pupils, and is off and running.

You now have two cliques bitterly opposed to each other and the club is split down the middle. The pupils of pro A will not speak to the pupils of pro B and the vibes can be felt as soon as one steps through the door of the rink. Now that there is a definite polarization, one group decides that it had better go the whole way and try to take over the running of the club. The following season, one of the groups, now consisting of almost half the club, decides not to rejoin and goes to a neighboring rink where they try (probably successfully) to form their own club, which means another desperate battle with the first group who now oppose the granting of a USFSA sanction for the formation of a new club in the area. Had the board acted promptly in the first place and stood firm in its declared policies, the whole affair would probably have died an early and natural death.

The Instant Lesson

The successful organization of instant lessons, i.e., those not booked in advance and taken on a casual, irregular basis, can present surprising organizational difficulties. As explained earlier, most skaters working on USFSA tests beyond the level of the beginners' badges take lessons on a regular basis. Even if a lesson is only taken once a week, it is customary to take it at the same time on the same day, otherwise it is very difficult for a pro to make sense out of a busy schedule. The problems arise when parents arrive unscheduled at a family or recreational-type session and want a lesson for their child right then and there. If it is at the height of the season, all the pros may be booked up, but by some lucky chance a pro may have a cancellation and can take the child. No further lessons are arranged, but a few weeks later the family turns up again for an instant lesson; this time, however, there is no vacant slot, so the child has to do without. Some other family experiences the same difficulty and complaints are made to the board, who are told that "people" can't get lessons— although it may, in fact, only involve a couple of families. The complaint appears to be a valid one, so the board, not wishing to lose members, decides to take the easy way out and bring in another pro.

Having read what has gone before, you will see that this can bring its own problems. But the board nevertheless determines that something has to be done. The club looks round for some young pro, perhaps teaching in the rink's public sessions, who is willing to attend club sessions on the off chance that someone will take a lesson, or perhaps two, for which they will be asked to hang about for a couple of hours. If this type of casual lesson-taking picks up during the height of the season, the extra pro can be fairly busy and everyone is happy.

But the problem is not really solved. One day during the busiest part of the season, three families turn up at the club on the same afternoon all wanting a lesson sometime between 3:45 and 4:15, as they all have to leave early for various reasons. The extra pro is booked until the end of the session (yes, she did have a cancellation at 3:15, but that doesn't help), and there you are with the same problem again. What are you going to do? Hire an *extra* extra pro?

There is no perfect solution to the instant lesson. The only way to make it work would be to have instant staff. Nevertheless, there are ways that will considerably improve the situation. First it must be made clear to the membership, particularly new members, that the club cannot guarantee that a lesson slot will always be available to them at whatever time they choose to turn up at the rink; but at the same time it should also be made clear that irregular lessons *can* be arranged provided that they are booked in advance—which is why most clubs give the telephone numbers of their pros in their newsletters—and that skaters must be prepared to take such times, within reason, as are available. Nevertheless, there may still be a number of skaters who would like to take a casual lesson on the spur of the moment, but because the problem has been explained to them, they will not be disappointed if it is not immediately forthcoming. Even if the pros are theoretically fully booked, the casual lesson may still be possible due to last-minute cancellations.

The procedure for getting such lessons should also be spelled out to skaters. As soon as the skater arrives on the ice he should go to the pro of his choice and ask, "Do you have a cancellation this afternoon?" The answer may be, "Yes, I do . . . come to me at four o'clock." It is now imperative that the skater does in fact report to the pro at four. It must not be left to the pro to track down the skater. There may have been no time to take the skater's name—remember that when you talk to a pro who is giving a lesson to someone else, you are doing so on that person's time, so there should be no idle chit-chat—and when the skater disappears into a crowded session, the pro may have difficulty in recognizing him again among all the others. (Sorry, parents, a lot of children do tend to look alike to busy pros.) Or the child may have gone to the toilet or be playing a video game in the lobby. By the time the pro has chased all over the building looking for him, five minutes of the lesson may be wasted.

Also, in the case of young children, it is usually better if an adult asks the pro for the lesson. Quite often a child is dropped off at the rink with instructions to ask the pro whether she has any lesson time free. It often happens that the child does not really want the lesson, and either does not ask the pro or exercises a little wishful thinking and assumes the pro has no time. When the child is picked up from the rink, the mother asks, "Did you get your lesson?" to which the child replies that she had *asked* but the pro didn't have any time free. Unfortunately a friend of the family is present at the session, and having noticed that the pro did have a free period, mentions the fact to the mother, who complains to the board that her child is being treated unfairly. When the pro is taken to task, she quite rightly says she has never heard of the child, but dark suspicions still exist. Fortunately it occurs to someone to question the child again, who finally admits that no, she didn't actually ask the *pro* but that she did ask a friend about getting lessons and had been told that the pros were nearly always booked up and so she didn't try any further. In all fairness to the child, it must be pointed out that some children are very shy of going up to unknown pros and addressing them, which is one of the reasons that lesson bookings are usually better handled by an adult.

One last word on cancellations: It should by now be firmly established that everyone benefits when lessons are canceled as early as possible. It frequently happens, however, that a skater cancels quite legitimately due to an illness of indefinite duration. It is most essential that when he has recovered, or feels he will be well enough to skate in a day or so, he let the pro know that he is coming back. The pro may be quite willing to resume lessons with the skater at the old time, but he cannot be expected to leave the slot permanently vacant until the student recovers. I am often astounded at the indignation of students whom I haven't seen for at least a month, who suddenly rise from their sickbeds and turn up at the rink without warning, expecting to take their usual lesson. The pro must be given time to cancel, if possible, the skater who is temporarily taking the lesson slot.

Judging Beginners' Tests

The judging of beginner-level tests and the awarding of badges frequently present clubs with difficulties. Chapter 3 deals with this problem to a certain extent, but mainly in the context of public session classes; the same principles hold good, however, for club tests at the beginner level. These are usually judged by members who are reasonably good skaters themselves and are interested in the children. It is sad to see how often these kind, dedicated people, who only have the skaters' interests at heart, are berated for what are normally very sound decisions. Naturally there will always be a few unsound decisions, but this is to be expected and must be accepted. Notice, too, that an allegedly wrong decision is rarely remarked upon when it involves a skater passing a movement that he should have failed. Pleasant though the result may be, the philosophy is weak. Taking part in a beginners' badge program should not be regarded as a game, in which winning is normally considered the prime object, but as a learning process. (See "Incentives" in chapter 3.)

Although the majority of parents are very reasonable regarding beginners' tests, it is not the easiest thing for one member to judge another member's child. However good a skater the judge may be, even if he is a former world champion, at some time or other aspersions may be cast on his motives and abilities. If the going gets really rough, it is sometimes better to hand over the judging to the pros, whose opinions always seem to be more readily accepted by parents. Above all, however, these beginners' tests should be kept in perspective. If a child is really Olympic material, the fact that his backward skating on one foot was a little faulty in the Intermediate Second Class badge is not going to prevent him from getting to the top. Make him work on it for ten minutes and let him try again next week; he'll be all that much better for the extra practice.

The Ice Show

It is with regret that I have to include the annual ice show in the catalogue of activities that can cause stresses and rifts within a club structure, but quite frankly there is nothing to equal a show for bringing out latent passions and ill feelings. This is a great pity, as ice shows can be enormous fun, just as amateur theatricals were in the past. In well-run clubs that have established a clear modus operandi, these performances can be, and frequently are, staged with a minimum of dissatisfaction. Even in the average show the majority of skaters, the rank and file, have a wonderful time, which is as it should be. Unfortunately, it often happens that among the higher-level skaters and their families, far too much time and effort are spent in jockeying for positions.

My wife and I skated for many years in professional ice shows and, later, when we decided to teach, choreographed numerous amateur shows. One of the great differences between professional and amateur shows is that in a professional show the skater has a contract that tells him what he is expected to do and what he can expect in return: whether he will be required to skate as directed or, if he is a top-rank performer, how many appearances he will make, how he will be billed in the program, and many other details. Everything is, or should be, cut and dried. He does what is in the contract or, if the terms are not to his liking, he doesn't sign it.

The fundamental and greatest difficulty in most amateur shows is the apparently arbitrary and loose manner in which the various roles and solos are handed out. It may seem clear to the show committee but seldom to the skaters and parents, which can lead to the most unbelievable political maneuvering. Even the question of whether some small child is going to be a daisy or a white bunny can lead to tense confrontations. After a particularly harrowing series of summer shows that left me with a racing pulse and extra systoles for many months thereafter, we decided that in the absence of contracts, the only successful way of casting an amateur show was to hand out roles, solos, and participation in numbers on the basis of the skater's level of competence as shown by USFSA (or ISIA) tests, competitions, or, for the lower-level group numbers, beginners' badges. The requirements can be adjusted from year to year according to the standard prevailing in the club and the number of solo spots, roles, etc., available. There are all sorts of ways in which this can be worked, but once the choice of level at which parts are to be assigned is made, everyone concerned must stick to it. As far as the elementary group numbers are concerned, decisions will have to be made, for example, that all girls having passed their Novice Second Class badge will be buttercups, or that Novice First Class skaters are to be snow maidens. Something appropriate, preferably involving a lot of activity, must, of course, be found for the boys. The achievement of qualifications should be subject to a cutoff date some days or weeks before rehearsals are due to start. The system works well provided everyone knows what is to be expected well ahead of time and the club has the courage to carry it through without wavering.

One other aspect of club shows must also be considered; that is, how much time is going to be devoted to rehearsals. This depends largely on the structure of the club. It is best not to disrupt too much the training schedule of the test and competitive skaters. On the other hand, if you don't have a show at all, you may upset skaters at the lower level or those who skate purely for recreation. As every club and the amount of ice time at its disposal is different, it is difficult to give specific advice. Nevertheless, there is one point that should be made. In the vast majority of amateur shows far too much time is wasted during rehearsals. The choreographer, or choreographers, should have their numbers planned in advance, and the music should have been selected, cut, and ready for use before rehearsals start. If possible, every number should have its own separate chairman whose duty it is to see that all skaters know the times of rehearsals and clearly understand that they must not miss more than a certain amount of rehearsal time.

The club should lay down a rule that after, let us say, two absences, a skater may be required to drop out of a number. Skaters who have missed a rehearsal should be expected to learn any new movements from their friends before attending the next one. The club must be firm about these rehearsals. There is nothing more calculated to enrage a choreographer than to be assigned twelve people with which to form a group number and then find that only six of them arrive for the first rehearsal and an entirely different six for the following one. This sort of thing does not simply double the rehearsal time necessary, it may quadruple it, and even then the number will probably look underrehearsed on the night of the show.

Starting rehearsals early in the season to compensate for irregular rehearsal attendance does not help and can, in fact, be counterproductive, as the lack of a sense of urgency causes time to be frittered away on the ice, and the skaters get bored and fidgety. You will probably achieve as much in six weeks as you will in nine or ten; there is nothing like a touch of panic for keeping everybody on his toes. By the way, if Easter intervenes during the rehearsal period, the club had better make some special arrangements, as it is pretty certain that there are going to be twice as many absent as normal.

The Test Chairman

Do not misunderstand me—the Test Chairman is not listed here as a problem (although I know some exceptions); I cite him here as a solver of problems. A good test chairman is usually in close touch with both skaters and pros and can forestall or smooth over many possible problems, not necessarily to do with the tests. The Test Chairman's job is highly important and clubs should see that the most competent person available is given this position and not assign it to someone just because he is willing and has time free. The job is best left to somebody who is a very good organizer, excellent at public relations, and possibly a judge himself, but the first two qualifications are the most important.

If one analyzes the roots of disharmony as described in this chapter, it will be found that many of them can be traced back to (1) lack of direct communication, (2) failure to enunciate and stand by club policies, and (3) common human frailty. The phrase *lack of communication* is in constant use to explain almost anything that goes wrong, but to my mind the trouble is not lack of communication but too much communication of the wrong sort. If only people would get their facts straight! This is why I stress *direct* communication. One must get to the source. So much is reported by third parties that is misheard, misconstrued, twisted to support a particular point of view, or repeated in the wrong tone of voice. All of which comes under the heading of human frailty, which also, alas, includes a few other and more damaging tendencies. If you think I have put a great emphasis on what clubs and their members do, or fail to do, let me assure you that I am well aware that many pros are not perfect either. But then, this is a parent's, not a pro's, guide and there are limits to its size.

17
Fair Play for Judges

The final results of the Regional Competition have just been announced, and for three-quarters of an hour an expectant crowd has been waiting in hushed silence round the entrance to the judges' room. At last the door opens, the crowd surges forward, and several judges emerge to be immediately surrounded by members of their own and other clubs patting them on the back and uttering excited cries of congratulation:

"Mrs. B., that was a fantastic performance!"
"Yes, you judged even better than last year!"
"You were so consistent—it's absolutely amazing how you and the rest of the judges got all the skaters in exactly the right order. . . ."
"That's right—everybody, particularly all the parents, agreed with you right down the line."
"How do you do it? With so little practice, too."

As the crowd mills round the group of modest, blushing judges, a small child seeking an autograph gets trampled underfoot, but feels it was well worth the try.

No, no, I am afraid it is all a figment of the imagination. It is a sad fact that judges perform one of the most thankless tasks in the skating world. Not for them the plaudits of the crowd, no storms of applause when their marks are put up, no standing ovations when some judge puts up 5.5 when all the others have 5.8. Boos, hisses, pounding of feet on the bleachers is their common lot. I know. I too have suffered. Can you realize what it is like to be booed by eight thousand people? Until one becomes hardened, it can be quite shattering to the ego. To make matters worse, here comes the referee, and you know you will have a lot of explaining to do, while visions of a nasty letter from the authorities canceling your appointment float before your eyes. There are, of course, compensations, and by and large, judges get great satisfaction from their self-imposed burden, despite the occasional hardships.

Let us consider the task with which a judge is faced when marking a figure test—and here I shall elaborate on some of the points mentioned earlier when discussing the marking system. He must take into consideration all of the following:

1. The shape, symmetry, and size of the circles. In order to do this he must pace out the figure, and then view it from various angles.
2. Whether the figure has been skated on clean edges. There must be no flats (double lines) anywhere round the figure. In the triple repetition of a two-circle figure made up of circles of sixteen feet in diameter the skater travels just over three hundred feet. Theoretically the judge would have to examine the whole length of the tracing, but fortunately he knows where flats are most likely to occur, so this process can be speeded up.
3. The quality of the turns and their placement. All turns should be clean, that is, they must be made directly from edge to edge and contain no flats, unwanted changes of edge, skids, or scrapes. The turns must be symmetrical, with their cusps pointing in the right direction. Having found an error, the judge must then assess its *degree of commission*, e.g., how far from the cusp does a flat occur? Is it one of, say, six inches in length, or is it just a small one about half an inch long in the cusp itself? Most figures have six turns to be examined, but the double threes have twelve, and the paragraph double threes in the Eighth Test contain no less than twenty-four.
4. The quality of the center (where the figure starts). Is it correctly placed in relationship to the axes of the figure? Is the thrust made from the flat of the blade? Is the strike-off in the correct direction?
5. The skater's carriage, flow, motion, and speed.

The first four items above are, of course, examined after the figure has been completed. During this examination the judge theoretically starts with the count of six in his mind and deducts points, or fractions of a point, for errors as he finds them. If the skater makes the error three times, then the deduction is multiplied by three. At the same time, these deductions must be modified or increased according to the degree of commission, something that must be left to the discretion of the judges. To do all this the judge is allowed approximately 1½ minutes. One hundred percent accuracy, please, and don't keep the referee waiting.

The amounts to deduct for errors are laid down in a book issued by the USFSA known as *The Evaluation of School Figure Errors,* but in actual practice it is highly doubtful whether a judge really goes through all these mathematical calculations in his mind, and quite frankly, if he did so in the short time available, he would most likely come up with some very bizarre marks indeed. Fortunately, experienced judges develop a very accurate feel for the standards required at specific test levels, and can assess fairly consistently whether a skater is above or below standard, a skill that requires many seasons of constant practice; hence the system of trial judging.

From all this you can see that there must inevitably be differences of opinion. In the figures, some judge may consider symmetry the most important aspect; a second may be more impressed by the quality of the turns; while a third may place considerable weight on the accuracy at the center. The really experienced judge—particularly one who has been a high-test skater himself—sees not only the errors in a figure but also the good points, which may account for apparent leniency at times.

When it comes to competition judging, there is the added difficulty of placing everybody in the correct order. The juvenile events are particularly challenging. Many of the competitors are so light that it is almost impossible to see the tracings. It would be easier if the figures were well traced, that is, all the tracings put nearly on top of one another, but at the juvenile level they are usually scattered, and one sees puzzled referees wandering all over the ice trying to decide which tracing—when, by a happy freak of lighting, he can find it—belongs to which figure, and where to put his markers. Added to this is the fact that at this level nearly all the figures contain major errors. So how are you going to judge a figure containing six flat threes but with good circles and lineup, against one with only two flat threes but with the lineup three feet out and circles of unequal size? The variables could be multiplied indefinitely.

Judging competitive free skating is difficult at all levels, since in most cases one skater's program differs so much from another's that the judge is being asked to compare entirely different things, and under a variety of headings. The sheer weight of numbers in a competition can be formidable.

Imagine having to place in correct order thirty to forty juveniles in a regional competition. Of course, dividing the competition into heats is the only answer—and the rules do provide for groups of not more than fifteen—but even so it may still be a very challenging task to make an accurate decision between as few as eight skaters of approximately the same level. Things are not so bad when it comes to the short program, in which everybody has to perform the same basic moves, but even here personal variation is permitted in the connecting steps. In the long free skating programs many judges resort to a personal system that has been in existence unofficially for years, that of awarding points for various moves on a scale worked out by themselves, and after adding them up, using them to arrive at a mark out of six; but even this method goes only part of the way, as so many other factors have to be taken into consideration.

Earlier I mentioned that when the open marking system is used, there is a tendency to revile the judge whose low (or high) mark seems to be out of line. Before you add your hisses to the general pandemonium, you must decide whether the judge in question is marking consistently high or consistently low. If his range of marks follows a uniform pattern throughout the competition, he may still arrive at the right ordinals, i.e., he may still place the competitors in the correct order, and since it is the ordinals that (except for the case of ties) decide the result, no harm will have been done. But if you have kept track of the marks and conclude that politics or favoritism has been the motivating factor, then, most certainly, a few disapproving sounds are in order.

Considerable thought has been given to better methods of judging modern skating—not by juggling the calculations but by making the judges' job on the ice easier. In addition to videotaping the whole event, an idea frequently put forward by otherwise intelligent people is that of running all the performances (not the marks) through a computer—no suggestions, of course, how this should be done or the data prepared. I suppose that by a wild stretch of the imagination a system might be worked out for the figures, but even then subjective judgments must be made in respect to style and ease of movement. It would certainly not be applicable to a combination of sport and art such as free skating. Can you imagine using a computer to compare a Beethoven symphony with a Chopin nocturne? No—I think we can forget that idea for quite a time yet. Much more practical in the case of the figures would be to adapt the system used for the freestyle in professional championships by giving each judge a certain aspect of the figure to evaluate—one judge for the turns, one for symmetry of circles, and so on. This is, by the way, not a new idea.

Now, having given the judges a fair shake, I must also be fair to the skaters they judge. There is, regrettably, another side to the coin, and it would be naive to ignore it. In all levels and forms of society (even among teachers of skating), there are those whose behavior is unacceptable, and the judging community is not immune. Fortunately, these individuals are remarkably few, but it is about time somebody brought the matter out into the open, and I am about to do so. A test judge's marks, or his behavior on the ice, are rarely questioned. Occasionally a pro takes a stand, but he knows it is going to make no difference to the test in question and may in the long run make matters worse. Even more rarely does a parent make a complaint. He does not have the knowledge to present his case, and most parents are, quite frankly, scared of judges: not personally, but because of the damage they fear a complaint might do to their child. Because they are never queried, a certain type of judge begins to think he is infallible and becomes puffed up with a sense of his own importance, pontificating to all, and writing the most utter rubbish on his marking sheets. These are the Toads of the skating community, and like the celebrated Toad in *Wind in the Willows*, do no great harm, but are wildly inconsistent and the most crashing bores.

The second group are the Scrooges, who seem to hate skaters and passing tests as much as Scrooge hated Christmas. Session after session they turn up, failing everything in sight, circumventing the majority system by giving a below-passing mark when they cannot get their way by any other means, doing their best to dominate panels, and generally upsetting all and sundry by their unnecessarily scathing and sarcastic remarks. These are the failing judges, and are known as such among the skaters. It seems that little can be done officially about this problem, but taking the reasonable view that the majority are probably in the right, I suggest that clubs, parents, and skaters get together with the club test chairman and insist that these consistently out of line failing judges be boycotted. There seems no other way.

The other side of the coin does, however, present another type of judge—a variety much easier to tolerate provided one is prepared to give his conscience temporary leave of absence. Such judges, relatively few in number, are sometimes known to their colleagues as patsies. The patsy, in his desire to be popular and in constant demand, can be depended upon to pass everything within sight. They provide a welcome relief from the Scrooges and their existence seems to be nature's way of evening things up. Nevertheless, an unrelieved diet of patsies does not over the long haul do much to improve the general standard of skating.

Well, it had to be said, but I regret having had to insert a jarring note. Certainly the vast majority of judges do an outstanding job, so I will end this chapter in a more cheerful key: Judges on the whole deserve our confidence and whole-hearted thanks for their time, skill, patience, and devotion. Human perfection is a rare quality wherever we may seek it.

18
Hints for Competitors

Much of what has already been said earlier in regard to taking tests applies equally to taking part in competitions. In competitive skating, however, there are additional problems, particularly in respect to the free skating. In a competition the skater is no longer just skating against a standard, he is also skating against other competitors whom, presumably, he wishes to beat. This means that he must not only skate better than everyone else, but he must look better and present himself better. Here are a few pointers, some addressed to the parent, others to the skater.

Which Level?

The level at which a skater competes must be given considerable thought. Should he, for example, take a test that, if passed, would put him into the Novice class, or should he hold back and compete at the Intermediate level where he may have more chance of success? A lot depends on which is more important to the skater's career: his passing a particular test or his success that year in competition. To do well in competition a skater's figures and free skating must be of a far higher standard than that required for the qualifying tests. It is a policy of many skaters to hold back, which means that a skater who scrambles through a qualifying test with just a bare pass is likely to come up against tough competition from skaters who have held back and possibly practiced their figures and required moves for a whole season longer than he has. On the other hand, if a skater is ready to take a certain test and has a good chance of passing, it may be as well to seize the opportunity, regardless of which group he will have to enter. Whether to go for a test or to hold back is often a matter of personal feeling and philosophy, and it is not uncommon for the pro and parents to be in disagreement as to the course to follow. Judging from the skaters we have observed over a period of many years, it would be our guess that more skaters have benefited from taking and passing a test than from holding back; but this is a generalization, and each case must be judged on its own merits.

Pre-Competition Training

The schedule of training before the event will, of course, be decided by the skater's pro, but there is one golden rule I believe every trainer would agree with: When a skater has to run through his program (as opposed to working on sections), he must put everything in. That sounds obvious, doesn't it? Nevertheless, a large majority of skaters (possibly as many as 80 percent of would-be competitors) will not put in their double jumps when practicing their programs. Any skater who, when required to do so by his pro, does not make a serious attempt during program practice to do all his most difficult jumps might just as well give up any idea of doing even moderately well in competition. Skaters who leave out their jumps in practice will leave them out, or miss them, in competition. We have seen skaters' careers ruined by failure to observe this rule. It is one of the most common causes of bad feeling between student and trainer. Few trainers will in their hearts blame a student for taking a fall, provided a genuine attempt has been made. But a skater who makes singles out of all his doubles makes a mockery of the practice session. There are times, of course, when there may be the legitimate excuse of some temporary hurt or injury that must be sympathetically dealt with, but there are, I regret to say, a number of skaters who only seem to develop these aches and pains when any great effort is demanded of them. A recognizable pattern usually manifests itself, and all trainers have their own methods of dealing with the situation; but it is noticeable that the skater who eventually does well in competition is the one who minimizes his ills rather than exaggerates them. Nor is any trainer fooled by the skater who, when running through his program, always seems to find someone standing in the exact place where he has to do his most difficult jumps—this is also a recognizable pattern, and one that does not augur well for the skater's future.

Let us now return to the sensible skater who really does try his best to cooperate. In the longer programs the skater may have to be gradually brought to the pitch where he can get through the whole 4 or 4½ minutes. Training theories differ, but it is generally held that if a skater skates to the point of complete exhaustion, he is not going to be worth much for the next two or three days. If it is decided that in the early stages the program should be skated in two parts with a short rest in between (usually consisting of stroking round the rink), then the break should be made at a predetermined part of the program, and not by the arbitrary decision of the skater while he is skating.

Programs must be run in, that is, they must have been practiced over a sufficient period of time for them to have become completely automatic; apart from other obvious advantages, this allows the skater to give some attention to how he presents the program. Many skaters, after they have had a program for a couple of months or so, get bored with it and start looking for new music. A complete change of music and program after a very short period of use is usually only justified in the case of very young skaters of pre-juvenile level whose skating is improving so rapidly that they need a better vehicle for its presentation; but the advanced skater with the more difficult program must buckle down to work and practice the program until it becomes second nature.

Dress and Makeup

For the figures nothing further need be added to what has already been said in chapter 9, "Hints on Taking Tests," but in free skating the competitor is trying to outshine everybody else, so something more striking in the way of costume is in order. For men and boys the choice is not difficult. At the present time the sleeveless jumpsuit is very popular, often in some pure, saturated color, worn with an open-neck shirt. Be careful, however, of this open-neck appearance; some shirts are cut so low and so wide that the skater looks as though he has just got out of bed—an unfortunate impression.

For the women and girls, it is important to remember the effect of distance. In a large arena busy patterns get lost, and even bold patterns tend to merge into one. Patterns, if they are to be used at all, must be very bold and simple; it is good to remember this even in the smaller rinks. Under the strong lighting used for most competitions pale shades can wash out completely. So we are looking for a costume of simple, good lines, made out of stretch material, with clear, saturated colors (never muddy), and a simple, bold pattern if one is to be used at all. The skater must be comfortable and able to lift her arms without hindrance. Find out what styles are in vogue; some of the color photographs in *Skating* magazine can be of great help.

Some makeup should be used (this includes the men), but it should not be overdone—just enough to take away the pallor. If TV lights are being used, makeup should be heavier, not for the benefit of TV viewers but for the audience and judges, who are the skater's more immediate concern.

Entries, Exits, and Presentation

The average skater's entries and exits onto and off the ice surface when presenting his program are simply appalling. The entry is usually a little better than the exit, but not much.

We are watching a regional competition: "And now, representing the ABC Figure Skating Club, Miss Wendy XYZ." Swinging her arms, head down, and pushing smartly with her toe rakes, Wendy XYZ advances to the starting place of her program bringing herself to a shuddering halt with a labored snowplow stop lasting at least fifteen feet. Turning to face down the rink, she strikes a position, feet spread, weight evenly distributed between them as though she is expecting to be charged from behind at any moment, head thrust slightly forward, and shoulders rounded; her arms are in some undefined semaphore position. Surprisingly, she skates quite well even though she does not once take her eyes off the ice during her whole program. As the final chord of her music sounds, she strikes a similar pose to that used at the beginning, except that now both arms are stretched toward the roof at an angle of 45 degrees from her body. The audience is all set to applaud—but Wendy has gone. She is already making her drooping way toward the exit, as though apologizing for her performance.

You think the description a little exaggerated? Not a lot, I am afraid. So now, instead of addressing you, the parent, I should like to have a word with your skater. I am sure that neither he nor she would ever look anything like my description, but I should still like to utter a few words of advice.

Step onto the ice confidently with your head up; after a few quick strokes approach the starting point of your program on one foot in an elegant, upright position; come to a stop, *but don't use a snowplow*—it makes you look like a beginner immediately. Strike an elegant pose with your back straight, head erect, chin up, and chest out. You must not relax your shoulders, or you will give that unfortunate impression of drooping. Stand with almost your entire weight on one foot—this is a good rule to follow whenever you have to stand with both feet on the ice—and try to give the impression of complete self-assurance. During your program try to look above the level of the barrier. You may find this the hardest thing to learn, but it becomes easier as you develop confidence in what you are doing. Professional show skaters acquire the skill rapidly, since without the ability to project, their contracts would probably not be renewed.

When I say look above the barrier, I mean precisely that; it is useless lifting your head and looking down with your eyes. Audiences are very conscious of a skater's eyes. You must actually *see* the public; it is not sufficient to direct a vague gaze toward them. Ideally, every so often you should pick out a different individual in the audience and smile, or at least cast a pleasant, direct look, at that one person. It is a strange fact that in this way you can establish a personal relationship, not just with a few individuals, but with the whole audience. Smiling is, unfortunately, another big problem. You must learn to smile naturally—not a broad, cocky grin, but as if you mean it. Practicing in front of a mirror helps—you will feel foolish at first, but it really helps. Smiling, looking above the barrier, and adopting a pleasant, natural expression is a skill that needs constant practice; you cannot just turn it on for a competition. This is another important reason why your program should be so run in that it is absolutely automatic. It is difficult to do all that I have been telling you if you are trying to think what comes next, or if you have to concentrate too hard on that tricky step you never got around to practicing sufficiently.

At the end of your program strike your final position and, for heaven's sake, stand still. It is a good idea to make it a rule to hold your position for at least three seconds, not just for competitions but every time you practice. After a short bow to thank the audience for their applause, move from your position and skate off backwards; try not to turn your back on the audience until you are about fifteen feet from the exit. Remember, you must always make a good finish to your program even if you have skated badly; it is no good apologizing at the end of a poor program by getting off the ice as fast as you can. That just makes matters worse, and can become a habit, even when you skate well. Skaters frequently get the impression they have skated badly when, from the judges' point of view, they have actually skated quite well.

If you remind him, your pro will be only too happy to show you methods of stopping and some good opening and finishing positions that will add distinction and polish to your performance.

The Day of the Competition

Immediately upon arrival at the competition, check the bulletin board for the practice and competition schedule. At competitions with many entries, which may extend over a period of several days, practice time is normally provided before and between events. Almost invariably this means that practice time has to be spread out among several rinks in the area, which may mean quite a lot of driving. The difficulty here is for the pro to apportion his time in such a way that he can be in several places at once: at rink A to oversee the free skating practice of his juveniles; at rink B to watch his intermediates practice their figures; and, of course, at the main rink where the senior event is just about to begin. Parents and skaters must be patient; it is a nerve-racking time for all. As a parent, it is in your own best interest to be the right-hand man of the pro, assisting him to get the skaters to the right places at the right times and watching out for schedule changes, not badgering him with problems that can best be solved by yourself. Keeping one's eyes open for important alterations in the schedule is particularly important. Notification of such changes can sometimes appear (not, of course, in the best-conducted competitions) on small pieces of paper pinned to some pillar or wall quite remote from the official bulletin board (it's true, I assure you), rather like legal announcements that appear in an obscure corner of a newspaper. So do keep your ears and eyes open—in this way the pro can feel free to concentrate on training his students. Particularly watch to see whether the competition is running ahead of schedule. This a frequent occurrence, and if you don't anticipate the possibility, your skater can be upset by urgent demands to "get ready quickly, we're waiting for you."

Fathers can be very useful in keeping track of the marks and working out the current standings. Most of them seem to enjoy the job, and it keeps them out of everybody's hair.

The Warm-up

Immediately before the free skating event each group (up to six skaters) is allowed a six-minute warm-up on the ice. The skater should already have warmed up in the dressing room and have decided approximately what he is going to do during this period. All too often the warm-up is regarded as a practice session or even as a mini-competition, which frequently results in the skater overexerting himself ("He finished sixth but won the warm-up"), particularly if he is first to skate. The most important function of the warming-up period on the ice is for the skater to accustom himself to the speed and hardness or softness of the surface, and to the feeling of being in front of the spectators. If he feels the necessity to show off, then it must be done by powerful stroking and a few of his best jumps and spins. Nevertheless, the final word on the strategy to be adopted must be left to the trainer, who knows his skater's abilities and psychology.

Having warmed up, the skater should not sit down and relax. If he does so, the body tends to go into a resting phase from which it may not recover for two or three hours. Most trainers find it best if the skater keeps up some gentle form of exercise until it is his turn to skate.

It is interesting to note that professional show skaters, particularly those who make only one or two appearances during a performance, get very little opportunity to seriously warm up on the small piece of ice remaining backstage; nearly all their warm-up is done off the ice.

Falls and Other Emergencies

Every skater must know exactly what to do in the case of a fall or difficulty with the music. If, when skating a figure, the skater falls or stops, he should immediately look to the referee, who will tell him how to proceed. If the referee decides that the fall was the skater's fault, he will direct him to continue from approximately the point at which he fell or stopped. If, however, the referee decides that the skater was interfered with, or fell because of bad ice, he will rule that it was not the skater's fault and will allow him to start the figure again, possibly after a period of rest.

If a fall occurs during the free skating or the short program and it is the skater's fault, he must get up as quickly as possible and continue the program; there is no extension of time. If the fall is not the skater's fault, or he is interfered with in any way, then the same rule holds as for figures, i.e., he will be given the option of continuing from the point of interruption or reskating the entire program after a period of rest determined by the referee. This option is also granted the skater if something should accidentally happen to his clothing or equipment that might endanger his safety. The referee will stop the performance until repairs can be made. A distinction should be drawn, however, between problems that are caused accidentally and those caused by carelessness. For example, for a blade to break is an accident, but for a blade to come off is almost invariably due to carelessness in the care of the equipment. Carelessness in such matters is inexcusable, and although the skater may get away with it once, he will not be popular if it happens a second time.

It is not uncommon for a mix-up to occur in the music room, which results in the wrong music being played, or the right music at the wrong tempo. Should this happen, the skater must inform the referee within 30 seconds of the start, in which case the skater is permitted to start the program again. If there is a stop or interruption in the music after the first 30 seconds, the referee will stop the skater and give him the option of restarting the program or continuing it from the point of interruption. It is, however, important for the skater to remember that he is not allowed to complain about the tempo or quality of the music after the first 30 seconds have elapsed. If, through no fault in the skater's tape, the music suddenly becomes almost inaudible, this would presumably be counted as an interruption in the music, and the referee would act. Nevertheless, in most cases it is wise to keep skating until the referee blows his whistle to stop.

Equipment

Skates should always be kept in a safe place. If they are left around in the dressing room, somebody could pick them up instead of his own. And the skater's name should always be marked inside the boots, so that if anyone does pick up the wrong pair, he at least knows where to return them. Moreover, if equipment is left around unattended, accidents can happen. Quite unintentionally, of course, but don't take any chances.

Psyching Out

Skaters must beware of any attempt to "psych them out." The following example is probably one of the most effective ploys in this type of gamesmanship.

Just prior to the free skating event the junior ladies are supposedly admiring one another's costumes in the changing room:

"Lisa, I *love* that dress—turn round—yes, it's . . . do you think it'll be all right?"

"Why, what's wrong?"

"Well, just that—do you really think you'll be able to skate like that? I mean—it's a little tight, isn't it?"

Actually the dress is perfectly okay, but the effect on Lisa is disastrous. From that moment until she has to skate her program, she spends most of the time tugging at her pants and wondering what on earth is going to happen when she tries her double Axel. Skaters are not usually as mean as that, but one must be prepared for all eventualities.

19
Higher-Level Instruction

Finding a Suitable Teacher

As soon as a skater is out of the beginner stage and thinking seriously about tests and competition, the choice of a suitable teacher becomes more difficult than at the earlier level. Most pros nowadays tend to specialize in either figures and freestyle on the one hand, or ice dancing on the other, but there are a number who are equally qualified in both. In some large, competitive clubs specialization may be carried to a great degree, so much so that a student might take figures from one teacher, jumps and spins from another, and have his program put together by a third. This is known as *team teaching.* But be careful: This method usually works very well when performed by a husband and wife team, or by a small group of pros who get along very well together, but in other circumstances splitting up the training of a skater among several pros can cause more problems than it solves (see "The Anchor Pro" later in this chapter).

A good criterion of a teacher's competence is his local reputation. Even in the case of a teacher apparently lacking formal qualifications, he must be doing something right if his students are passing tests and doing reasonably well in competition. When, however, a new instructor moves into an area and little is known about him, one must look for some form of official qualification. This may consist of what he personally achieved as an amateur or, if he is a member of the Professional Skaters Guild of America (PSGA), how they rate him as a teacher. It is not compulsory for a teacher to be a member of the PSGA, and in all fairness it should be pointed out that there are a number of top-rank trainers who are not members of the Guild; nor is it mandatory for a PSGA member to be officially rated, but if he does have a rating, or classification as it is sometimes termed, you will usually find that he knows what he is doing and is interested in his work. If he has no rating, amateur qualifications will at least reveal his ability as a skater himself, but this is no indicator of his ability as a teacher.

Very few figure or freestyle instructors attempt to teach entirely by demonstration. One does not have to be able to do a triple jump in order to teach it; in fact, as some of the world's top-rank trainers are well into their seventies, it would be unreasonable to ask them to demonstrate single jumps, let alone triples. Teaching is a separate skill that is acquired over a period of many years, by practice, observation, and learning to express the complex dynamics of skating in a clear and simple manner. The knowledge of techniques is in itself not sufficient: over the years the best teachers have evolved increasingly better and faster methods of teaching the skater to achieve these techniques. It is not always realized by the general public that, compared with other sports, there is relatively little written material in existence on figure skating techniques. Most trainers have to work out their own system of teaching by individual experiment; one trainer's methods may not produce the same results in the hands of another, perhaps not even in the hands of a former pupil, unless he was taught the rationale behind the method.

One last word of advice when choosing a teacher: It is not always wise to judge a pro entirely by his current students. He may have come into an area where he is faced with the correction of long-standing bad habits —a very difficult task. And always take into account the material with which he has to work: to put it bluntly, even the greatest teacher cannot make a silk purse out of a sow's ear, particularly if the latter happens to be lazy and uncoordinated.

The Attributes of a Good Teacher

One of the greatest attributes of a good teacher is his ability to relate to his students, which really means that he should be sympathetic to their problems and be able to talk to them according to their intelligence or level of mental development. I do not interpret relating to a student as being buddy-buddy with him; in fact, having watched a number of young pros new to the business fall into this trap, I can say without reservation that in 99 percent of cases this approach just does not work. A time is sure to come when the student gets balky and needs a firm hand to get him, for example, to run through his program properly, that is to say, without leaving most of the important moves out. Then the young pro is in sore trouble. Friendly, yes; buddy-buddy, no.

Much teaching involves the diagnosis of faults, some of which may be very obscure, making it easy to mistake a symptom for an underlying cause. The good pro must, therefore, be an astute and experienced analyst of movement. Patience is also a virtue—as I write this I can hear certain parents who know me well bursting into gales of derisive laughter; but I must point out that a certain amount of playacting goes into teaching, and as often as not the pro is not really as impatient or as angry as he may sound. Very often something has to be done to get the student's adrenaline flowing, on the same principle that a gun fired behind an athlete just before an event is said to increase his performance.

Over the years the experienced teacher has acquired a knowledge of all the sound and logical variations of the basic techniques. These accepted variations have running through them the golden thread of sound dynamic principles, and are used either because the instructor is more familiar with a particular method, or because he feels it will suit the pupil better. Techniques used by high-test skaters are not necessarily suitable for weaker, less experienced skaters. The good instructor understands this and will vary his teaching accordingly.

At some time during his career it may be necessary for a student to take lessons from another teacher on a temporary basis before returning to his regular teacher. A typical case occurs when a skater goes away to a summer school. It would be most unwise—even unethical—for the temporary teacher to condemn all that the new student is doing simply because it does not fit in with the techniques he is currently teaching. Regrettably, however, this situation occurs all the time. The good, experienced pro can, however, usually make an intelligent estimate of the method the skater is supposed to be using, even though the skater's movements may suggest that he has not completely understood what his regular pro was telling him. In fact, when describing the methods of their previous teachers, students are apt to make wildly exaggerated statements that occasionally make the absent pro sound downright lunatic.

Listen to the two pros talking when they get together at a seminar or convention:

Pro A: "I had your little student Susan for a month last summer."

Pro B: "Yes, that's right—she told me you helped her a lot—nice skater, isn't she?"

Pro A: "Mmm—yes; I was very interested in your new method of teaching the forward outside bracket."

Pro B (nervously): "What do you mean?"

Pro A: "Well, she says you make her twist her left ankle round the back of her right calf, place her left forearm in the small of her back, and point her right shoulder down toward the ice to make the turn. She said it was supposed to help the flow of the movement. You were most insistent upon it, apparently."

Pro B: "Oh, come on! You know I wouldn't tell anyone a load of garbage like that. . . ."

Pro A: "Well, we all have our methods."

Pro B: "What I said was . . ."

And there follows the description of a sane and logical movement bearing little or no relationship to Susan's interpretation.

Ethics

Good ethics on the part of a professional are, of course, a must, and a strong effort is made by the PSGA to make its members aware of certain guidelines, which include neatness of dress and self-discipline. Two very important principles are that no professional should criticize another professional's methods of teaching or his personal habits, nor should any professional solicit, either personally or through third parties, another professional's students. When one pro is better or more successful than another, it is understandable that there should be a flow of pupils in his direction. But active solicitation is another matter entirely and can, when it occurs within a closed organization such as a rink or club, wreak the most devastating havoc, even to the point of causing a splinter group to break away from the main body and form their own club. Praising a professional is one thing, but solicitation on his behalf is another, and it is sometimes difficult to draw the line. The best way of dealing with this problem is for all the pros to have a thorough understanding amongst themselves that they will discourage all attempts at solicitation, particularly via students or students' parents. In passing, it should be noted that the happiest clubs and rinks are those in which all the pros get on well together—a rather rare situation, but fortunately such clubs do exist.

If you see an instructor teaching in stadium boots instead of skates, do not assume that it is laziness on his part. When a student has reached the point where he does not have to be placed manually into position, most good instructors have sufficient powers of explanation to make skates unnecessary. Indeed, they can be a distinct handicap when teaching figures, since by the time the instructor has skated up and down the patch looking at turns, the ice is in such a mess that it discourages all attempts at neatness on the part of the student. Moreover, when a teacher spends many hours on the ice without being able to take his skates off, his feet may suffer. The muscular tension of simply standing for hours on blades can be very wearing, so much so that it can take the teacher's mind off his lessons. You will get more out of a pro with happy feet than from one who suffers from muscle fatigue and corns.

The Anchor Pro

When more than one teacher is involved in the production of a skater, it is advisable that one be designated the anchor pro responsible for the final product. In singles skating four main aspects are involved: the figures, the technical side of the freestyle, the choreography, and the dance movements (taken from ballet, modern, jazz, etc.) designed to enhance and embellish the choreography. The standard of skating is now so high that, as mentioned earlier, it is not always easy to find a pro who can handle all phases, although there are pros whose knowledge is wide enough to do so quite successfully. It is in the dance (and we are speaking here of stage, not ice, dancing) that outside help is most frequently needed. In fact, the stage dancer who has learned to adapt his or her art to the needs of free skating is now becoming a much sought-after specialist. But however many teachers finally get into the act, it is the anchor pro who should have the final say, and he is usually the one who teaches the skater the figures and technical aspect of the free skating. The anchor pro can see the overall picture. If the teaching is spread among too many pros with no single pro finally responsible, the parents will have no one definite authority to turn to for final advice. Worse still, when competition time comes round, it may happen that no single pro feels he has sufficient stake in the competitor to give the individual attention needed throughout all phases of the event.

The American Professional

Having observed training and trainers in many countries, I have come to the conclusion that the overall standard of the American professional ranks very high indeed. Some countries designate one professional as national trainer, a system which may well be sound if no mistake has been made in the selection. But it is likely to have a discouraging effect on other excellent trainers, who know that eventually the product of several years' hard work will be taken out of their hands and channeled through the national trainer, and it is he who will take all the credit if a student does well in competition. In such an event, the professional who has laid the groundwork well, and who is himself a fine trainer, may feel that he will never be given a chance to make it to the top—a predicament that can lead to feelings of bitterness and frustration. In all fairness to national trainers, however, it must be said that on occasion they have to take over some totally untalented skaters out of whom they are expected to make world-beaters; so the job may not be quite so enviable as it might seem.

In the U.S. we have no official national trainers. We work by the free enterprise system, in which it is possible for any trainer, if sufficiently knowledgeable and given the opportunity, to rise to the top. Professionals are judged by their results, which in itself pushes the standard ever higher. Nevertheless, in order to produce a champion, a trainer's high competence is not sufficient: he must have talent to work with, a skater whose parents can assume the financial burden of training and traveling, and he and his student must be in the right place at the right time. There are hordes of would-be champions all over the U.S.; approximately a thousand girls start on the official competitive ladder at the Regional level every year. Of these, only three can represent the U.S. in the World Championship or Olympic Winter Games. Theoretically, the judging system selects the best three, but it can and does occasionally happen that a few good skaters are lost in the shuffle, or their time has not yet come.

Success breeds success, and as soon as a trainer manages to produce a champion, he and the city where he teaches may become a glamorous

Mecca for the competitive skater. This is all very fine, but for the lesser skater a trainer's success can become the student's dilemma if the rink or rinks involved become overpopular or the trainer in question has very little time open. In such cases the individual tends to get lost in the crowd. What you, the parent, must realize is that it is not always necessary to pick up house and home and move to the ends of the earth to get good training and good training facilities. The impression that the grass is greener a thousand miles away may prove to be an optical illusion; you may well have a pro who is capable of training a skater to the topmost level right on your own doorstep. And if anyone approaches you with the promise of guaranteed results, either you are being sold a bill of goods or something very strange is going on.

So do not overlook or underestimate some excellent trainer in your home location, a trainer who is deeply interested in your child and can give him or her more personal attention than he might get elsewhere. Not every pro can locate himself in the more popular training centers. He or she may be locked into one area by family responsibilities or other circumstances. Nevertheless, it does do a skater a lot of good to train occasionally on a rink where there are better skaters than he; but weigh the pros and cons dispassionately and don't get carried away. Discuss the matter openly with your regular pro and don't burn your bridges behind you.

How Many Lessons?

When a pro is asked how many lessons a week a child should have, he often finds it a difficult question to answer. If he suggests a number that the parents consider too much for their pocket, they may be embarrassed or think the pro is money-grabbing; whereas if he thinks the parents are short of cash, he may suggest what he thinks is the bare minimum, which in the long run may prove to be insufficient. As a skater progresses, parents should become more willing to allow the skater increased lesson time, not only because he needs it but because his progress demonstrates a dedication to the sport and he probably has an attainable goal within reach.

It is almost impossible to be specific about the lesson time a skater should be given, but as a rough guide an average singles skater at the intermediate level should do well on a weekly schedule of one hour for figures, one hour for freestyle, and a half-hour on the freestyle program. An hour could be divided into two half-hour, three twenty-minute, or four fifteen-minute lessons. Personally, I feel that the fifteen-minute lesson is too short—I would tend to favor the twenty-minute lesson. A skater might manage on less if he is intelligent, creative, observant, gifted physically, a hard worker, and skates at a rink having a high standard; but this does not mean he would not do better on more. So much depends on the mental receptivity of the skater, which, together with the physical coordination, may vary from day to day. If I can fit it into my schedule, I will often extend a lesson if I feel that I am about to get a point across, or cut a lesson short if things are going badly. The skaters are, of course, informed of the time added or subtracted so there can be no misunderstandings.

Up to a point, the more lessons the better, but even with a receptive child there must come a time when lessons become merely supervised practice, resulting in a drop-off in return for money spent. Supervised practice is a luxury, and one that should not be necessary for a skater genuinely interested in getting to the top. Nevertheless, there are skaters who lack psychological drive and who benefit from having someone just to watch them; in such cases it is often helpful for skaters of the same level to work together at the freestyle, provided they are genuinely interested in what they are doing, are taught by the same pro, and do not use the occasion for idle conversation.

The total number of hours the skater has available on the ice must also be taken into account. A skater must have time to himself for practice. It is, for example, bad economics to have three half-hour figure lessons a week if he only has three patches during that time. Part of the training of a skater is to get him to think and work by himself.

If you still have difficulty deciding how much time to give your skater, talk to a number of families at different rinks; you will soon get an idea of the average lesson and practice schedules followed by the better skaters. But do not be bound by what you hear. If you feel you can better your competitors' schedules, you may be that much ahead of the game.

One last and very important word: Never skimp on the technical side of the training. It takes many years to refine techniques, and the skater who can produce the jumps and spins consistently will always beat the skater with the sophisticated arm and body movements who spends most of her time on the ice sitting on it. That is not to minimize the dance aspect of free skating, which is of tremendous importance nowadays, but quite futile without faultless jumps, spins, and footwork as the foundation.

20

The Professional Skaters Guild
of America

Just as amateur skaters in various countries have banded together into national associations and federations, so have professional teachers in the major skating countries formed their own national associations. The largest of these, and the only one in the U.S., is the Professional Skaters Guild of America (commonly referred to as the PSGA or, by its own members, as the Guild), which, at the moment of writing, has over seven hundred members and is still growing.

Aims of the Association

The aims of the Guild are *(a)* to increase the knowledge of the sport, *(b)* to improve the teaching skills of its members, *(c)* to award ratings (classifications) showing the degree of skill of a teacher, *(d)* to set up standards of ethics by which members will abide in their dealings with their colleagues and the general public, and *(e)* to provide suggestions and technical advice to other bodies, both amateur and professional. In addition the Guild provides its members with services such as health and accident insurance, legal counsel, a job placement service, and an excellent newsletter that is fast reaching the status of a magazine.

Organization

In order to accomplish all the above, the Guild is organized along conventional lines with officers, board members, and seventeen committees, five of which (the liaison committees) deal with the maintenance of relations with the USFSA, the ISIA, the PSAC (Professional Skaters Association of Canada), the IPSU (International Professional Skaters Union), and with the managements of ice shows and the professional skaters engaged therein. Secretarial work and coordination is carried out by an outside professional management company whose head office is in Buffalo, New York (see chapter 29, "Where to Go for Further Information").

Because of the size of the U.S. it would seem a difficult task to coordinate the efforts and thinking of members spread over so vast an area. The problem is solved by a system of conventions and seminars and, when possible, by meetings at the Regional, Sectional, and National Championships. Whereas Guild conventions and seminars deal mainly with the technical side of skating and allied subjects, meetings at competitions consist largely of discussions of the official rules of skating and how they may be modified or improved. Suggestions are put into the form of motions, those made at the regional and sectional levels being sent on to the national meeting, where they are put into their final form and then passed on to the USFSA for consideration; when they have relevance to international competitions, recommendations may also be sent to the International Professional Skaters Union.

Although the Guild is not officially allied to either the USFSA or the ISIA, Guild members are now invited to sit on certain USFSA committees, and many ISIA members, particularly managers who teach, are also members of the Guild. The only organization to which the Guild has any official alliance is the International Professional Skaters Union. All professional associations are, however, autonomous, and the IPSU cannot dictate policies to member associations. It does, however, form a very useful function in correlating ideas from professional bodies all over the world, and passing them on to the controlling International Skating Union.

One of the Guild's valued honorary members (you will find him listed in the PSGA Membership Directory) is Snoopy, who, with the encouragement of Charles Schulz, has contributed so much to the understanding of the coach/student relationship. May Snoopy long continue to set trainers so fine an example in the handling of difficult pupils.

PSGA Conventions and Seminars

Since its introduction in the sixties, the PSGA annual convention has made steady growth in importance, efficiency, and value. With the expansion of the Guild it had long been felt that the meeting of a handful of pros once a year at the National Championships was totally inadequate to further its cause: such a meeting might provide some good suggestions but could in no way disseminate or improve knowledge among its members. To improve the situation an annual convention was inaugurated, a step that has proved highly successful. Nowadays conventions are held at some pleasant resort hotel accustomed to catering to such gatherings, and having a rink within easy reach where on-ice demonstrations and discussions may be held. Conventions run five days with an extra two days often added to take care of board meetings and rating examinations. Nonmembers are always welcome, and of late many USFSA judges and officials, as well as ISIA rink managers, take the time and trouble to be present at these professional gatherings. Lectures are given by experts in their fields, not only in ice skating, but in a multitude of relevant subjects; related topics covered include equipment, music, makeup, grooming, costuming, diet, skating injuries, psychology, biomechanics, stage dancing, ballroom dancing, and public relations—the range is enormous.

Conventions are held during May and are rotated through the three sections of the country, one year in the East, the next year in the Midwest, and the third on the West Coast. When practical, the dates and location of the PSGA and the ISIA conventions are made to coincide, or approximately so.

In this way, exhibitors at the ISIA trade show can also provide a trade show for the PSGA, giving the pros a most valuable opportunity to compare blades, boots, and a vast array of other types of skating equipment. PSGA conventions can be quite costly affairs, and it is a great tribute to the excellence of their content and organization that so many members continue to support them year after year at considerable personal expense.

Seminars follow similar lines to conventions. Originally, only three seminars, normally lasting two days and for which a fee was charged, were held during the year, but they have become so popular that the PSGA is now offering a dozen or more free one-day seminars spread across the country in addition to the regular full-length seminars. Subjects tend to be aimed at the technical aspect of skating, which is usually handled by Master-rated pros, the object being to provide not only high-level information but also information for the professional teaching at the lower test level who may not be in a position to attend the Annual Convention.

How Instructors Are Qualified

One of the most valuable services the PSGA has rendered the skating public is that of rating instructors according to their teaching skills. This is of particular assistance to clubs and rinks in outlying districts who wish to engage a professional and have no knowledge of his qualities except his own estimation of himself or what he has accomplished as an amateur, none of which is any particular indication of his ability to teach. The price he charges is no indicator, since in most areas there are insufficient differences in fees to distinguish a teacher at the beginner level from one who is Master-rated. The PSGA is not in a position to set standard lesson fees —it can only make recommendations. Setting uniform fees is made particularly difficult because of the variation in living costs from one part of the country to another.

Before continuing with an outline of the rating system one thing must be made clear: the PSGA is not a union; it is not a closed shop, and no professional teacher is under any obligation to join the association. Nor is it mandatory for a Guild member to be rated: It is purely voluntary. A teacher who is not a Guild member or, being a Guild member, has not elected to be rated, is not necessarily a poor teacher; he may, in fact, be excellent. In actual practice, once a pro has established himself in a particular part of the country, his abilities become generally recognized by the results he produces; his reputation spreads by word of mouth and, if his results are good, he is rarely asked about his qualifications either inside or outside the Guild. But if he moves to another area where he is less well known, he may be required to produce formal qualifications. I do, therefore, urge any professional reading this who is not a member of the Guild to join and become rated. It may turn out to be a very good investment in the long run.

Ratings are not easy to get. Details of the requirements are set down in a small book, *Rating System Requirements,* issued by the PSGA and subject to periodic revision, which is why I have not gone into all the finer points here. Very briefly, the general principles are that a candidate applying for a rating in any of the branches of figure skating (see below for Group Instructor and Program Director ratings) must have taught for a specific number of years; must have passed the test for which he is to be rated, or had a pupil pass that test; and must pass a very stiff oral examination.

PSGA Rating System

For the sake of simplicity the phrase *Skating Instructor* (as in *Master Figure and Free Skating Instructor*) is omitted. The word *Free* standing alone denotes *Free Skating*. The letters in parentheses following each rating are the rating code, which appears in the PSGA Membership Directory immediately after the names of those professionals possessing such a rating. The left column indicates the rating passed, while the right column indicates the level of teaching ability demonstrated by passing that particular rating.

Rating	Demonstrated ability to teach up to the level of:
Figures and Free Skating	
Master Figure and Free (MFF)	*8th Figure and Senior Free
Master Figure (MF)	*8th Figure
Master Free (MFS)	Senior Free
Senior Figure and Free (SFF)	6th Figure and Junior Free
Senior Figure (SF)	6th Figure
Senior Free (SFS)	Junior Free
Certified Figure and Free (CFF)	4th Figure and Novice Free
Certified Figure (CF)	4th Figure
Certified Free (CFS)	Novice Free
Registered Figure and Free (RFF)	2nd Figure and Juvenile Free
Registered Figure (RF)	2nd Figure
Registered Free (RFS)	Juvenile Free
Pair Skating	
Master Pair (MP)	Gold Pair
Senior Pair (SP)	Silver Pair
Certified Pair (CP)	Bronze Pair
Ice Dance	
Master Dance and Free Dance (MDFD)	Gold Dance and Gold Free Dance
Master Dance (MD)	Gold Dance
Senior Dance (SD)	Silver Dance
Certified Dance (CD)	Bronze Dance
Group	
Master Group (MG)	
Senior Group (SG)	see text below
Certified Group (CD)	
Program Director	
Master Program Director (MPD)	
Senior Program Director (SPD)	see text below
Certified Program Director (CPD)	

*The Gold Medal is awarded to a skater when he has completed both the Eighth Figure (Gold Bar) and the Senior Free (Gold Bar).

These orals are the biggest stumbling block for the candidate. They are normally held at the annual convention, occasionally at seminars, and on an average each examination lasts an hour. That is a long time to be under the gun when faced by five Master-level pros who really know their business. There are no trick questions, and there are rarely questions about matters that can be looked up in the *USFSA Rulebook*. A professional must have a thorough knowledge of techniques and, most important, an understanding of the dynamic principles behind them. If, for example, he says that he tells pupils to drop the free shoulder going into a bracket, the examining board will want to know *why* he tells them to do this. If his answer is that that was the way his own trainer always told him to do it, his reply is not going to impress anybody. If no further explanation is forthcoming, he is not going to last long. The examiners are not necessarily demanding that the candidate teach a specific technique—there are many dynamically sound variations, particularly in the figures—but he must be able to defend logically the techniques he describes. He must also know the common faults, their causes, and how to correct them. His explanations must be easy to follow—if the examining panel cannot understand him, it is hardly likely that his pupil will. Candidates are also questioned on such subjects as music, program construction, the learning process, ethics, and relations with pupils and parents.

You may be assured that any pro passing a PSGA Master oral really knows his stuff and that those awarded a less advanced classification are highly competent to teach up to their rated level. Indeed, there are many pros who are quite capable of teaching at a considerably higher level than their ratings suggest. It must be pointed out that rating examinations can be quite costly affairs. If, for example, an East Coast pro has to travel to an annual convention on the West Coast to get his rating, he not only has fares, convention fees, hotel, and living costs to pay for, but on top of that a fee for taking the examination, not to mention possible loss of teaching income while he is away. He is putting a lot of money on the line to back up his feeling that he will succeed. He may elect to wait, therefore, until he can take the examination nearer home. My wife and I have sat on many examining panels, and it is our experience that any instructor who should not be taking the exam reveals himself very early in the questioning. But the exams are very fair, and examiners bend over backward to put candidates, most of whom are very nervous, at their ease. More and more pros are taking these rating exams; at a recent convention eighty-one rating exams at all levels were held, out of which there were fifty-seven passes.

The last two types of rating mentioned above, Group Instructor and Program Director, are primarily of interest to rink managements, but they deserve mention to show the wide range of PSGA interests. The Master Group Instructor must be conversant with both the USFSA and the ISIA Basic Test Programs and be able to handle classes of toddlers, school children, adults, power skaters (practicing basic hockey skills), and have a sound knowledge of lower-level figures, free skating, and ice dancing. He must also have taught groups for a certain number of years during which time he must have logged up a specified number of hours. He must pass a stiff oral and submit a résumé of his teaching experience, which is examined very closely. The requirements for the Senior and Certified levels follow the same general lines as for the Master but differ in the number of years and hours of experience required and the strictness of the oral examination. The Master Program Director should have all the knowledge of a Master Group Instructor plus the ability to organize programs of all types (such as group lessons, summer schools, and promotional activities as they affect rinks, clubs, and communities) and to handle all the business and publicity aspects involved.

21
Music for Free Skating

I think every professional has had the experience of a pupil coming up to him and saying, "I need some music for a program—do you have any ideas?" We would all like to be able to answer right off the bat somewhat along the following lines: "Yes, now let's see—you need two and a half minutes, right? Okay—there's a very good opening on the HMV recording of selections from *Giselle;* I think it starts about half an inch in, on the second band of the first side; that must be a full minute; then there's a very beautiful slow part halfway through the first side of *Swan Lake* put out by Melodiya—that's about three-quarters of a minute—and then for a good strong ending I advise the last part of the third band on the second side of the latest recording of *Carmen,* without vocal—that should just about do it. You might be a couple of seconds over, but that'll be all right. I should be able to get that on tape for you by tomorrow."

But I am afraid it does not work like that. Although the production of a piece of music is somewhat easier at the lower levels, the more advanced skater with the longer program must have music of good quality containing a suitable opening, ending, and variations of character and tempo, something which can be very time-consuming to produce. (Incidentally, the locations of the pieces of music mentioned in the above conversation are entirely fictitious.)

Much more goes into putting together a piece of music than is apparent at first sight. The following processes are involved:

Research   Listening to a wide range of music and deciding on the type suited to the skater.

Selection	Choice of the various sections that may lend themselves to the editing process.
Editing	The various sections must be visualized as forming a continuous whole and then transferred to a master tape or directly to a cassette. This latter process is now usually referred to as *cutting* the music.
Timing	Part of the editing process. The various sections must be timed so as to produce the correct total length.
Counting out	Part of the editing process and dealt with below. Very useful in the subsequent construction of the program.

The actual research and choice of selections can be the most time-consuming part of the process, often requiring hours of listening to dozens of records. Having chosen the various sections, they must be timed and an estimate made as to whether they can be cut in such a way as to produce a final piece of the required length. It is very rare that one finds a suitable piece of music with an adequate opening, middle section, and ending that needs no editing, although this may occasionally be possible with light music for programs of very short duration (1½ or 2 minutes).

How the Parent Can Help

If you as a parent can assist in the various processes, you may save yourself considerable expense. If a professional researches, selects, and edits the music and puts it into a final form on a cassette for you, he will, or should, charge for the service. Many pros do not charge nearly enough given the hours they spend researching the music and the time they spend in all the ancillary processes, not to mention their financial outlay in gathering together a record library.

In order to be of material assistance, you must have access to a large number of records, an appreciation of music, and a considerable amount of free time. In the early stages of a skater's career my wife and I often describe the process of producing skating music to the parents and ask them whether, before we get into the act, they would like to see what they can do themselves. Sometimes this results in the parents doing a good job, in which case they usually get better and better and can be very helpful. But just as often, after a week or two has passed, a frustrated father turns up at the rink and says, "I sat up till four o'clock this morning trying to cut that music—I think perhaps you'd better have a go at it." But it is all most helpful in giving parents and skater a knowledge and appreciation of what and how much goes into the job. In case you wish to try—and I sincerely hope you will—the following sections give a brief outline of the processes.

Choosing Suitable Music

When skating a singles freestyle program, a skater is marked—among a host of other considerations—on his ability to keep time to the music, whether his skating conforms to the music chosen, and the way in which he expresses the character of the music. The skating program as a whole, and therefore the music to which it is skated, must be harmonious in composition and varied in content. If the music is such that it does not allow the skater to demonstrate these qualities—that is, if the music itself does not possess harmony, character, and variety—it will clearly be unsatisfactory. To use a rather grandiose term, a skater is supposed to be able to interpret his music, which may be a little above the heads of the younger ones. But they should at least be able to move in time and harmony with the music.

Other desirable qualities are melody, rhythmic phrasing, and suitability to the skater's talent and style of skating. The music must, therefore, by neither too heavy nor too light for the skater: a minuet by Boccherini would scarcely be appropriate for a hulking six-foot boy; nor would one expect a little girl of five to perform to the crashing chords of Sibelius's *Finlandia.* Reverse the choice and you might have something suitable.

Another important consideration, often ignored, is that the music should have "first time impact" and universal appeal. The judges and audience are going to hear the skater's music once, and once only; the music should not, therefore, be such that it needs to be listened to several times for full appreciation. It should be assumed that a judging panel is reasonably well educated musically—you may even have a few music connoisseurs among them. Skaters come and skaters go but judges go on forever, or so it may seem; beware, therefore, of yielding to contemporary musical fads. A piece of music from the latest popular film may seem just the thing to your young skater, but it may have appealed to dozens of other skaters in the same way, and if your skater is the sixth within half an hour to skate to the same piece of music, the judges are liable to be prejudiced against him after the opening phrase.

So, what type of music are we looking for? Is it going to be classical, taken from works by such composers as Beethoven, Bach, or Mozart; light classical from overtures, ballets or orchestral adaptations of operas; pop music (which seems to mean different things to different generations); contemporary music; music from film scores; rock, disco, or jazz; or perhaps even "music concrete," which, I presume, consists of those peculiar series of noises such as I once heard in a work titled "Amplified Plant Music" used by a modern dance group. The best advice I can give to amateur competitive skaters is, don't try to convert the world, particularly the judges, to your way of thinking—leave that to the pros. They may be more able to get away with it. When skating in amateur tests or competitions, never present anything in your music, skating, or costume that might cause controversy or offend somebody. Play it safe—keep your innovations for show numbers.

The above range of music is very wide, so let us discuss some of the options. Some years ago the bulk of the music used for singles and pair skating consisted of selections from overtures and ballets, much of it written between 1840 and the turn of the century. Occasionally a skater would come along with heavier classical music taken perhaps from a Beethoven symphony, but only for the longer senior programs. (The selection of a logical and aesthetically sound two-minute period from a work such as Beethoven's Seventh is not an easy task, to say the least.) Then with the explosion in popularity of rock music, and perhaps in reaction to the overuse of light classical recordings, rock and disco began to dominate the field. This trend was intensified by the fact that the vast majority of younger skaters entering the ranks never seemed to have been exposed to any other kind of music. Even the more serious freestyle training periods at some clubs became disco sessions. Most musical styles have a place somewhere in skating, but it should be kept in mind that figure skating is an artistic sport, in large measure composed of extended flowing and gliding movements. In order not to be accused of personal bias or value judgments, I cannot do better than to quote from Ricky Harris's excellent book, *Choreography & Style for Ice Skaters* (New York: St. Martin's Press, 1980). The italics in the passage are my own.

> If you are going to use jazz, disco, or other contemporary forms, one thing to consider is the sameness in dynamics. When you use music that has the same qualities, tempos, and accents in every measure, you end up skating

to a background of music, rather than being able to interpret the music. *. . . Good* rock, disco, and jazz *that have the necessary qualifications* for interesting movement and interpretation can be effectively used for competitive programs.

Quite recently there has been an increase of interest in classical, light classical, and melodic, rhythmically phrased contemporary music containing variation in tempo and meter. A considerable amount of classical music has reappeared in new arrangements for modern instrumentation —the electronic synthesizer, for example—and Bach has been rediscovered. The irony is that many young skaters, who put on a nauseated expression whenever classical music is mentioned, happily skate to it without being aware of the fact. The availability and vast resources presented by the "older" music, coupled with a greater stress on the aesthetics of skating (a reaction to the overemphasis on the triple jumps), is causing many of the more experienced senior skaters, and in particular leading professional show skaters, to return to the more classical works when they are permitted a choice and feel it suits their style. It will be interesting to see how far the pendulum swings.

So much for a general overview of skating music. But what if the reader has a little five-year-old daughter who is about to take part in her first competition at the pre-Preliminary level and requires a program lasting only 1½ minutes? Programs of such short duration are not expected to contain the variations of tempo and mood that would be looked for at the higher levels; at the elementary stage the requirements of both skating and music are pretty minimal. In such a case something simple like "The Lonely Goatherd" from *The Sound of Music* might suffice. Such pieces are not hard to find, but they still may have to be edited so that they have a beginning and an end; you cannot solve the problem by simply lifting the needle off the record. This is considered gauche in the extreme and will result in killing any applause your skater may deserve at the end of his program, and he will leave the ice and the audience in surprised silence. Fortunately, however, there are usually so many repeated sections in this type of simple music that editing presents no great problem. You will, of course, realize that the piece of music I have mentioned is only an example, and I am not suggesting you use it. Otherwise, after the publication of this book, I can imagine having to sit through scores of programs of little girls skating to "The Lonely Goatherd"—perhaps thousands of little girls all over the country—a terrifying and lugubrious prospect. Which brings us to the question of originality.

At all levels one does, of course, try to keep from using music that some other skater in the same club is using, but it is impossible to know everybody's choice in the whole region. So the indignant and frequently heard cry, "She's using my music!" is almost invariably unjust, although it must be admitted that instances of mysteriously disappearing cassettes are not unknown. Originality does not lie simply in the music chosen but also in how it is put together. When two or three selections are used to construct a whole program, it is unlikely that another skater will choose exactly the same selections and in exactly the same order. In bygone days, when taping was not so common and editing difficult, more serious clashes did occasionally occur, and then the situation resembled that of two ladies arriving at a cocktail party in identical dresses. But now, when so many different selections are used, such total conflicts are statistically very unlikely. It is, however, only natural that skaters would like exclusive use of any music they have chosen, particularly within their own club. One large club at which we taught used a system of registration: As soon as a skater had chosen and recorded a piece of music, he registered it with the music chairman, and no other club skater could use the same piece while the original skater was still using it. Provided it is not subject to abuse, the idea seems a reasonable one.

Making the Selections

Please note that in order to avoid infringement of the Copyright Act when recording copyrighted music, you should check with ASCAP or BMI (see chapter 29) before proceeding.

The average program of two minutes and above usually brings in several changes of tempo and character. The number of changes and their complexity depend on the length of time available and the desirability of bringing out the skater's strong points. A very common and relatively simple arrangement is the fast/slow/fast format or perhaps some combination such as slow/medium-slow/fast. Various constructions are possible provided they do not chop the program up into too great a number of sections of different character for the time available.

Although it is quite in order to start a program slowly, very few amateur skaters have the necessary beauty of skating to sustain the interest of the average audience during a slow ending; it is most important not to risk an anticlimax. During a very short program, say, 1½ minutes, there is barely enough time to get in one change of tempo and, as I mentioned earlier, a medium pace throughout may be quite adequate. A good alternative is a slow/fast format if the young skater can handle it.

Before starting your research, discuss the format and the type of music with the pro and, if he is competent to make this type of decision, with the skater. Once you have the format (for example, fast/slow/fast) it helps to know approximately how much time should be devoted to each section. But here you may have to be guided by the music available and, as the old saying goes, "cut your coat according to your cloth." It is also very important that both the skater and the pro who is to do the choreography like the music; this will save a lot of valuable ice time and unnecessary argument.

Try to choose music of similar type and orchestration, preferably from the same composer. It is unwise, for example, to switch from an overture by Rossini played by a symphony orchestra to a fugue by Bach on the synthesizer, or to mix violently different types of music, such as classical and disco. It is essential to avoid the impression that the program consists of a jumble of music, which means keeping to the minimum number of selections necessary to construct the final format. I have known skaters who have used six pieces or more, all of conflicting character and taken from as many different records. One extreme case was of a young student who arrived with a 2½-minute program consisting of no less than thirteen pieces; there were marches, polkas, waltzes, nocturnes, fractions of overtures—you name it, that tape had it. This was not a case of bad editing by whoever put the music on the cassette—there was no editing at all. It was simply a straight 2½ minutes taken from a record bearing some such title as "Moments with the Maestros," each moment being distressingly fleeting. Such medleys, when used for skating, are extremely disturbing and choreographically impossible.

Before we go further, the term *cutting* should be given a short explanation. Originally this referred to cutting the grooves in a disc, but it was subsequently applied to the splicing together (involving cutting) of various sections of reel-to-reel tape to form a harmonious whole. This method is now seldom used except by sound studios or skating professionals interested in this type of work. The simplest method of editing music is directly onto a cassette by means of a pause button (see "The Mechanics of Cutting" below). Nevertheless, the process is still frequently referred to as cutting music.

There is a great variation in the ease with which certain types or arrangements of music can be cut. Classical symphonies are particularly difficult because of the length of time usually required to develop a musical theme, the constant changes of key and, apart from the conclusion of specific movements, the difficulty of finding the end to a phrase of music where one can cut in with another section. Although successful cutting of classical symphonies is quite possible, it presupposes a good musical background on the part of the editor and can take a tremendous amount of time. The next most difficult are the full scores of certain well-known ballets such as *Giselle*. Just as you come to the end of a melodic phrase and are about to push the pause button, some instrument comes in on the upbeat and off you go again on a new section, possibly in a different key. On the other hand, if you can find prerecorded selections from these larger works, or abridged arrangements, things will be much easier as the various sections will have been arranged with logical endings. Short ballets, known as divertissements, used at one time between the acts of operas, as well as orchestral selections of well-known operatic works, without vocals, may also be a source of suitable music.

Finding a good ending is very important and presents surprising difficulties. One often discovers what promises to be a good strong finale only to find that it wanders off into something quite unsuitable. It frequently helps to find the ending first. Having found a good ending, place the needle about a couple of minutes back on the record and explore what has gone before. Occasionally, particularly when putting music together for the shorter programs, you may find a beginning that leads right into the selected ending, and which contains sufficient variation in tempo and character that no editing is needed. One is indeed lucky to find such sections, but they are well worth looking for.

Having made your selections, write them down immediately. If you do a lot of cutting, keep a special book for your notes; pieces of paper can get lost very easily. Write down the name of the piece, all details of the record including number and company, description of the selection (slow, fast, etc.), how long it lasts and, above all, where it begins on the record, that is to say, how many inches in from the edge. If the final tape is ever lost, trying to reconstruct the music without these details, even if you made the cut yourself in the first place, can be an absolute nightmare. You think you remember where everything started, but nine times out of ten you just can't find it again.

Skaters are constantly mislaying their tapes, and the resulting panic, particularly if the loss occurs just before a competition, is a sad thing to see. We advise all parents to have at least one duplicate—lock it up in a safe place and *do not tell your child you have it.* It may sound cruel, but more often than not, losing a tape is the result of thoughtlessness, and the consequences can be dire. If the only copy of a tape is lost and no record has been kept of the sources of the music and how the cuts were made, it is almost impossible to construct an exact replica. This awful possibility should be allowed to sink in before you come to the rescue with a duplicate tape.

If you move to another rink, see that your notes accompany the tape. Many times a new student from some other part of the country has come up to me or my wife and said, "I was using this music last year but I need another thirty seconds—could you add something on for me?" If the music already has a definite start and finish, you can't just add something on at either end, something has to be inserted in the middle of the recording. Not a simple matter if he doesn't know what the music is, what orchestra is playing it, or what record, or records, it was taken from. More maddening still is the skater who hands you a tape saying, "My brother was messing about with this and erased the first twenty seconds." If we cut the music ourselves, we probably have it on a secret master tape, but if we didn't make the tape and don't have all the details, it will be just as quick, and possibly quicker, to start afresh with new music.

Duration of Programs

Before starting to research the music you must know the length of program required. For official USFSA competitions in the singles category, the requisite times are as follows:

Senior Men	4½ minutes
Senior Ladies	4 minutes

Junior Men	4 minutes
Junior Ladies	3½ minutes
Novice Men and Ladies	3 minutes
Intermediate Men and Ladies	2½ minutes
Juvenile Boys and Girls	2 minutes

Nonqualifying competitions below the level of juvenile usually require 1½ minutes.

All the above times are subject to a latitude of 10 seconds either way, which makes editing a little easier. This means that a 2-minute program could last 1 minute 50 seconds or 2 minutes 10 seconds. This is a big percentage difference in a 2-minute program, and if the skater has a lot to offer, there is a strong temptation to extend the music to the full 2 minutes 10 seconds. Be warned, however, that despite what manufacturers say, tape recorders do not always run at the exact speed they are supposed to, especially those that have been in constant use in cold, damp rinks; so you might end up with a program a few seconds too long. A whistle is blown at the end of the 10-second grace period, which is a signal for the judges to stop marking immediately, so that if the tape has been playing a little slowly, your skater's beautiful spin combination at the end of the program may be wasted. It is advisable, therefore, to aim for the precise time rather than try to stretch the program to the limit.

The referee begins timing the program from the moment the skater starts to skate and not from the beginning of the music. Starting to skate is usually interpreted as the moment at which the skater moves from his starting spot; but to avoid any misunderstanding the skater should play it safe and stand absolutely still until he hears the precise point in his music where he should start to actually move his feet. Normally a skater arranges to start moving two or three seconds after he hears the beginning of his music, but some skaters like to start on the very first note. To do this they may arrange for a beep to be heard a certain number of seconds before the beginning of the music; but I have always felt that this is aesthetically clumsy and smacks of waiting for the sound of the starting gun in a track event.

The fact that a skater's program is not timed until he starts to move gives a little latitude in the editing. It may happen that after the final cutting, a program is found to exceed the grace period by perhaps five seconds. If no alteration can be made, there is nothing in the rules to prevent a skater from standing still for six or seven seconds after his music has started and thus compensate for the extra length of his program. Nevertheless, this should not be overdone, as too long a wait gives the impression that the skater may have forgotten his program or lost the courage to take the first step.

For the more advanced singles skater it should be pointed out that the ten-second latitude does not apply to the short program, which must not exceed two minutes under any circumstances. But it may be as short as the skater wishes, provided all the required elements are included.

Counting Out

So, you have collected your possible selections and have timed them only to find that the whole thing comes out about thirty seconds too long—not an unusual situation. What are you going to do? Go back and look for other bits and pieces that may come out to the right length? No, the first thing to do is to find out whether the existing piece can be shortened; and the best way to do this is to count out the music. Counting out is also very helpful to both skater and pro when the choreography is being set, as it provides a mental map of the piece as a whole. On page 218 there is a very simple example of how this may be done. It may not be the way in which a top-rank musician would tackle the job, but the method is very practical. The music is the slow waltz from the Pas de Deux in Tchaikovsky's ballet, *The Sleeping Beauty.* It is from the full score (happily one of the easier ones to cut) played by the National Philharmonic Orchestra, Richard Bonygne conducting (London CSA 2316). The album consists of three records, the selected piece starting ¾ of an inch in from the edge of the sixth side.

The diagram shows how the music is counted out in eight-bar phrases, three beats to the bar, the principal melodies and their repeats being marked A, B, C, and D. The three phrases of the introduction are marked a, b, and c. The whole piece runs on my machine about 1 minute 54 seconds. Let us say you want to bring it down to within the 1½ minute range (10 seconds either way). As you can see, the music starts with an introduction lasting 14½ seconds, followed by the main melody (A1), which repeats in almost identical form three more times (A2, A3, and A4), followed by two other melodies (B and C); then the main melody repeats two more times (A5 and A6) but in a considerably slower tempo, leading

Plan of Worksheet for *Sleeping Beauty* Waltz

Introduction (14½ secs.)

a	3		A4	3		A6	3
	3			3			3
	3			3			3
	3	4 secs.		3			3
b	3			3			3
	3			3			3
	3			3			3
	3	4 secs.		3	9 secs.		3	11 secs.
	3	silence	B	3		D	3
	3	2 secs.		3			3
c	3			3			3
	3			3			3	slowing to
	3			3			3	finish
	3	4½ secs.		3			3
A1	3			3			3	13½ secs.
	3			3	9½ secs.			
	3		C1	3				
	3			3				
	3			3		Approximate total		
	3			3		playing time:		
	3	9 secs.		3		1 minute 54 seconds		
A2	3			3	9½ secs.			
	3		C2	3				
	3			3				
	3			3				
	3			3				
	3			3				
	3	9 secs.		3				
A3	3			3	9½ secs.			
	3		A5	3				
	3			3				
	3			3				
	3			3				
	3			3				
	3	9 secs.		3				
				3	10½ secs.			

into the final section (D). Starting at A1, the duration in seconds of each section is shown at the conclusion of each eighth bar.

There are several ways of shortening this piece, all very simple, but they are sufficient to show the general principles involved. The actual mechanics of the cutting will be dealt with in the next section. Just to cut out the 14½ seconds of introduction is not quite enough as it brings you dangerously close to the edge of the time limit, and the local machine at the competition might run a little slow. You could leave the introduction as is, cut out A1 and A2 and start again at A3. That eliminates 18 seconds and you are down to 1 minute 36 seconds. That should be all right, but it's your little girl's first appearance in public and she's a rather weak skater, so perhaps you want to shorten it just a bit more. To do this, cut out the first 10 seconds of the introduction and start at c, then go once again to A3 and continue to the end. This removes 28 seconds and you are down to 1 minute 26 seconds, with a very safe margin.

Why would it have been unwise to have cut out A3 and A4 instead of A1 and A2 since they are of the same duration and similar melody? The reason is that the last two notes in the very last bar of A2 are not quite the same as those of A4, which lead into the different melody, B. If you went straight from the end of A2 to B, it just would not sound quite right, and one of the things you are trying to do is to disguise the points at which the cuts are made. These little groups of notes that occur at the end of a preceding bar and introduce the first note of the following bar are often referred to as upbeats and can be a source of great frustration to anyone first trying his hand at cutting music. You have to listen very carefully to decide whether you are going to make the cut at the end of a bar or on the upbeat just preceding it. Ideally one would work with the musical score in hand, but it is not necessary to be an accomplished musician or to be able to read music to make these cuts; a strong feeling for beat and musical phrasing, coupled with plenty of practice, is all that is required.

It must now be quite clear that with all this chopping and changing around it is highly improbable that the final mixture will prove to be musically correct. The elementary examples of editing given here are nothing compared with the mayhem frequently committed on music of longer duration. But we do our best, in the knowledge that the original composers are hardly likely to hear our efforts—although they may be turning over in their graves.

The Mechanics of Cutting
Cassette or Record?

Your next task is to put your selections into permanent form. Until quite recently there was still a choice between the use of cassette tapes running at 1⅞ inches per second (ips) and 7-inch records running at 45 revolutions per minute (rpm); very occasionally 33⅓ rpm records were used. More and more, however, cassettes are superseding records, and in many recent competitions cassettes have become mandatory. The great advantage of a record is that if a speed dial (see "Strobing" below) of the type shown in figures 23–25 is attached to it, the record can be played at exactly the same speed all over the country, whereas many cassette players vary slightly from the standard speed and, unless they are of the rare type that has a speed adjustment allowing for a variation of about 10 percent either way, nothing can be done about it. The demise of the 7-inch record was brought about by its vulnerability. Young skaters tend to jam them with no protective covering into skatebags, causing bending and a multitude of scratches. I have even had them handed to me with chewing gum stuck to the playing surface. On the other hand a cassette does protect the tape to a large extent, the only disadvantage being that occasionally, in the case of some of the very cheap ones, the tape may wind itself round the capstan—an unmitigated disaster. Use a good brand; it does not necessarily have to be ultra-this or ultra-that because the subtle dynamics may be lost in the average rink PA system, but the cassette must be sound mechanically.

Choose a cassette that has as short a running time as possible. The most readily available are C60s (30 minutes on each side), but C15s (7½ minutes a side) are now manufactured specifically for skaters—enquire at your local skate shop, as your local music dealer may never have heard of them. The C15 has several important advantages over the longer tapes: because of its shorter length the tension is more even, you are not paying for so much tape, less time is spent on rewinding it if it is allowed to run on, and the tape's relative thickness makes it more resistant to stretching and malfunction. Never use C120s or C90s, as the tape is much thinner than that used in C60s or C15s. Thin tape just does not stand up to the constant stopping, starting, and rough handling that the average skating tape undergoes.

Making the Recording

The following is not intended to be a full technical explanation but simply a rough guide; you will learn the subtleties as you practice.

If you took your music to a professional sound recording studio, they would first transfer it by means of a reel-to-reel recorder onto a tape running at 7½ or 15 ips. The editing would probably be done by actually cutting the tape and splicing it together again. From this master tape the music would be rerecorded onto a disc or cassette. The final job would be very professional and the joins smooth, but it could be expensive. It is quite possible, however, to do an excellent job by recording directly onto a home cassette recorder, provided it has a pause button and a sound level meter. It is very difficult to cut and splice cassette tape, so most editing is done by means of the pause button, which instantly stops both the recording and the movement of the tape across the recording head, but does not switch the machine off. When buying a recorder with the idea of cutting music, always test the pause button to see that it functions instantaneously.

You will need a record player from which you can run a lead directly to your cassette recorder. Never attempt to record via a microphone; the quality will suffer badly and it is very difficult to cut out background noise.

You should make a trial recording to see whether the combined selections are the right length and to make sure that the music blends in together without too much jarring or unsuitable changes of key. Get everything ready to go: record on the turntable, cassette in the recorder, power on, the tape adjusted so you can start recording immediately after the end of the leader tape. Depress the pause button and then the record buttons; the tape will not move and nothing will record, but you will have activated the sound level meter. If you now play part of your first selection, you will be able to check the recording volume by the needle on the meter. In most setups the volume of the recording on the tape is independent of the volume coming through the record player speakers, so the volume must be controlled from the recorder itself. This means that you can record at the required volume on the tape while still keeping the speaker volume low—very useful if you are spending half the night on the job and don't want to wake up the rest of the house. It is also possible to make excellent recordings by taking a lead into the recorder directly from the speaker terminals by means of alligator clips, in which case the volume and tone coming through the speakers will have a direct effect on the recording. If everything seems to be under control, you can now start your recording. Ideally it helps to have your sheet with the music counted out at hand, with all the proposed cuts marked in with pencil.

Unless your first selection starts right at the beginning of the record, play the preceding music over several times so that you know exactly where to start recording. When you think you are ready, play the preceding music again, press your finger on the pause button and then release it just as the required section of music starts. Be ready for the end of the section and cut the music off by once again using the pause button. When stopping a recording, particularly when there is a natural pause in the music before the next section begins, a good alternative to the pause button is to use the volume control on the recorder. If done properly, this can result in smoother transitions. As you hear the end of the music arrive, swiftly turn the volume control knob on the recorder to zero and let the tape continue to run for two or three seconds. Now play back the recorded section to see that you have not chopped it off too soon.

If you don't want to make any changes, set up for the following section by getting your next selection ready on the turntable. Adjust your tape to the point where you want to start recording again, and once more press the pause and record buttons. Now repeat the process as you did before and then listen to the two sections to see whether you have made a good cut. There should be no clicks or undue pauses between the sections, and ideally the join should be unnoticeable. Repeat the whole performance for any other sections you wish to add. You now have a preliminary recording that can be timed. If by some miracle it has come out to the right length and the recording has been smooth, you may not wish to tempt fate by doing it over again. But you'll usually discover room for improvement—the length may need adjusting, the transitions may be a little rough.

Stopping the recording by use of the volume control is most effective when used to make transitions from one major part of the music to another, e.g., from fast to slow or vice versa. It is at such points that natural pauses are most likely to occur, and cuts can become very obvious if the length of the pause is incorrectly timed. There are, however, certain types of cuts, such as the removal or insertion of repeats within the same section of music, where it is necessary to come in toward the end of a bar on the upbeat, and the pause button must be used.

Always try to record at a volume that does not have too great a range —that is, the difference in volume between the loud and soft sections should not be too great. To do this you will have to adjust the sound level while actually recording. In most rinks the acoustics cause soft sections to get lost. Practice sessions present a particular problem as there is always a lot of background noise and in order to hear the soft sections the music has to be played far too loudly unless adjustments have been made in the recording. The bellowing roar of such recordings does not seem to worry the younger generation, who regularly risk deafness listening to hard rock, but it may disturb older persons who, despite their age, have managed to retain their hearing.

Having made your recording, it should be regarded as a master tape and two copies should be made, keeping the original in a safe hiding place. If you have a second recorder, you can make the copies yourself, but it is sometimes difficult to get good quality. It is not expensive to get copies made professionally and the results are usually very good. I specify two copies because most competitions now state on the entry form that skaters should have an extra copy with them in the building. Quite apart from the possibility of loss, tapes do occasionally malfunction and they are extremely difficult to repair, particularly at a moment's notice. Mark the skater's name indelibly on the tape and, for competition purposes, add the event, length of program, and home club.

Most tapes nowadays have a leader of about five seconds before the tape itself starts. If one tape is going to be used for practice and one for competition, the practice tape should have the start of the music delayed to give about twelve seconds before the start. If the music system is within the ice area, it is then possible for the skater to put on his own music and still have time to get into position on the ice; otherwise somebody else has to stop skating and do it for him. On the competition tape the music can start immediately after the leader.

Every time a practice tape is used it should be wound back after use. Many rinks hold practice sessions where time is short and it is difficult to get everyone in. If a skater presents a tape that has to be wound back all the way while others are waiting their turn, he should immediately be put back to the end of the list and the next skater allowed to start.

A skater should collect his tape immediately after use, or at the latest at the end of the session. Failure to do so is the number one cause of lost tapes.

Strobing

At many major competitions the organizers collect all the individual cassettes and transfer the music onto one long reel-to-reel tape, which is used for the actual performance. This is all very fine in theory but is only successful when the organizers put first-class equipment in the hands of an expert who really knows what he is doing. There have been some regrettable lapses in which too many machines have been involved and the quality of the sound and particularly the timing have suffered. Nevertheless, the method can be successful. Some organizers who are equipped with variable speed record players will still accept 7-, 10-, or 12-inch records running at 45 or 33⅓ rpm, provided they have a speed dial (also sometimes known as a strobe disc) attached. In case records should ever come back into favor, this chapter would be incomplete without some mention of the strobing process.

Strobing is a well-known technique—mechanics use it for timing car engines—and the principle has been adapted to discover whether the turntable of a record player is rotating at precisely the right speed. The speeds at which the turntable of a home record player will rotate are 33⅓, 45, and sometimes 78 rpm, with nothing in between. Most machines are accurate in their speeds, but some are not. To check the accuracy of the speed of rotation of a turntable you can obtain at most hi-fi stores a speed dial made of a light card that fits snugly over the spindle of the turntable so that it rotates at the same speed (figure 23). You will see that it has four sets of radiating black lines corresponding to 16⅔ (a rarely used speed), 33⅓, 45, and 78 rpm.

If you set your turntable to 33⅓ rpm and view the dial by a source of electric light, the lines of the third ring out from the center should appear to stand still. They will not look as black or as sharply defined as they normally do, but will appear rather fuzzy and gray; nevertheless, they will still look like lines. If the turntable is rotating a little too slowly, these lines will appear to be moving gradually backward, i.e., in the opposite direction to that of the turntable. If, on the other hand, the turntable is running too fast, the lines will appear to be moving forward.

This optical effect is the same as that sometimes seen in a movie when the spokes of a wheel seem to move slowly in comparison with the speed of the vehicle. In the case of a speed dial a similar illusion is caused by the fact that in the U.S. alternating current reverses polarity sixty times per second (sixty cycles); this causes the light by which you view the dial to go on and off sixty times a second, thus providing an absolute constant by which measurements can be made. The speed at which this occurs, coupled with the persistence of human vision, makes this on-off action of the light quite invisible to the naked eye. When the light is on, the mind registers a picture of the lines in one particular position; during the period when the light is out there is just time for each line to move into the position previously occupied by the line ahead before the light goes on again, so that the position of the lines appears unchanged. The distance between each line and the number of lines to the circle can be calculated in such a way that combinations can be produced that will make the lines appear to stand still at any speed for which the speed dial may be designed.

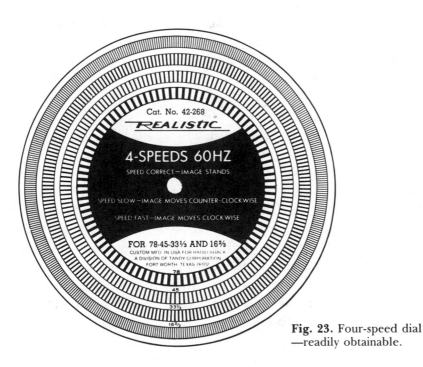

Fig. 23. Four-speed dial —readily obtainable.

Fig. 24. 45 rpm dial for 7-inch records.

Turntables with infinitely variable speeds differ from regular record players in that they can be adjusted to play at any speed from just below 16 rpm to a little above 78 rpm. If, therefore, you use a record with a strobe dial attached (it should be firmly fixed to the record with adhesive), you may be assured that it can be made to play at exactly the right speed in any rink in the U.S. that has such a variable-speed turntable available.

The dial shown in figure 23 is of a combination type; that is, it may be used for any of the standard speeds. Small dials made just for 45 rpm records (figure 24) are difficult to find nowadays but are still available at the time of writing from the PSGA head office (see chapter 29, "Where to Go for Further Information").

Although the cassette reigns supreme in almost all clubs, there is still a good case to be made for the use of 45 rpm records for ice dancing, when absolute accuracy of tempo is required. In tests, competitions, and serious practice sessions, dance music must be played at exactly the correct official speed—no latitude is permitted. Quite frequently ice dancers indignantly complain during club sessions that a certain dance is being played at slightly the wrong tempo, which may well be the case when one considers the damp, the cold, and the rough usage to which most rink cassette players are subjected. Unless one has a rulebook and a metronome on hand, the charge that the music is off tempo is very hard to refute. On the other hand, if the club is using records with speed dials attached, there can be no argument.

If you can locate a source of supply, the 45 rpm dial can also be

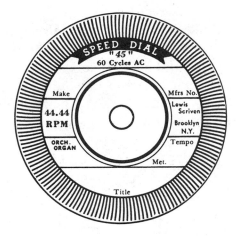

Fig. 25. Dial allowing adjustment of variable-speed record players to 44.44 rpm. This type of dial is very difficult to obtain nowadays.

obtained in sets containing supplementary dials calculated to enable an infinitely variable-speed turntable to be adjusted a small percentage above or below 45 rpm (figure 25). This means that records can be slightly slowed down or speeded up, not in an arbitrary fashion, but in such a way that guarantees the revised speed at every playing. In this way adjustments can be made to freestyle music that may need a couple of seconds either way to make the time just right; and fast dances such as the Kilian can be slowed down to a "social" tempo to make them a little easier for the not so advanced skaters. If your club uses cassettes, they have probably been recorded from records in the first place, so there are probably some dance records stacked away in a closet somewhere. If the music chairman has no objection, you should practice strobing some of these records as it is something all parents should be able to do if the need arises. But one word of warning: You must remember to look at the speed dial under a source of electric light, never under daylight. I have often watched parents who have forgotten this and, after having desperately tried to make the lines stand still, have said, "You know, I just can't seem to do this. I think there must be something wrong with my eyes."

Further Information

The May, June, July, and August, 1982, issues of *American Skating World* (see "Skating Magazines" in Chapter 29) contain outstanding articles by Malcolm Bender on the use of cassettes for skating music. He deals with their mechanics, repair, and the actual process of editing at far greater length than space allows in this book. Rather surprisingly, Mr. Bender favors actually cutting and splicing the tape rather than using the pause button method. I say surprisingly because the narrow, somewhat fragile tape used in cassettes is considered to be much trickier to handle than the wider, tougher tape used on reel-to-reel machines; but it appears to present no difficulty to Mr. Bender, and he gives very explicit instructions regarding how it should be done. As neither I nor my wife (who does nearly all the cutting for our students) have ever attempted splicing cassette tape, I can offer no opinion except that my impression is that it might be better to familiarize yourself with the pause button method first and then see how you get on with the cut and splice method.

In the June issue, Mr. Bender gives some highly valuable instruction on the repair of tapes, to which I can only add one piece of advice. If you ever succeed in getting a cassette open, for heaven's sake don't drop anything! It's bad enough looking for tiny screws on a shag carpet, but if you drop the tape . . . I did that once, so I know. As soon as it hit the floor between my feet, it seemed to take on a life of its own. Every move I made to salvage the situation seemed to make matters worse until its twisting and writhing had created a mound nearly a foot high around my ankles. I eventually threw the whole lot into the trash can. But don't let my experience discourage you—just hold the cassette over the table and I'm sure you'll be okay.

22

The Special Place
of Figures

Why do we skate figures? I am sure many parents have been asked that plaintive question on the way to the rink in the dark hours of the early morning. It is highly likely you have asked yourself the same question many times. To anticipate what I hope to be able to demonstrate in this chapter, let me start by saying that we would be in bad shape without them. To understand their place in the scheme of things one must have a rough idea of how they came into being. The history of skating is highly complex; the description given here is the briefest of brief summaries, but sufficient for the present purpose.

How Figures Arose

During the latter part of the eighteenth and most of the nineteenth century skaters were engaged in discovering exactly what could be done on skates. It was in this period that the main movements such as threes, brackets, rockers, counters, loops, changes of edge, mohawks, and choctaws were invented. Most of these movements took their names from the marks they made on the ice. One of the first of these movements to be discovered was known as "The Figure of a Heart on One Leg," described in *A Treatise on Skating* by Robert Jones in 1772. The "heart" was, in fact, a simple forward outside three made on a small circle. A primitive form of forward outside eight—considered very difficult in those days—was also mentioned. Since both these movements resembled numerals, they were given the name of *figures,* a generic term that from then on was applied to all the movements irrespective of the appearance of their tracings on the ice. But during all this time it was not just the turns that had occupied skaters' minds: a number of moves, such as spreadeagles, spirals, pivots, simple half-turn jumps, and spins, which we would now consider as constituting elementary freestyle, were being developed. But freestyle was not as yet a separate category, and all these moves were referred to as figures, a term that was used very much in the same way that a modern skater would use the word *move*. Although the forward outside eight was already known, as yet nobody had thought of incorporating the various turns into the figure-of-eight form. Admittedly the British had devised a definite schedule of patterns for their own particular type of combined skating in what was known as the English or Victorian style, but this was a totally different concept of skating from that practiced across the Channel and had very little bearing on the direction the sport was soon to take.

In the latter part of the nineteenth century order was finally brought into the existing chaos. An American, Jackson Haines, visited Europe where he gave a number of exhibitions. As well as being a powerful skater, he was a very accomplished dancer and created a sensation, particularly in Vienna, by the way he linked the various moves together to music in a flowing and harmonious manner—a totally new concept. His skating was greatly assisted by his invention of an all-metal blade that could be screwed to the boot—hitherto skates had consisted of metal blades set in wood and attached to the boot by straps. Another of his inventions was the sit spin, which until well into the twentieth century was still known as a Jackson Haines spin. His skating so impressed Demeter Diamantidi, a member of the Vienna Skating Club and an avid technician, that he and another member, Max Wirth, made a careful study of Haines's movements and put them into the two- and three-circle form similar to what we use today. Nigel Brown, in his book *Ice Skating: A History* (London: Nicholas Kaye, 1959), writes:

> Among Jackson Haines's most ardent disciples was Diamantidi who was a great believer in theory. It was Haines's mastery of skating that impressed him. His lightning turns performed with ease and beauty of movement could only be performed in Diamantidi's estimation by adhering to the basic scientific figures. Mastering these, the skater was ready to interpret in his own personal manner, like Haines did, the higher expression of the art which included spirals, spins and jumps.

In 1881 these new figures (then known as *school,* and later as *compulsory,* figures) were published in a book bearing the title *Spuren auf dem Eise* (Tracings on the Ice) which in the following year formed the basis for the Vienna Skating Club's first international competition. Subsequently other figures were added, and at the first congress of the International Skating Union in 1892 a schedule of forty-one figures was adopted, a selection from which was to form a part of all future international championships that came under ISU jurisdiction. The same schedule is still in use today.

Nevertheless, competitions were not to consist solely of the official compulsory figures. A separate part of all competitions allowed skaters to present other movements, combinations of movements, or designs of their own invention. This caused a problem as soon as it came to serious international competition. At the 1882 competition, Theodor Langer skated a very intricate four-pointed star figure (figure 26), Leopold Frey presented a spreadeagle into a back outside eight concluding with a sit spin, and Axel Paulsen stepped onto the ice and did his newly invented one-and-a-half rotational jump into a back spiral. Other miscellaneous moves were presented, which did not help matters.

How could one judge such variety? Did you judge the tracing on the ice or the physical movement? Everyone—public, judges, and skaters—

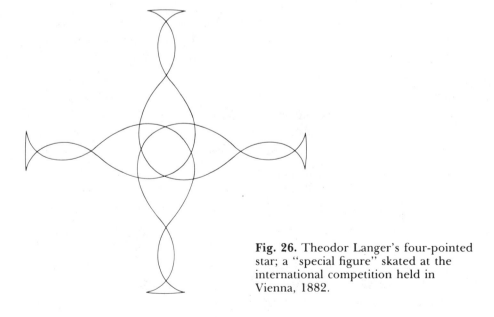

Fig. 26. Theodor Langer's four-pointed star; a "special figure" skated at the international competition held in Vienna, 1882.

was highly impressed by Langer's four-pointed star, but his manner of executing it looked awkward; nor did it have the spectacular quality of some of the other presentations. The result was that Langer ended up fourth, the first three places going to the skaters who presented what we would now call freestyle moves. From then on three official categories were recognized: compulsory figures, special figures (consisting of original designs on the ice, such as Langer's star), and free skating (commonly known as freestyle in the U.S.). The special figure event continued for some years side by side with the other two categories, but after a time special figures were allotted their own competitions. Gradually the special figures became more and more intricate and difficult to execute until they were finally abandoned, partly because of the awkward positions the skater had to adopt, and partly because of increased interest in the freestyle.

Why Do We Still Skate Figures?

For over a hundred years ISU and qualifying USFSA singles competitions have consisted of figures and freestyle (the third category of the short program is simply compulsory freestyle). In view of the less than enthusiastic attitude of most young skaters toward figures, why do we still skate them? There seems to be a widely held opinion that they are an antiquated and moribund form of the sport just waiting for a long overdue coup de grâce from the authorities to eliminate them entirely. Indeed, there was a very strong move a few years ago by the Eastern bloc nations to eliminate figures in international competitions but the move was defeated and they still remain part of all major ISU championships, admittedly in an attenuated form and carrying less weight in the total marks than formerly.

The reason for this persistence almost certainly lies in the dimly perceived fact that they serve a dual purpose—one that Diamantidi had in mind when he first laid out a basis for the ISU schedule: The figures should be part sport and part an interesting (at that time) system of training that would allow the skater to interpret the "higher expression of the art," i.e., the free skating. The endurance of figures in their dual capacity as a system of training and as an interesting sport is perpetuated by the fact that nearly all countries taking part in international competitions use a series of graded tests in figures as an essential part of the qualifications necessary to compete at the national level.

I cannot call to mind any other competitive sport or art (solo musicians also have their competitions) in which the technical elements are grouped into formal patterns to serve as part of the competition itself. The pianist has keyboard exercises, the ballet dancer has exercises at the barre and practice at the center, all of which are traditionally recognized methods of developing good technique. The skating layman does not, however, see figures in this light—but no other traditionally accepted series of skating exercises is as yet available. Ballet and other dance forms are nowadays an essential ingredient in freestyle and of immense help in acquiring body control, but they do not teach the balance unique to skating, which can be learned in no other way than by practice on the ice. Tradition may not yet be strong enough to require competitive skaters to practice certain necessary exercises as a matter of course, but the mandatory nature of qualifying figure tests effects a similar result.

Figures—An Evaluation

It is doubtful whether any informed skater would regard figures as having reached their ideal form either as a sport or as a system of training. But since they carry with them so many advantages—examined more closely below—we can afford to take a frank look at their shortcomings. As a sport the skating of figures has long since become sterile and unprogressive. Admittedly, over the years, the use of better techniques, equipment, and sharpening has brought about an enormous improvement in the actual tracings, but we still skate the same forty-one figures adopted in 1892. Any attempt to introduce new figures to relieve the monotony has been rebuffed. The former world judge and Olympic team member Captain T. D. Richardson did get as far as proposing a series of new figures, and variations on older ones, which was accepted by the National Skating Association of Great Britain to form a separate test schedule. But these were largely ignored, even though listed and diagrammed in the official NSA handbook. A proposal to adopt new figures was actually put before the ISU some years ago; the objection was raised, however, that there would then be far too many for the practice time available to the average skater—a plausible but unsound argument had the matter been given a little thought. Instead, the ISU went in the opposite direction: They reduced the number of figures to be used at competitions and, by putting them on an annually rotating schedule, ensured that the figures to be skated would be known years in advance. The idea seemed to be that the skater would now need to spend less of his time practicing them. The actual result was that he spent just as much time as before, but on fewer figures. What a recipe for boredom!

Nevertheless, it must in all fairness be said that many skaters actually like figures. As a relaxation they appeal to adults who may not be able to progress very far in the freestyle, and as an intellectual challenge they often fascinate those who, by profession or inclination, are interested in scientific subjects such as mathematics, engineering, and photography. Among the younger skaters the change of heart from boredom to interest frequently occurs at about the Fourth or Fifth Test level, when the tracings on the ice begin to look neat and the designs become apparent. The skater may get quite fussy about her patch (it is usually, but not invariably, the girls who become the more enthusiastic figure skaters), which is one of the reasons that many pros teach the high-test figures wearing stadium boots. To examine the centers and turns of a figure a pro must move all over the patch, and if he is wearing skates it can soon look like a disaster area. I have often heard skaters complain bitterly about a pro that "he always comes and messes up my patch."

Apart from the execution of perfect circles, most skaters derive considerable satisfaction from getting their turns clean and putting one tracing exactly on top of another. Placing three well-executed brackets within a tiny area gives a skater the same feeling of accomplishment that a British dart player gets when he puts three darts into the triple twenty—quite an amazing feat when one considers the amount of beer consumed during a game.

Having dealt with the criticism most often leveled against figures as a sport, we must now examine their use as a means of developing body control. To the layman watching a freestyle session it may seem inconceivable that the spectacular jumps and flying spins could derive the slightest help from the slow, careful, earthbound movements of the figures. But the top-rank jumper does not make careless, uncontrolled movements—the degree of control of the individual edges into and out of a jump is enormous. This edge control is one of the prime skills taught by figures. Consider, too, that during a jump a strong male skater is in the air an average of approximately 0.65 seconds. Let us suppose that in a senior freestyle program lasting 4½ minutes he puts in ten major jumps; this means he is in the air a mere 6½ seconds or, if you count minor jumps and flying spins, 10 seconds at the most. The remaining 4 minutes 20 seconds is spent on the ice stroking, spinning, and executing footwork and other miscellaneous movements. A few minor slips or moments of lack of control are to be expected in the jumps, but not when the skater is in contact with the ice performing the major part of his program.

Any expert watching a free skater either in practice or during a program can immediately sense whether the skater has had a background in figures. The free skater with sound figure training is smooth, executes his turns with minimum effort, usually has excellent footwork, and gives a satisfying impression of complete control over any edge he strikes. The skater lacking such a background is choppy, unnatural in his movements, one-sided in his footwork (such as it is), and clearly has difficulty in controlling the natural rotation set up by the edges.

Any pro who has ever tried to teach freestyle to a powerful skater who has never done a figure in his life will tell you how very difficult it is. Not only is all control over the edges lacking, but so is any understanding of the way in which his body works. If he is asked to pass the free leg forward and at the same time press the free hip back, he will look at the teacher as though he is out of his mind, and probably tell him it can't be done. Teacher and student are just not on the same wavelength.

Dancers with classical training have a refined knowledge of body movement, and one might think they would be much easier to train as a result. In a sense they are, but only if they have already spent many seasons on the ice acquiring the balance so unique to skating. Many professional theatrical performers have fallen into this trap. Many years ago my wife and I were working as a pair in a large stage show in Spain. There were three ice numbers; the rest were floor acts that included a pair of exhibition dancers. A few days after the opening, the man in the dance act came to us and with a disdainful wave of the hand and a curl of the lip, said, "My partner and I will have our act on the ice in three weeks— you will see." Clearly the implication was that when this happened, we would be out of a job—very kind of him to warn us. Well, they got themselves some skates—I can't think where in those days in Madrid—and went to work. I am afraid the story has no real ending because after a couple of weeks they had obviously given up the whole idea and didn't come near us for the rest of the run. But it is a good example of the layman's total misconception of the skills involved in figure skating and the time necessary to acquire them.

To be a good freestylist it is not necessary for a skater to have passed the Eighth (Gold) Figure Test; one has only to watch the Intermediate or Novice free skating in a Sectional championship to see that this is so. Nor does the passing of the Gold Figure Test guarantee that the skater will be a good free skater, but it does supply some very important tools, if he can use them. There are many skaters, top-rank in the figures, who, because they lack the necessary power, courage, and artistic flair, are hopeless in free skating. The really fine freestylist must have all these qualities *plus* the body control; it is useless having one without the other.

Just how high up the figure test ladder a skater must go to achieve his maximum potential in the freestyle is almost impossible to say, but it does seem that, among the better free skaters, those who have gone highest in the figures show the greatest degree of quality in their freestyle. This quality is difficult to define. The skating of a high-tester shows strength, confidence, and flow, accompanied by the ability to hold the body and limbs absolutely still when required. Those who have achieved the Eighth Test have spent countless hours practicing turns (particularly the difficult bracket) at high speed and on tight, hard edges. Not only do they have all their turns completely under control but they are equally adept on either side, which gives them a tremendous advantage in the footwork. For the ice dancer, footwork is just as important as for the singles skater, if not more so, because it forms so large a part of free dance programs. Next time you watch a free dance program, see if you can spot which one of the couple does the more complex footwork—it is highly likely that he or she is the more advanced in the figure tests.

What Exactly Do Figures Teach?

To clarify what has been said, the following is a list of the major skills taught by figures; most of these skills have direct application to freestyle and ice dancing. Following the list is a short discussion of the individual elements.

1. Ability to hold an edge in various positions without losing control of the rotation.
2. Ability to move various parts of the body in isolation, together, and in opposition.
3. Ability to strike onto a true curve in the correct direction in relation to the preceding curve.
4. Ability to execute all turns, fast and slow, with complete control.

5. Development of equal ability on both sides of the body.
6. Development of a physical point of reference.
7. Sense of pattern round an axis.
8. Stillness in the upper part of the body.
9. Concentration.
10. Discipline.
11. Ability to execute well-shaped turns.
12. Development of the run of edge.
13. Ability to execute all turns cleanly.
14. Ability to trace in triple repetition.

The first skill on the list, control of edge rotation, is of extreme importance in almost every aspect of skating, particularly so in the approach and landing of jumps, a fact that is seldom appreciated. If, for example, the body starts to rotate in an uncontrolled manner on the forward outside edge into an Axel, or on the back inside edge before a Salchow, overrotation may force the skater into the jump too soon and timing will suffer. Similarly, if the rotation is not controlled on the landing edge, the skater will either "fall out of the circle" or be forced to step off onto the other foot before he has had time to demonstrate control of the landing position.

From here on the numbers in parentheses refer to the numbers of the skills in the above list. Because of the natural rotation set up by the curve of the edge, the various parts of a skater's body tend to move together in the same direction as one unit. Through analysis and practice the skater must learn to move limbs, shoulders, torso, and hips independently of one another; he must also learn the totally opposite skill of moving several parts of the body simultaneously (2). It must be understood that these skills are only of use if they can be performed in the presence of the complex dynamic forces peculiar to skating, which is why skating can be so frustrating to many trained dancers and athletes. At the moment figures, when correctly taught, are the only accepted method we have of teaching these skills; it is, therefore, fortunate that they are incorporated into a compulsory test schedule.

When passing from one foot to the other it is very important that the new foot is placed on the ice so that the direction of the new curve at the moment of transition is the same as that of the end of the previous curve (3). On skates this is a totally unnatural action, the natural action being to turn the new foot out as it is placed onto the ice. When this action appears in freestyle or ice dancing, it gives the skater an ugly, splay-footed appearance. This turned-out look of the feet is particularly prevalent in young, untrained roller skaters when they first try ice skating. The correct action is most easily learned by practicing a simple forward outside eight under the eye of a competent teacher, who will insist that the skater make the two circles tangential at the point of transition from one foot to the other.

Execution of *all* turns with complete control (4) implies equal ability in both directions (5). Both these abilities enable the skater to attain the highest degree possible in the realm of footwork, a field that will take on increasing importance when the multi-rotational jumps have become commonplace.

The necessity for a point of reference within the body (6) was stressed by John Jerome in his book *The Sweet Spot in Time* (New York: Summit Books, 1980). He quoted the brilliant choreographer Twyla Tharp in answer to the question whether she preferred candidates with classical or modern dance training for her type of work. "Classical," she replied. "People with ballet training are more centered. I don't mean this in any mystical sense—they just know where their center is. They know how to get their weight between their feet and keep it there, how to arrange their limbs around a central body core. They have a reference point. When you work with them you have some place to start from." When changing from one position to another in, for example, the approach to a difficult turn, the skater must move his limbs carefully round his center of gravity (his reference point) in such a way that he does not disturb it in the slightest degree. The most minute unnecessary shift in the center of gravity will show immediately in the tracing and the figure will suffer. This is the devastating thing about figures: every fleeting moment of instability leaves on the ice a trail of incriminating evidence that only the healing passage of the Zamboni can erase.

The skating of symmetrical circles properly aligned in the rink gives the skater a sense of how to place curves in proper relationship to a long axis (7). This is surprisingly important in many freestyle moves, particularly footwork, where the skater must visualize the correct pattern in the rink if he is not to find himself on the wrong edge. It is of even greater importance in compulsory dances, where such curves (known in this context as *lobes*) must be placed, starting at the correct angle, around the "continuous axis," an imaginary line parallel to the rink barrier.

The ability to hold the upper body still (8) when it is not being used for any specific purpose gives the impression of great control; this ability is shared by many great artists and athletes. When the skater has achieved this skill it means that the control of his balance is located in the correct muscles, predominantly those of the thigh (quadriceps) and, to a lesser degree, the ankle. If you watch a beginner when he first learns to skate forward on one foot, you will see that he balances with the upper part of his body assisted by his arms and free leg. In the natural course of events these movements will disappear as the correct muscle groups take over, but the last movement to go is that from the waist; the instructor must pay particular attention to this during figure lessons. I have had skaters at the Fourth and Fifth Test level come to me who still had traces of this very slight waist movement. Lack of firmness in that part of the body not only creates technical problems in the figures but can give the disturbing impression of a slight lack of control or looseness in the freestyle.

The value of concentration and discipline (9 and 10) is self-evident. These virtues not only are of prime importance in any type of competitive activity but bring great benefit to the skater who has not been fortunate enough to acquire good work habits in his educational environment. Concentration and discipline are seldom developed in a permissive atmosphere, however, and among other things this means that good patch rules (see chapter 10) must not only be set up but enforced. We have never found any serious competitor who resented this approach.

The ability to execute turns in good shape (11) may on the face of it seem of little importance in freestyle but, in fact, it has considerable relevance to footwork. If a skater regularly produces turns badly out of shape—very common in poor figure skaters—it means that he is out of position during the turn, i.e., his point of rotation is not quite over the turn, or he is skating asymmetrically across it. The result is that if a section of footwork requires several turns in quick succession, he will either look awkward and clumsy or, most probably, make a complete botch of it.

Run of edge (12) means that with a given amount of initial thrust the skater travels the maximum distance possible. Most moderately good figure skaters will have developed all the run of edge necessary for their freestyle. Maximum run of edge becomes extremely important in the Seventh and Eighth Figure Tests, however, because without it the skater may just fail to reach center in the slow section of a paragraph figure (one containing two circles, possibly with turns, that must be executed on one foot). Even if he stops only a foot before he reaches the point of initial thrust, he will be heavily marked down. In this context run of edge assumes much greater importance than in the freestyle.

The final two skills, namely, the ability to execute all turns cleanly (13), and the placement as accurately as possible of one tracing on top of another (14), have a very high priority in the skating of competitive figures, but a comparatively low priority in promoting skills for free skating and ice dancing. Nevertheless, I must continue to emphasize very strongly that the development of the first twelve skills in the list are essential for all branches of figure skating and, as things stand at the moment, are best developed by practicing the figures themselves.

Perhaps a concrete example will make the effect of lack of figure training clear. Normally I am adamant in my refusal to teach any student wearing hockey skates. I am not against hockey, it is a fine game; my son plays, and I am delighted to report that he still has a full set of teeth, real ones. I have even had a lot of pleasure myself fooling around the rink with stick and puck, but that is as far as I am prepared to go. Nevertheless, a year or so ago a distraught mother begged me to try to do something about her hockey-playing son's stroke. His times (speed) were lagging behind those of the other players, and even she could see that something was technically amiss. She stooped to a little flattery, which in this case did get her somewhere. I rose to the bait, thinking to myself that if anybody could do anything about the poor fellow's stroke it was I—anyway, *noblesse oblige,* and I obviously had a moral duty to discharge.

The young man and I had never met, but I set some morning ice aside when there would be nobody else around. At the appointed time a gangling, slender youth in hockey skates appeared. He was about fourteen years old, wearing rather dilapidated jeans, a loosely flying T-shirt bearing some strange insignia, and was attempting to get his mouth round an enormous wad of gum. He mumbled "good morning," and when I suggested that he might like to warm up a little he immediately went into an imitation of a hockey player, or rather his conception of one. Off he skated down the straightaway, hunched over, chest concave, arms loosely swinging, first one shoulder in the air and then the other, blades dragging across the ice after the stroke—if you could dignify it by such a name—producing a grating, tinny sound that set my teeth on edge. My first concern was that his simian crouch might cause him to trip over his own hands, but he avoided this and went round the corner with that strange chopping run peculiar to novice hockey players.

All this time I was trying to analyze what might be wrong with his stroke. He had his weight centered all right, right between his feet, but this did not do for him what it might have done for a ballerina because it completely prevented him from skating on one foot or even keeping his weight over it for a distance of more than two or three inches at a time. This is not a technical book, so I cannot go into the details of stroking as I should like to, but it is sufficient to say that one of the prime requirements of a long powerful stroke (as opposed to a fast run) is that the weight should be transferred from one foot to the other relatively slowly, during which time the thrusting blade generates power in a sideways action. The thrusting blade can, however, only deliver power while it is in contact with the ice: take the weight off the thrusting foot and the source of power is lost. Not only had the boy never been shown this technique, he had not even been taught the basic skills that would have made such a technique possible. If you push against something, whether it be with your foot or hand, there has to be some weight or inertia at the point where the push starts, which means that a leg or arm must be attached to a body before it can exert pressure, and that body must form a firm base, or point of origin; precisely the same problem that astronauts have to deal with. Nothing in the boy's training had ever been directed to the way in which he should control his body so that it would form a stable base of operation. He was so lacking in control that his body was never consistently in the same place at the beginning of any stroke. Even if the stroke had started correctly, the body was so loose and free that there was no weight behind the thrust to generate any power. It was impossible to make any correction in his stroke until some degree of body control had been developed. To address oneself to his leg action would have been starting at totally the wrong end.

Despite my aversion to his skating, I found him a pleasant young man and managed to make him dimly perceive what was wrong. What he should have done was learn some of the basic skills on figure skates so that he was not always trying to imitate what he thought hockey players did. He then could have mastered some of the elementary figures, such as the four eights, which would have given him the necessary steadiness in his torso. The whole situation arose in the first place because another young man at the same rink had done precisely that and had learned to handle himself equally well on both types of blade. He had advanced to approximately the Second Test figure level and was fast becoming a powerful free skater, with the result that when he put on his hockey skates he skated rings round the rest of the team and had the fastest times by far.

This anecdote points up very clearly the necessity for some type of training in the fundamentals of body movement and carriage as a prerequisite for any branch of skating, including hockey and speed skating. At the moment the figures, embodied as they are in a series of mandatory tests, are the best form of on-ice training. The system is not perfect, but it is effective.

Any new system that might be devised would be very like the existing one, except that the priorities would be different. The tracing would still be important since it reveals so much about the skater's control, but there would be much more emphasis on posture. The present rules contain many laudable requirements in this respect, but with the necessity for accurate triple repetition (provided the first tracing is a good one), these cannot always be carried out. Take for instance the rule "The head should be carried in an upright position, relaxed and held naturally." If a skater is to put lines, turns, and loops one on top of the other he must look down —mind you, a great majority of skaters make the worst of this necessity and develop round shoulders or an ugly crouch—but I have never yet seen perfect figures put down by a skater looking all the time above the barrier level, which is where they should be looking in all other branches of figure skating. Nevertheless, because figures carry with them so many advantages we must for the moment accept this, and teach posture during the freestyle lessons, or by off-ice training such as classical dancing. Ice dancing itself is very helpful since it demands good upper body posture in the compulsory dances, at the same time that it helps the skater to develop a sense of pattern. Even for the dedicated singles skater some exposure to ice dancing is beneficial, even if it is only up to the Bronze Test level.

By the same token, and for the reasons given earlier, figures help the ice dancer's control. At this point it is important, however, to distinguish between posture, which implies a static position such as we should like to see in figures and ice dancing, and elegant movement, set off by periods of good posture, which is appropriate to freestyle. In the compulsory dances the upper body is held in an upright posture throughout, whereas in the freestyle the skater is allowed almost unlimited freedom of movement of torso and limbs, provided an aesthetically pleasing effect is created.

23
Recognizing Turns
and Figures

All parents of test or competitive skaters, even if they never set foot on the ice, should be able to recognize the basic turns, figures, and freestyle moves. Knowing what skaters are trying to do does help to while away those otherwise unproductive hours you may have to spend watching patch or freestyle practice. It will also increase your status among other parents if you can distinguish a *three* from a *bracket;* more still if you know the difference between a *rocker* and a *counter,* or between a *double toe* and a *double flip.* But until you really understand what you are looking at, be wary of using any newly acquired knowledge in the presence of a competent skater—a blunder is easy to make and difficult to live down, especially if committed in front of your own child, who may well bar you from all future practice sessions.

It is assumed that by now the nonskating reader is acquainted with the concept of the fundamental curves, or *edges.* The abbreviations are: RFO (right forward outside), LFO (left forward outside), RBO (right back outside), and LBO (left back outside). The inside edges are shown in the same way: RFI (right forward inside), and so on.

The Turns

A turn is any movement made on a curve, or curves, from forward to backward or backward to forward, the skater remaining on one foot throughout or changing from one foot to the other. Those turns in which

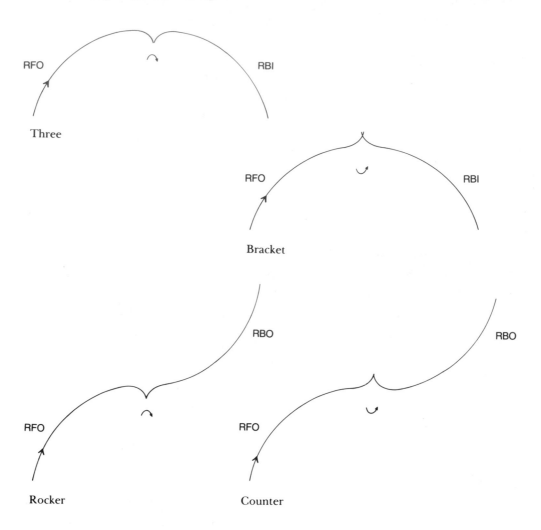

RFO   RBI

Three

RFO   RBI

Bracket

RBO   RBO

RFO   RFO

Rocker   Counter

Figs. 27–30. Turns on one foot. All the turns in figures 27 through 30 are shown as being entered on the right forward outside edge (RFO), but they may also be entered on any of the other three edges. The curved arrow shows the direction of rotation of the skating foot.

the entry and exit are made on the same foot are *threes, brackets, rockers,* and *counters* (figures 27 through 30). Those that involve a change of feet are called *mohawks* and *choctaws* (figures 31 and 32). Only the turns on one foot are used in figures (strictly speaking there is a choctaw at the center of the figure known as *threes to a center,* but it is not generally recognized as such).

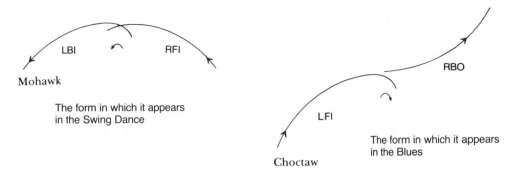

Figs. 31 and 32. Turns involving a change of feet. The mohawks and choctaws are shown here as being entered on the right and left forward inside edges (RFI and LFI), respectively, the forms in which they are most commonly met. They may, however, be entered on any edge. The tracings differ slightly according to the variety of the turn skated.

But all the above turns, some with variations, form part of the footwork in freestyle, pair, and ice dancing.

For the sake of simplicity the diagrams show the turns on one foot as starting on the RFO edge only, but they may be entered on any edge, forward or backward, which means that there are four versions of each of these turns—eight if you choose to count the left foot as well. The mohawks and choctaws are shown as starting on the FI edge only since this is the form in which they are most commonly seen. There are, however, many varieties of these two turns: Not only can they be entered on any of the four edges, but differences in position of the free foot and leg before or after these turns give rise to further labels, namely, *open, closed, swing,* and *crossed.* More detailed descriptions of all the turns mentioned above, as well as certain steps used in ice dancing, are to be found in the *USFSA Rulebook.* The tracings on the ice of the one-foot turns remain basically the same whatever the entry edge, but in the case of mohawks and choctaws the tracings may differ somewhat at the point where the change of feet takes place according to the variety of the turn being skated.

It is almost impossible for a layman to tell a rocker from a counter just by looking at the tracing on the ice because if he has not watched the turn being made, he will have no way of knowing in which direction the skater was traveling unless the whole figure has been skated, and the direction can be deduced by examination of the centers; but ten chances to one the casual onlooker will not have access to the ice surface. If you look at the diagrams you will see that if the skater enters the turn from the opposite direction to that shown by the arrow, the rocker becomes a counter and vice versa. To distinguish these two turns in movement, always remember that in a rocker the body starts the rotation in the direction of a three whereas in a counter the direction of initial rotation is that of a bracket.

The best way to become familiar with the one-foot turns is to watch a patch session. Threes occur in all figure tests from the Preliminary up through the Eighth. If you watch a Second Test, you will see all the threes in their simplest form. Look for the brackets in the Fourth and Fifth Tests (also in the Sixth and Eighth), the counters in the Sixth Test, and the rockers in the Seventh. Examples of mohawks or choctaws or both are to be found in various forms in most of the dances (not, fortunately for the weaker skaters, in the Dutch Waltz or Canasta Tango). To familiarize yourself with these last two turns it is best to have a dance professional demonstrate and explain them. I say a dance professional because, although good freestylists can execute most of these turns, they are not always as familiar with the nomenclature as the ice dancers. Even the best freestylist may have to think hard when suddenly asked to produce a back outside closed choctaw (it occurs in the Rhumba) even though he may unknowingly use it in some of his freestyle footwork.

All the turns have been diagrammed as if executed on large, extended curves, but when used in fast footwork or ice dancing, these turns are most frequently made on short, fast edges, making it very difficult for anyone except an expert to see at a glance exactly which turn is being used.

There are two other moves, *changes of edge* and *loops,* which, while not in the category of turns, are in such frequent use in the figures that they should be dealt with here.

Changes of Edge

A change of edge—usually referred to simply as a change—is the action of rocking over from one edge to the other without actually turning (figure 33). For example, the skater might start on the RFO edge and rock over to the RFI, but a change may be made from any of the four edges. This movement is in common use in all branches of figure skating, particularly

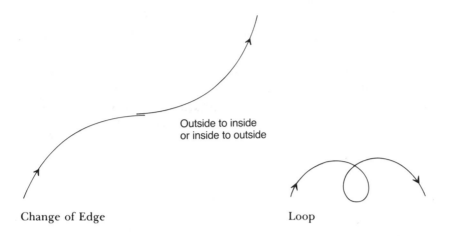

Outside to inside
or inside to outside

Change of Edge   Loop

Figs. 33 and 34. Changes of edge and loops. These moves may be skated on any of the four edges. The separation of the tracing at the point of rockover of the change of edge represents the width of the blade. The actual size of the loop is one and a half the skater's blade in length and one in width.

in the figures. Many years ago a change of edge was known as a *serpentine* or *serpentine line,* but nowadays the word has almost gone out of use except in the phrase *serpentine step sequence.* which is the official description of a snakelike sequence of footwork sometimes required in the short program. It is also occasionally heard as the name of the three-circle figures occurring in the first and second tests, i.e., *forward serpentine* and *back serpentine* instead of *forward changes* and *back changes.*

Loops

Like a change of edge, a *loop* (figure 34) does not involve what is technically known as a turn: If you start on a forward edge, you exit on the same forward edge; and the same applies to the back edges. Because they can only be executed slowly, the only time you are likely to see loops skated is when they are part of a figure. Very occasionally you may see a loop used in the slow section of a freestyle program, but it is most uncommon; they are never used in any of the compulsory ice dances. Loops are always skated on much smaller curves than other regular skating moves (a loop figure is only one-third the diameter of a normal figure), and because the balance is tricky and difficult to sustain throughout the whole movement, loops usually take a long time to learn to do well. Furthermore their geometry and dynamics are generally less understood than other movements used in figures—they make a fascinating study for the scientifically and mathematically minded. Loops bedevil skaters from the Third Test up, with the exception of the Sixth Test, at which point a skater's first reaction is usually a delighted and unbelieving, "What! No loops?"

The Figures

For those of you who may have skipped chapter 22, "The Special Place of Figures," I shall start with a brief summary.

Many years ago the International Skating Union decided that in order to facilitate the judging of international competitions, only certain designs on the ice should be skated. Those chosen were all based on the two-circle and three-circle form, and the use of the various one-foot turns, changes of edge, and loops already mentioned gave scope for considerable variation. Each of the chosen designs, or figures as they were now called, was assigned an official number and collectively constitute what is known as the ISU Schedule of Compulsory Figures, from which are selected those figures to be used in national and international tests and competitions. At one time those who prided themselves on their skating knowledge and memory had the irritating habit of referring to individual figures by their official number rather than by name. A great friend of mine would, for example, make a remark such as, "I always find number 21 an awkward figure after the first turn, don't you agree?" He would then cock an eyebrow at me in a challenging manner while I groped desperately to remember whether number 21 referred to rockers or counters (or was it brackets?) and whether it started on the outside or inside edge. (Actually number 21 is the inside rocker figure.) He always annoyed me intensely when he pulled this one, but as he was an international judge, I refrained from comment.

If you ask exactly how many figures there are, you will probably get several different answers—the reason will become clear as you read on. As shown here (figures 35 through 53), the figures are grouped according to their three basic forms: two-circle, three-circle, and paragraph, the

TWO-CIRCLE FIGURES

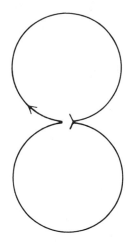

Fig. 35 Eight

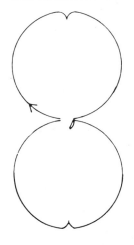

Fig. 36 Three

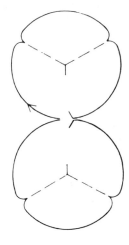

Fig. 37 Double Three

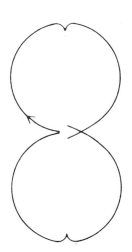

Fig. 38. Threes (to a Center)
This figure is unique in
the schedule (see text).

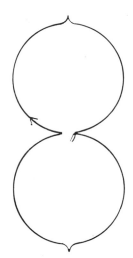

Fig. 39 Bracket

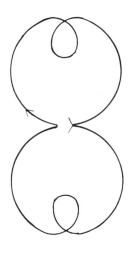

Fig. 40. Loop
The overall size of the
loop figure and its
variations is one-third
that of other figures
(see text).

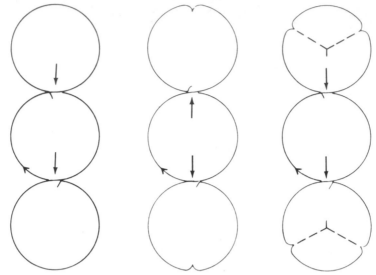

Fig. 41 Serpentine   **Fig. 42** Change Three   **Fig. 43** Change Double Three

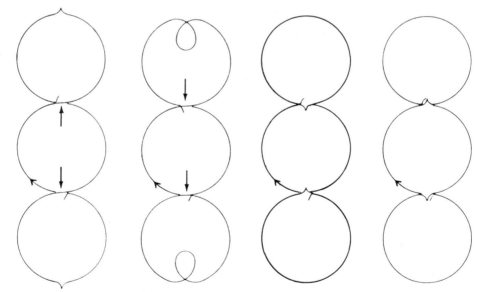

Fig. 44 Change Bracket **Fig. 45** Change Loop   **Fig. 46** Rocker   **Fig. 47** Counter

Figs. 41–47. Three-Circle Figures. In the following diagrams a change of edge is denoted by a vertical arrow directed at the point where the change of edge takes place.

PARAGRAPH FIGURES

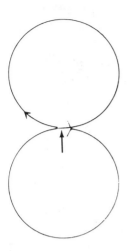

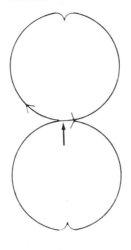

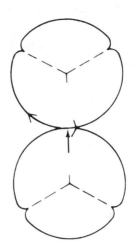

Fig. 48 One-foot Eight

Fig. 49 Paragraph Three (Three Change Three)

Fig. 50 Paragraph Double Three (Double Three Change Double Three)

PARAGRAPH FIGURES

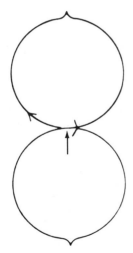

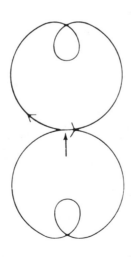

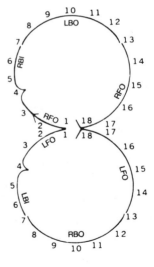

Fig. 51 Paragraph Bracket (Bracket Change Bracket)

Fig. 52 Paragraph Loop (Loop Change Loop)

Fig. 53. Waltz Eight This figure is not included in the ISU schedule (see text).

last-named being a special type of two-circle figure which I shall explain later. There is one figure, the waltz eight, that, although included in the diagrams, is only skated in the U.S. and does not form part of the ISU schedule. For the moment we shall ignore this figure, which leaves us with eighteen basic designs. The *USFSA Rulebook* gives the complete numbered listing of the figures as it appears in the ISU schedule.

Numbering the Figures

You will not miss a lot if you skip the next three paragraphs; it is an attempt to make clear in as few words as possible the somewhat peculiar system by which the figures are numbered—a rather dull subject, but I feel the interested parent is due an explanation. To understand fully what I am about to say you should have a *USFSA Rulebook*—you are going to need one anyway, sooner or later. If you turn to the Table of Compulsory Figures at the end of the chapter on Test Rules (TR), the first thing you will notice is that each of the eighteen basic designs is accompanied by a list of numbers marked *a* and *b,* each of which denotes a variation of the basic figure, bringing the total to forty-one *a* figures and forty-one *b,* for a whopping grand total of eighty-two (omitting the waltz eight).

The general principle is that the first number on the list accompanying any of the basic designs refers to the figure when started on the right forward outside edge—this is the *a* form. If the figure is to be started on the *left* forward outside edge, the figure has the same number but is marked *b.* However, if the figure also exists in variations starting on the right forward inside, the right back outside, or the right back inside edges, each variation is given a separate number, the right foot variation being marked *a* and the left *b.* Nevertheless, there is one anomaly that did not exist until a slight change was made in the system a few years ago. In certain two-circle figures, namely, the simple eights (numbers 1 through 4), the double threes (10 through 13), the loops (14 through 17), and the three (number 7, usually referred to as threes to a center), it really doesn't matter whether you start on the right or the left foot; in either case you are doing the same figure, because the second circle starts on an edge of the same character as the first.

Up until a few years ago those figures in which the edges and turns were the same whether started on the right or left foot were always started on the right, never the left, and these figures were not marked either *a* or *b*. The change in the system was, to the best of my knowledge, initiated in Europe. In order to save time in competitions a draw is made by lot for the starting foot of the first figure to be skated, after which the starting foot alternates. Thus, if the first figure starts on the left foot, the next figure starts on the right, the third on the left, and so on. This was fine while all the figures in a competition had *a* and *b* forms, but some confusion arose in lower-rank competitions which contained some figures that only needed to be started on the right foot, mixed up with others that had both the right and left version. It was therefore decided that *all* figures should be liable to a right or left start, whether it made any practical difference or not—to my mind an illogical and unnecessary tampering with a practice that had worked satisfactorily for years. In the U.S. all figure tests are still conducted on the old method; in the Preliminary Test, for example, everything is started on the right foot only. Competitions, however, are conducted under the revised rule.

Observations on the Figures

The size of the circles in all the figures except the loops is *approximately* three times the height of the skater in diameter, but skaters of the same height tend to vary somewhat in the size of circle that comes naturally to them. In the case of loops, the circle is much smaller, the width usually corresponding to the height of the skater, while the length is somewhat reduced according to the skater's technique (a tricky and much disputed matter that I do not intend to discuss here).

The waltz eight (figure 53) is of purely American origin and is not included in the official ISU schedule. It is unique in not really being a figure in the accepted sense but more of an exercise. Its original purpose was to prepare the skater for the American Waltz and for some reason it found its way into the Preliminary Figure Test. As can be seen from the diagram, the circle is divided into three parts, the first third being occupied by a forward outside three, followed by a back outside edge in the second third, and a step to forward in the final third. Each third is intended to represent six counts of the American Waltz, which presumably the skater is supposed to count to himself. Except for possible practice purposes, counting in this figure has long been discontinued. It is a figure concerning which I have very strong and adverse feelings. For skaters at the Preliminary Figure Test level it is a very difficult figure to do well, and requires certain techniques in the execution of the three that are not in accord with present-day figure techniques. It is my personal opinion that this figure is no longer appropriate and should be removed from the figure test schedule. However, for the moment we are stuck with it, and skaters must do the best they can.

Threes to a center (figure 38) deserves special mention. It is unique in the ISU schedule as being the only figure containing single turns on the axis in which both circles start on a forward outside edge. It is therefore in the class of figures just discussed where it does not make much difference whether one starts on the right or left edge. It is a most awkward figure—occurring, unfortunately, at the First Test level—which requires the skater to step at the center from a back inside edge to a forward outside edge on the other foot. This contortion is technically a choctaw, a movement that does not occur in any other figure in the ISU schedule. I suppose the simple bracket figure could be executed like this, but I have never seen anyone foolish enough to attempt it.

The counters, in the Sixth Test, were originally considered to be more difficult than the rockers, a Seventh Test figure; their position in the ISU schedule reflects this. The reason probably stems from the fact that in the early days the hollows used in figure blades were much deeper than we use today, with the result that the edges were more likely to get caught in the ice. Counters were more dangerous, because if the edge caught in the ice on an outside turn, there was no friendly free foot to put down, and the skater almost invariably fell flat on his side. With modern techniques and shallow hollows the chance of the edge catching is not nearly so great, and the rocker is now considered to be the more difficult turn to get clean.

Finally, the word *paragraph* requires some comment. A paragraph figure is a form of two-circle figure in which the skater, by means of a change of edge at the center instead of a change of feet, executes two whole circles on one foot without pause; he is thus required to travel double the distance that he would have to travel in a simple two-circle figure. Not only does the skater need considerable speed at the start, but he must also have a great delicacy of balance to make the edge flow and prevent himself from coming to a dead stop some feet before the center is reached—a most embarrassing situation when it occurs in a test or competition. The simplest form of this type of figure is the *one-foot eight* (figure 48), which is the more usual way of referring to it than paragraph eight. However, when threes, brackets, or loops occur within the figure, the customary expressions are paragraph three, paragraph double threes, paragraph bracket, and paragraph loop, rather than the more cumbersome three-change-three, bracket-change-bracket, etc. The back paragraph bracket (i.e., starting on the back outside edge) is, incidentally, considered by most skaters to be the most difficult figure in the schedule.

I have never been able to track down with complete certainty the origin of this strange use of the word *paragraph,* but it is probably connected with one of the many forms of fanciful symbol used at one time by book designers and printers to draw attention to the beginning of a paragraph. In books about fifty years old I have seen such a symbol in a serpentine-like form that could, by a stretch of the imagination, suggest the skating figure.

24
Recognizing
Free Skating Moves

The aim of this chapter is to help nonskating readers recognize the more common jumps, spins, and miscellaneous moves that make up modern free skating. To accomplish this it is not necessary to go deeply into techniques; all that is required is that the onlooker be familiar with certain typical positions and be able to identify moderately quickly all four edges. Although an important part of freestyle, footwork must be omitted here. Footwork is composed of step sequences consisting of complex combinations of turns and fast, short edges that are very individual to the skater and consequently difficult to classify. The best way to familiarize yourself with footwork is to ask a good skater to do some for you. It may not mean a lot unless the skater can slow the sequence down and demonstrate the component parts—something that most skaters find very difficult to do— but even the most exacting skater will not expect his parents to know how a step is constructed. He may, however, be justified in expecting that a snappy piece of footwork will at least be recognized as such.

The Jumps

Standard skating jumps are in the form of rotation around a vertical axis. The back somersault has now, quite rightly I believe, been banned from amateur competitions. As applied to skating the somersault is not as modern a concept as most present-day youngsters seem to think; it had already been performed in ice shows many years ago by Skippy Baxter and Adele Inge, who also did the forward version.

Jumps fall into two basic categories: The skater may jump directly from one edge to the other, in which case it is known as an edge to edge jump, or he may assist himself by the free toe at the take-off, in which case it is known as a toe jump. Jumps may also be classified by the amount of turn or number of turns in the air; thus, they may be half-revolution, single (one turn), double, triple, or quadruple (very rare). A few jumps exist in a one-and-a-half form. The Axel, although it requires one and a half turns in the air, is classified as a single to distinguish it from the double Axel. (The Axel will be defined in the section dealing with individual jumps.) Every jump has a name, sometimes taken from the skater who is generally acknowledged as having invented it, sometimes from the position in the air, and less frequently from the edges involved. There are many more jumps possible than are normally seen performed on the ice surface. In the late thirties an extraordinary English skater, Patrick Low, published a table in which all takeoff and landing edges and directions of rotation were combined to produce every possible combination of jump. He then methodically attempted to perform them all, in many cases very successfully. It is therefore very difficult to invent an entirely new jump. Many of Pat Low's jumps were highly interesting, but with one exception they are rarely seen nowadays. We are concerned here with the standard jumps that make up the major part of the modern-day skater's repertoire.

Learning to Identify Jumps

With the possible exception of the stag jump, it is impossible to identify any jump with absolute certainty unless you have watched the skater at the takeoff, in the air, and at the landing. Of these three phases the takeoff is the most important. It is essential to be able to recognize which edge the skater is on, the position of his body just before he leaves the ice, and whether or not he assists himself with the free toe, because the combination of these three things signals the basic type of jump he is about to do. Then, by observing the skater in the air and at the landing, with practice you will be able to say which variation, if any, of the basic jump has been executed.

By constantly watching skaters during a freestyle session you will soon learn when to expect a jump. Skaters get speed and set themselves up for a jump in a way that is usually typical for that particular type of jump. At the end of this approach, as it is called, the skater will strike onto his takeoff edge either by a turn or as a continuation of the approach. It is important to remember that however typical the approach, it is not an official part of the jump but simply a convenient method of getting onto the takeoff edge and assuming a suitable position of the body to execute the jump. Any approach is legitimate. Many young skaters who have not had this explained to them become confused, when asked to use another approach, as to what jump they are doing.

The majority of skaters (an educated guess might be 80 percent) jump to the left, i.e., counterclockwise, although there have been several world champions who jump to the right. There is nothing wrong with jumping to the right, except that in a crowded session it can be very difficult for a right-jumper to practice his jumps freely if everyone else is jumping to the left—he is forced to move against the crowd. Some years ago a few skaters did introduce into their competition programs some of the jumps in both directions, but this ability never seemed to be reflected in the marks they received, and the trend has for the moment died out. At this stage, however, it is important that skaters learn to jump and spin in the same direction, otherwise they may have difficulties with the flying spins, i.e., those spins that are entered from a jump. But it is not difficult to learn to spin both ways, and the combinations that can result can be very interesting and attractive.

With regard to the landings, the most commonly used edge is the back outside; then comes the forward inside landing assisted by the toe of the other foot, followed by the rarely used back inside edge landing. In the case of counterclockwise jumpers these edges will be the *right* back outside, *left* toe and *right* forward inside, and *left* back inside, respectively. Reverse *right* and *left* for clockwise jumpers. A few minor jumps and some one-and-a-half-revolution jumps land on the forward outside edge as- sisted with the toe, but these jumps are rather rare and not included in the list of standard jumps. It is quite possible to land directly onto a forward outside or forward inside edge without an assist from the toe, but such jumps rarely exceed more than half a turn. Nevertheless, full turns onto a forward edge (e.g., forward loop jumps) have occasionally been used. Such jumps are interesting fill-ins but do not normally constitute highlights in a program.

You must, of course, watch the position in the air. Half-rotation jumps in positions such as the stag give no problem, but be careful when you see a split position because, apart from the regular split jump, this position may occur in several other jumps; these will be explained later in this chapter under the heading "Description of Individual Jumps." However, when a split position does occur, you will at least know that the jump will very rarely be more than one turn in the air, so you will not be dealing with a multi-rotational jump. If, however, the jump is closed, i.e., the skater is pulling his arms and legs in close to his body, according to the degree of closure you may be dealing with a single, double, or triple. Doubles are easy to distinguish from singles, but to differentiate well-executed triples from doubles needs a practiced eye.

Table of Standard Jumps

A quick reference table of the standard jumps is provided on page 261. The order in which they are given is somewhat arbitrary, but the first six in the table might be considered minor jumps in that they do not normally lend themselves to great height or speed. Nevertheless, there have been exceptions, notably the enormous "falling leaf" of Richard Dwyer when skating for Ice Follies, Toller Cranston's stag jump, and Dr. Tenley Albright's mazurka.

Those jumps marked with an asterisk regularly appear in the single, double, or triple form (very occasionally, a quadruple has been performed, but I do not want to complicate the list). All the jumps listed have appeared at some time or other in competition within the last few years; a few, like the triple flip, less frequently than others. Several of the numbered jumps have standard variations, which are listed under the numbered basic form of the jump. The variations, where they exist, all have the same takeoff edge as the basic numbered jump under which they are listed. When this is not the case, as with the inside Axel, or when a toe assist is omitted, as with the toeless Lutz, the jump is listed separately.

For greater clarity it is assumed that the skater is jumping in a counterclockwise direction; in this way the right or left foot can be specified. For the clockwise jumper, *right* and *left* must be reversed.

Whether the rotation of a jump is "natural" or "counter" has no direct relationship to the skater's normal, chosen rotation. A jump is natural in rotation when the lift-off from the takeoff edge is in the same direction as the rotation of a three turned on that edge. A jump is counter in rotation when the lift-off is against the natural rotation, just as if the skater were executing a counter in a figure. If you are in doubt, reference to the previous chapter dealing with the recognition of turns and figures may help. You will see that in the majority of jumps the rotation is natural.

Theoretically minded skaters often query the amount of turn actually executed in the air, and quite rightly so. Nearly all skaters do curl the edge somewhat before takeoff, particularly in edge-to-edge jumps such as the loop jump or Salchow. Provided no actual "three" is made on the ice, this curling is generally accepted. Thus, if the skater jumps from a back edge to a back edge, as in a single Salchow, the jump is considered to have one turn, even if some of it occurs on the ice. This curling of the edge is least in evidence in jumps that are counter to the natural rotation, such as the Lutz.

The abbreviations should by now be obvious. The reader will be aware, for example, that RBO stands for right back outside. The presence of the word *toe* means that the takeoff or landing edges have been assisted by the toe of the other foot.

The table is not quite the same as that printed in the *USFSA Rulebook,* the major part of which is reproduced from the ISU list. The ISU list contains several jumps that are, to say the least, more theoretical than practical. The criterion on which the table is based is the likelihood of the jump being used in competition with the state of the art as it is at the moment. It is known, for example, that a double Walley has been done, but you just don't see them around, so I have not included it. A very practical list appears at the end of another USFSA publication, *The Evaluation of Errors in Figures,* frequently referred to simply as the *Evaluation.* This list shows the mazurka as described here rather than the very difficult form shown in the *USFSA Rulebook.* One other difference is that, when describing rotation against an edge, the *Evaluation* uses the term *reverse,* whereas I (and the USFSA Rulebook) prefer the word *counter.*

As you look through the list you may have noticed that sometimes the word *jump* is used, and sometimes not. In the ordinary day-to-day parlance of skaters, *jump* is only used when the meaning would otherwise be unclear. To do a loop is very different from doing a loop jump; but if a skater is asked to do a double loop, there is normally no other interpretation

Name of Jump	Number of Turns	Takeoff Edge	Natural or Counter	Landing Edge
1. Mazurka	½	Toe/RBO	N	Toe/LFO
2. Ballet jump	½	Toe/RBO	N	Toe/RFI
3. Half flip	½	Toe/LBI	N	Toe/RFI
4. Half Lutz	½	Toe/LBO	C	Toe/RFI
5. Stag jump	½	Toe/LBI	N	Toe/RFI
6. Falling leaf	½	RBO	N	Toe/RFI
7. Waltz jump	½	LFO	N	RBO
8. Salchow*	1, 2, or 3	LBI	N	RBO
One-foot Salchow	1	LBI	N	LBI
9. Flip*	1, 2, or 3	Toe/LBI	N	RBO
One-and-a-half flip	1½	Toe/LBI	N	Toe/RFI
Split flip	1	Toe/LBI	N	RBO
10. Loop jump*	1, 2, or 3	RBO	N	RBO
Half loop	1	RBO	N	LBI
11. Toe loop*	1, 2, or 3	Toe/RBO	N	RBO
Split toe loop	1	Toe/RBO	N	RBO
12. Split jump	½	Toe/LBI	N	Toe/RFI
13. Axel*	1½, 2½, or 3½	LFO	N	RBO
One-foot Axel	1½	LFO	N	LBI
Open Axel	1½	LFO	N	RBO
Delayed Axel	1½	LFO	N	RBO
Tuck Axel	1½	LFO	N	RBO
14. Inside Axel	1½	RFI	N	RBO
15. Walley	1	RBI	C	RBO
16. Toe Walley*	1, 2, or 3	Toe/RBI	C	RBO
17. Lutz*	1, 2, or 3	Toe/LBO	C	RBO
Split Lutz	1	Toe/LBO	C	RBO
18. Toeless Lutz	1	LBO	C	RBO

possible. Another common abbreviation is *double toe* for a double toe loop jump, but if the skater were simply to say toe loop, he would be referring to the single. And if you hear a skater talking about his double sal, he means, of course, his double Salchow; but this smacks of slang and is never used officially. It should also be observed that except where context dictates otherwise, in the full name of a jump only the word that is derived from a proper noun is capitalized: thus, "double Axel," but "double toe loop."

Description of Individual Jumps

The object of this section is to expand upon the above list with short descriptions, illustrations, diagrams, and a few interesting facts. Where possible the full sequence for the single jumps has been given from takeoff to landing, but in a few cases an attempt of complete explanation and illustration would be more confusing than helpful. In the case of multirotational jumps, for example, the difference between the single and the double or triple is largely a case of timing combined with very precise posture and control in the air, making recognition a question of constant observation.

All the illustrations show the skater jumping in a counterclockwise direction, as shown by the curved arrows in the diagrams. With the exception of Walleys and Lutzes, takeoffs and landings occur on a section of a large general circle. Whether the sequence runs from left to right or right to left across the page depends on whether it was necessary for technical reasons to photograph the skater from outside or inside the jumping circle. The curvature of the takeoff and landing edges are hardly ever symmetrical, and the diagrams have been drawn to reflect, as far as possible, how the tracing actually looks on the ice. Note that the asterisks in the diagrams indicate where the skater places a toe into the ice.

Mazurka. Figure 54 A, B, and C shows the mazurka in its most common form, but it can be performed in a multitude of ways. The skater could just as easily have finished on a LFI edge, in which case she would have made a serpentine pattern on the ice; another serpentine pattern would be created if she took off from a RBI and finished on a LFO. It is, therefore, a very useful little jump if the skater wishes to change direction on the ice. The mazurka also makes a very pretty entry into a waltz jump or Axel. The toe work in all the variations is the same, only the edges are different. A beautiful but difficult version is to cross the right leg behind instead of in front of the left at the top of the jump, as shown in figure 55. To produce even greater variety some skaters simply bring their feet together at the top of the jump and do not cross at all. I even found an old photograph of myself doing just that (figure 56), so I have taken the opportunity of making a discreet entry into this book rather as Alfred Hitchcock used to do in some of his films.

Fig. 54. Mazurka

A. Skater on RBO about to place left toe into ice.

B. Jumps one half turn to forward, crossing right leg in front of left.

C. After landing on right toe, skater finishes on LFO edge.

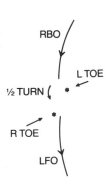

Ballet jump. As in the mazurka, the ballet jump consists of a half-turn in the air with an assist from the toe at the takeoff and landing, but unlike the mazurka the skater lands on the same toe as that used at the takeoff; for this reason the jump is sometimes known as a ballet hop. From a RBO edge the left toe is placed in the ice and the jump is made, but the position in the air now requires the skater to stretch the left leg straight down and the free leg out behind, using as graceful a position as possible. The landing is made on the left toe and RFI edge. It is a difficult jump to do with any speed and, quite frankly, is very little used except by beginners.

Fig. 55. Mazurka Variation
Alternative position at top of jump; right leg crosses behind left. Quite difficult.

Fig. 56. Mazurka Variation
Or the feet may be brought together; author demonstrates.

Fig. 57. Half Flip
D. RFI edge to complete jump.

C. Landing on left toe and . . .

B. One half turn in air with feet together.

A. Skater on LBI entry edge about to place right toe into ice.

½ TURN

RFI   L TOE   R TOE   LBI

Half flip. Figure 57 A, B, C, and D shows the half flip. The skater starts on a very shallow LBI edge, places the right toe into the ice and makes a half-turn in the air, landing on the left toe and RFI edge. The approach and takeoff are identical to that of the normal flip, only the amount of rotation is different. See the description of the flip for further details.

Half Lutz. The half Lutz bears the same relationship to the regular Lutz as the half flip does to the regular flip. Figure 58 shows the pattern on the ice, which is in the serpentine form. The only difference between a half Lutz and a half flip is that the former takes off from a BO edge and the

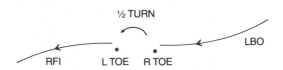

½ TURN

RFI   L TOE   R TOE   LBO

Fig. 58. Half Lutz
Tracing on ice of half Lutz.

latter from a BI. The toe action and landing of both jumps are identical. Notice that the skater takes off against the natural rotation of the edge—the turn is in the direction of a counter. Remember that whether a skater jumps against the edge (counter) or with the edge (natural) has nothing to do with the skater's regular direction of rotation: In the case of the half Lutz the clockwise jumper would simply have to take off from a RBO instead of a LBO. See also the description of the Lutz.

Stag jump. The stag jump is identical to a half flip with the exception that a stag position is assumed in the air (figure 59). This can be an awkward jump to do fast but can be used to great effect in photographs, in which case the skater usually enters the jump quite slowly or may even take it from a standing position.

Falling leaf. With the falling leaf (figure 60) we meet for the first time a jump that takes off directly from an edge without assistance from the toe. After a half-turn in the air (60 B), the landing is made as in a half flip on the left toe and RFI edge (60 C and D). The falling leaf is a very useful jump, not only for inclusion in footwork but as an entry into a forward inside three from which other jumps such as the double toe loop or spins like the flying camel can be taken.

Waltz jump. The waltz jump is the first completely edge-to-edge jump in the list. Figure 61A shows the skater on the LFO edge about to take off. The free leg is swung easily forward and upward, assisting the skater in her rise toward the peak of the jump (61 B), making a half-turn in the air and landing in a firmly controlled position on the RBO edge (61 C)—truly

Fig. 59. Stag Jump
Same edges and use of toes as in the half flip, but skater assumes "stag" position at top of jump.

Fig. 60. Falling Leaf
A. Skater on RBO take-off edge.

B. A half turn in the air in semi-split position.

C. Landing on the left toe and . . .

D. RFI edge to comple[t] jump.

a beautiful jump when done in the manner shown. This jump is easy to do badly and difficult to do well. In relationship to its simplicity it is, paradoxically, very often a skater's worst jump from a technical and aesthetic point of view. Notice in 61B the erectness of the torso and the carriage of the head. Next time you get an opportunity to watch a number of skaters doing waltz jumps, pay particular attention to their position in the air. The majority of skaters will buckle at the waist and appear to be looking at their feet. Only by the lift of the body and head as shown in the illustration can full height be obtained. Watch also how the average skater lands the jump. Can he hold the landing edge under control without swinging off it? If so, he is probably on the way to becoming a good jumper. Although this is not intended to be a technical book, it does make it much more interesting for the spectator if he knows a few of the important points to watch for. But don't make any comments to the skater—unless you are a very fine freestylist yourself, they will be resented, and it is hardly fair to the pro, who may be well aware of the faults and doing his best to correct them. The problem is that many skaters learn waltz jumps at a very early stage and often without proper supervision, so bad habits may become stubbornly ingrained. It is quite common to find that a skater will execute an Axel (the same edges but one more turn in the

Fig. 61. Waltz Jump

C. Landing on firmly held RBO edge.

B. A half turn in air. Note excellent position.

A. Skater on LFO take-off edge.

½ TURN

RBO   LFO

air) technically much better than a waltz jump, simply because he has learned the technique under supervision from the start.

The waltz jump gets its name from its similarity in action to one of the oldest ice dances, in which a FO three is followed by a BO edge on the other foot. Outside the U.S. the waltz jump is often called a three jump.

Salchow. The Salchow is named for the nine-times world champion Ulrich Salchow, who skated for Sweden. The pronunciation is "sal-cow" in the U.S., and "zal-coh" in England, where names are not anglicized to the same degree as they are over here. The single jump consists of one complete turn in the air, taking off from a LBI and landing on a RBO edge. Figure 62A shows the skater on the LBI preparing to take off. She has arrived on this edge following a LFO three, which is the most common approach. The free leg is then brought forward rather wide and the BI edge starts to curl in to initiate the rotation (62B). In 62C the skater is in the air halfway round the jump, and 62D shows the skater just after the landing on the RBO edge. The approach and takeoff is almost identical for the double and triple, the main difference being that for the multirotational versions a little more vigor is put into the free leg action. From

Fig. 62. Salchow

A. Skater on LBI take-off edge.

B. Moment before take-off; LBI curves sharply, free leg is brought forward and round for impetus.

C. Halfway round jump.

D. Skater lands on RBO edge in excellently controlled position.

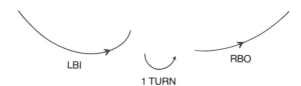

LBI   1 TURN   RBO

then on, the extra rotation is largely a matter of being able to hold a tight, closed, and very erect position in the air. The double is the most commonly seen multirotational jump.

One-foot Salchow. The takeoff for the one-foot Salchow is almost exactly the same as for the regular Salchow, but in the one-foot version the skater lands on the same foot and edge as that from which she took off, the LBI. Figure 63 shows the tracing on the ice. A back inside landing is shown in figure 66C of the half loop, but make allowance for the fact that the skater is moving from right to left across the camera. Both the double and the triple have been done but are not often used owing to the awkwardness of landing on the back inside edge.

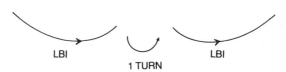

LBI   1 TURN   LBI

Fig. 63. One-foot Salchow
Tracing on ice of one-foot Salchow.

Flip. The flip is actually a Salchow assisted at the takeoff with the toe. The ISU lists the jump as a toe Salchow, adding the word *flip* in parentheses, which is certainly far less time-consuming than the German *getupfter ein-gehakter Salchow,* under which extraordinary name the jump is also listed. The name *flip* arose in the U.S. when it was found that this jump was most effectively entered on an almost straight line, making it look so different from the curved approach of the regular Salchow that it was felt a new name was needed for the toe version.

Figure 64A shows the skater immediately after having executed a LFO three on a relatively flat curve to arrive on a shallow LBI takeoff edge; the right toe strikes the ice (64B), one turn is made in the air (64C), and the landing is made on the RBO edge (64D). Even though the takeoff edge is comparatively straight, the skater is still on a slight curve, so the edges are the same as for a regular Salchow. Compare the similarity of the entry with that of the half flip (figure 57A). The entry for the double is essentially the same as for the single. The triple flip is considered one of the more difficult triples and at the moment of writing is rarely seen even among top-rank skaters.

One-and-a-half flip. For the one-and-a-half flip an illustration and diagram are unnecessary. The jump is exactly the same as for a half flip except that

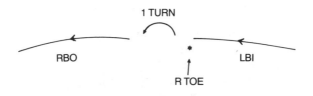
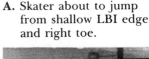

Fig. 64. Flip

| **D.** Landing on RBO edge. | **C.** Skater at top of jump. | **B.** Right toe strikes ice for take-off. | **A.** Skater about to jump from shallow LBI edge and right toe. |

an extra turn in the air is added. This was quite a popular jump at a time when techniques had not reached the stage to make the double flip as common as it is today. Nowadays, if a skater does a one-and-a-half flip in his program, there is often the sneaking suspicion that he meant it to be a double but couldn't quite make it.

Split flip. The split flip is quite a difficult jump but can be very effective if done well. Takeoff and landing are exactly as for the regular flip, but the skater inserts a momentary split position in the air before closing the position to complete the turn. To explain it another way, imagine a regular split jump (figure 68) in which the skater, instead of landing forward on the left toe and RFI edge, suddenly pulls his arms and legs close to the body, completes an extra half-turn and lands on the RBO edge. Unless the skater gets great height, it is extremely difficult to get a full split position and still have time to pull in to get the extra half-turn: the action of splitting slows the rotation down and uses up a lot of valuable time in the air. If you can imagine opening and closing an umbrella within the period of half a second, you will have some idea of the difficulty.

Loop jump. The loop jump is an edge-to-edge jump in which the skater lands on the same foot and edge from which he took off. Figure 65A shows

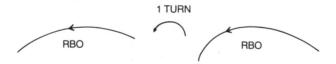

Fig. 65. Loop Jump

C. Landing on RBO edge— the same edge from which she took off.

B. Skater at peak of jump.

A. Skater on sharply curving RBO take-off edge, left foot about to leave ice.

the skater on a RBO edge two or three feet before the takeoff just prior to the left foot starting to leave the ice. Figures 65B and 65C speak for themselves. The takeoff for the double and triple is the same, with similar reservations to those mentioned for the double and triple Salchow. The triple loop is quite difficult but is more frequently seen than the triple flip. The loop jump gets its name from the similarity of the action of the body to that of a back outside loop as used in a figure.

Half loop. Unlike the half flip and half Lutz, which only make a half-turn in the air, the half loop does actually go from a back edge to a back edge, i.e., from the RBO to the LBI. But because the free leg does not travel so far as in the full loop jump, the skater does not feel that he has rotated more then half a turn, and this was probably the origin of the name—which only goes to show how illogical skating nomenclature can be. Figure 66 shows the three phases of the jump. If you compare the position in the air with that of the full loop jump, you will see at the peak of the jump how the skater has transferred her weight over to the left foot in preparation for the landing, whereas in the full loop jump the weight remains over the right foot. The double is not regularly performed but I have seen it. I have not yet seen the triple but I have no doubt that it is possible. Whether, however, these triple jumps landing on a back inside edge are

1 TURN

LBI   RBO

Fig. 66. Half Loop

C. Landing on LBI edge; see text and compare figure 65C of the loop jump.

B. Skater shifts weight to left foot while in air.

A. Take-off from RBO as for loop jump; compare figure 65A.

Fig. 67. Toe Loop

D. Continuing on to the RBO edge.

C. Moment of contact with ice on landing . . .

B. Leaving ice from left toe; note erect position of body.

A. Skater on RBO edge about to place left toe into ice for take-off.

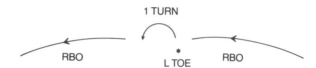

1 TURN

RBO   L TOE   RBO

worth the time spent in acquiring them is open to question as the landings seem to lack the flow of those on the back outside.

Toe loop. As its name suggests, the toe loop is a loop jump assisted with the toe, but as with the toe Salchow (flip), the free leg has to stretch along the line of intended travel before the takeoff. Figure 67A shows the skater on the RBO edge just before her toe makes contact with the ice for the lift-off (67B). Figure 67C shows the moment of impact with the ice, and 67D the final position on the RBO edge after the landing.

Although this simple little jump is a requirement for the USFSA Basic Tests and the Preliminary Free Skating Test, it is rarely used in its single form. It is, however, very popular as a double and is usually learned at the same time as the double Salchow. The usual method of getting onto the takeoff edge is to execute a FI three, in this case the RFI. So if you see a skater setting herself up for a jump by a FI three, probably down the side of the rink almost parallel to the barrier, you can take it as a signal that the most likely jump to follow is a double toe. The triple toe and triple Salchow are the most frequently executed of all the triples.

Fig. 68. Split Jump
Position at peak of regular
split jump.

Fig. 69.
Russian split, in which the
skater splits sideways and
slightly forward, trying to touch
her toes she does so.

R TOE L TOE

LBI   RFI

½ TURN IN SPLIT POSITION

Split toe loop. Although the regular single toe loop is seldom seen in an advanced program, you may occasionally see the split toe loop. This is exactly the same as the regular toe loop except that as the skater lifts off she assumes a momentary split position in the air before the landing. It is, however, difficult to get as strong a position or as much height as the regular split (see below) because the right leg leads the split position and thus creates more rotation than in the regular split, in which the left leg leads—presuming, of course, that the skater is turning counterclockwise.

Split jump. The simple phrase *split jump* denotes the jump in its most common form, as opposed to other jumps which may also include a split position, such as the split flip or split toe loop. The entry edge, takeoff, and landing are exactly the same as for a half flip, the only difference being that the skater assumes a split position at the top of the jump (figure 68). Unlike the flip and its variations, which most commonly use a three or mohawk to get onto the BI takeoff edge, the split jump is usually approached by a series of back crossovers in a counterclockwise direction; as soon as the skater has enough speed he finishes his last crossover on the LBI edge and makes the jump. Many years ago the split jump was

Fig. 70. Axel
A. Take-off from LFO edge.

B. Lift-off from ice.

C. One turn completed.

D. After a further half turn, skater lands on RBO edge.

commonly taken from a LBO exactly like the entry to a Lutz (figure 75), in which case the use of the toe at the takeoff and landing was precisely the same as in a half Lutz. This made a very attractive serpentine pattern on the ice, but this entry is seldom seen nowadays, probably because the back crossover entry makes it easier to do several split jumps in succession.

The split position itself can have two forms: the regular split position as shown in figure 68, and the Russian split (figure 69), in which the split is made sideways and slightly forward, the skater trying to touch her toes as she does so. This latter form was at one time considered a man's jump, but many women now perform it with great effect. Notice that in the case of counterclockwise jumpers it is the left leg that leads in the air in the direction of the line of travel.

Axel. The Axel is named for the Norwegian skater Axel Paulsen who, under the circumstances related in chapter 22, first performed the jump in competition in 1892. It consists of one-and-a-half turns in the air, starting from a LFO edge and landing on the RBO, as shown in figures 70A through D. It can be seen that the jump is actually a waltz jump with one turn added. Because of the forward takeoff, many skaters find this jump more difficult to do well than the double Salchow. The Axel is a remarkable jump in that it lends itself to many variations, which all look totally different although the edges are exactly the same. Even the regular Axel, with no frills attached, differs in appearance from skater to skater, all of whom may have been taught by the same pro using the same basic technique.

Although the Axel consists of one and a half turns, it is classed as a single jump. One might think that since the single consists of one and a half turns, the double would have three turns, but this is not so. To execute the double the skater simply adds an extra turn, so that once again he can land on that comfortable back outside edge. The triple consists of three and a half turns, and the quadruple, four and a half—a very rare jump indeed, but it has been performed. On this basis the single Axel might well be called a double waltz jump, but here again, logic in terminology is not skating's strong point.

One-foot Axel. For the one-foot Axel the skater takes off from the LFO as for the regular Axel, but instead of landing on the RBO, he lands on the same foot from which he took off, on the LBI edge (figure 71). It is a tricky jump because the technique in the air is somewhat different from that of the regular Axel in that the axis of rotation has to be transferred over to the left foot before the landing, just as in the half loop. Once this is understood, the jump becomes much easier to perform. This jump is very useful in a series or combination of jumps. The double has been done but, like other multirotational jumps landing on the back inside, it is very awkward.

The next three variations of the Axel all consist of the same edges but differ in position or action in the air. Because they all require an open, time-consuming position in the air during the major portion of the flight, none, to the best of my knowledge, has ever been performed as a double.

LFO   1½ TURNS   LBI

Fig. 71. One-foot Axel
Tracing on ice of one-foot Axel.

Open Axel. The open Axel is only occasionally seen nowadays but is a most spectacular jump if done well. Immediately after the takeoff the skater assumes a wide position of the legs in the air, rather like the skater in figure 70B, but even more so, and then remains in that position right up to the landing. In the true open Axel the skater does not close the position to obtain rotation but relies purely on power and height. The point of rotation stays right between the feet until just before the moment of contact with the ice on the landing. It is not a jump you are likely to see on the local rink, but many skaters execute a very attractive compromise in which they start in an open position and close somewhere round the peak of the jump for the final rotation—this might be called an open-type Axel.

The most astounding exponent of the true open Axel I ever saw was the Austrian world champion, Felix Kaspar, whom I watched perform it many years ago at Queen's Club, London. I was happily practicing some minor jump of my own, thinking how good I was, when a little man I had never seen before stepped onto the ice surface, got up immense speed in a few strokes round the end of the rink, and then took off down the center of the ice in this enormous leap, rotating so slowly that I still have a clear picture of the white triangle of his breast pocket handkerchief (we were natty dressers in those days) as he sailed round to land some fifteen feet from his point of takeoff. "If this," I remember thinking to myself, "is what he is doing for openers, I had better take my skates off and get out of his way." He was, of course, way ahead of his time, and the fact that he was a gymnast also helped. Until then we had never seen anything like it, and it was many years before I saw it performed again in anything like the same manner.

Delayed Axel. At one time quite popular, the delayed Axel seems to have gone out of fashion for the moment. As with the open Axel, the skater starts the jump with a very wide position of the legs, but in this case the passage of the free leg takes a much straighter path in the line of travel, and the skater looks directly ahead until the peak of the jump is reached, or just after. The onlooker may well think the skater is doing a waltz jump but then, just when it seems too late, the skater pulls his arms and legs in to his body, makes a quick turn of the head, and converts the jump into an Axel.

Tuck Axel. I first saw the tuck Axel performed by a male Russian skater at the 1975 World Championship in Colorado Springs. Since then I have seen it a few times in competition, and it looks as though it may eventually become a standard variation. Immediately after takeoff the skater is in an open position but as he rises to the peak of the jump he pulls his takeoff leg (the left if he is jumping counterclockwise) up under him and assumes a sit spin position in the air. The free leg swings round his axis of rotation until during the descent the skater resumes a normal position for the landing. I can't say it is a pretty jump, but it is highly spectacular.

Inside Axel. I have been unable to obtain a satisfactory sequence for the inside Axel, but figure 72 shows the tracing on the ice. Although the name Axel is used, it is an entirely different jump from any of the preceding variations as it takes off from a different edge. From a RFI edge the skater lifts off, turns one and a half times, and lands on the RBO as for the regular Axel. You will notice that takeoff and landing are on the same foot. The inside Axel is the only standard major jump to take off from a forward inside edge. Because there is almost no assist from the weight of the free leg, it is difficult to get height on this jump, but it can be useful as part of a series.

It is easy to get the names of the one-foot Axel and the inside Axel confused. Just try to remember that the one-foot Axel takes off like the regular Axel and that the inside Axel takes off from the forward inside edge. The jump was invented and first performed in competition by another Austrian skater, Willy Boeckl, who won the world championship four times in the 1920s. It would be more convenient if we named the jump for him.

Walley. In the U.S. the jump known as the Walley is named for the American skater Nate Walley, who won the world professional title in London

RFI   1½ TURNS   RBO

Fig. 72. Inside Axel
Tracing on ice of inside Axel.

Fig 73. Walley
A. Take-off from RBI edge; skater will turn to the left.
B. Halfway round jump.
C. Landing on RBO edge, the total jump forming a serpentine pattern on the ice.

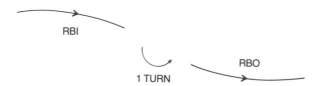

in the late thirties (the original world professional championship that is now held in Jaca, Spain). In Britain, however, Pat Low is credited with the invention of this jump, and in that country it still bears his name. It is a most unusual jump—little height, but very neat and effective. In figure 73A the skater is seen on a RBI edge about to jump to the left, i.e., counter to the natural rotation of the edge; after one turn in the air she lands on the RBO, the same foot from which she took off. The takeoff edge is quite shallow, and, once the skater has the knack of it, the jump can be performed at top speed. It is quite common to see a skater do two or even three Walleys in succession. This is accomplished quite simply by changing edges from the RBO to the RBI after the landing—a little swaying action that brings the skater back onto the takeoff edge again. It is a jump that once learned is almost never missed, but many skaters have great

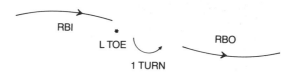

Fig. 74. Toe Walley
Tracing on ice of toe-Walley.

Fig. 75. Lutz

A. Skater about to take off from LBO edge assisted by right toe; she will turn to the left.

B. Three-quarters of a turn completed.

C. Landing on RBO edge, having described a serpentine pattern across the ice.

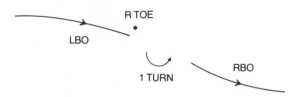

difficulty in acquiring the trick (a question of placement of weight) and give it up in disgust as being quite impossible. A double has been done in practice, and I firmly believe that if persevered with, the double could become a standard jump.

Toe Walley. The toe Walley is simply a regular Walley assisted at the takeoff with the toe (figure 74) and bears a remarkable resemblance to the toe loop, particularly when performed as a double or triple. The reason for this resemblance is that very few skaters, when executing the multirotational versions, can actually stay on the back inside edge at the takeoff; instead they rock over onto a short back outside edge as they place the toe into the ice, so that they are actually performing a double or triple toe loop. To take off from a clean back inside edge seems to put the body into such an awkward position that it hardly seems worth the effort, but it can be done. Nevertheless, for these reasons it is not a popular jump, and I shall leave it at that.

Lutz. The Lutz is another of those few jumps that form a serpentine pattern on the ice surface and, like the Walley, take off counter to the natural rotation of the edge. Figure 75A shows the skater in the typical position on the LBO edge immediately before takeoff, and the accompanying diagram shows the pattern over the ice; 75B shows the skater three-quarters of the way round the turn, and 75C, the landing on the RBO edge. Among better skaters the double is relatively common, but the triple is rare. The Canadian skater Don Jackson, who won the world championship in 1962, was the first to execute the triple successfully in competition, a feat that created an absolute sensation at the time. The jump gets its name from yet another Austrian skater, Alois Lutz.

Unfortunately, many skaters are afraid of the double. This is very understandable as the takeoff has a very awkward feeling, one that makes the skater think he will never be able to get round the jump. This feeling of inadequacy may have some bearing on what I am about to say. Because of the serpentine pattern and speed required, the double Lutz (and the same applies to the triple) is usually practiced in the bottom or top half of the rink with the takeoff approximately on the midline of the ice surface, and the landing in the direction of one corner of the rink. When left to themselves, skaters tend to delay the takeoff so that the landing occurs very close to the corner of the rink. Nine skaters out of ten delay the takeoff more and more until finally they are practically jumping into the barrier. They get so close that they can with justification abort the jump and thus relieve themselves of the responsibility of doing it at all. This is rather like the skater who always happens to find someone in his way when about to take off in any jump he finds particularly difficult, even when the nearest skater is at least fifty feet away. Perhaps I have grown a little cynical, but all I can say is that this is my impression after watching skaters for more years than I care to remember. Watch for yourself and see if you come to the same conclusion.

Split Lutz. The split Lutz bears the same relationship to the Lutz as the split flip does to the flip: it is a regular Lutz in which the skater assumes a split position in the air and then suddenly pulls in for the extra half-turn to land on the RBO edge. If you understand the split flip, you will understand the split Lutz. Both these jumps are very effective and make a welcome change from the multirotational jumps; neither is used as much as it should be.

Toeless Lutz. In Britain the toeless Lutz is known as a "Lutz without the toe," which is exactly what it is. The entry, the position in the air, and the landing are almost precisely the same as for the regular Lutz. If you look at figure 75A and imagine the free leg sweeping round the skating leg without the toe touching the ice, you will understand how the jump is done. This jump was very popular at one time but now seems to have disappeared completely from the scene. Like the Walley, to which it bears a technical resemblance, it is difficult to learn but very easy once the knack has been acquired. The greatest problem is that the natural action of the free leg causes the skater to change edge before the jump and convert it into a very obvious Salchow, which entirely destroys the effect. Nevertheless, if the skater can do Sixth Test back outside counters and relies for rotation on a quick hip twist rather than the weight of the free leg, the jump can be done without the rockover. The ISU lists the double version, but I have never heard of anyone having done it. If such a claim were made, I should be very suspicious and need to see the tracing of the takeoff on the ice with my own eyes to convince myself that it was not in fact a double Salchow. As a single, the jump is just as attractive and useful as the Walley and should, therefore, be given more attention than it is given at present.

The Spins

As with the jumps, the terminology of spinning can be confusing, but the vocabulary is now so ingrained that it is unlikely that much can be done to improve it. The main function of the name of a spin is to describe the position of the skater's body while executing it; to this name the terms *back* or *reverse* may be added to denote the foot on which the skater is spinning, and this is, for the nonskater, where most confusion arises. A skater may also spin on his toe rake or on the flat of his blade, but there is considerable latitude in this.

The easiest way to explain the above points is to do so while describing the individual spins. It is important to remember that in all illustrations the skater is rotating counterclockwise, whether she is on the right or left foot.

Scratch spin. The scratch spin is the first spin learned after the simple beginner's two-foot spin (not described here, as it is abandoned as soon as learned). Figure 76A shows the skater on a deep forward outside edge, which forms a tightly spiraling curve while the free leg is brought round high and wide (76B) until the spinning point is reached, after which the hands and free foot are brought into the body and pressed downward for maximum speed. Some skaters bring the clasped hands above the head, which has the same effect of increasing the rate of rotation as pressing them down. However, none of these positions are mandatory, the prime requirements for a scratch spin being that the skater is in an upright position, is spinning on the toe, and rotating at least at a moderate speed —the faster the better. When watching beginner skaters, do not expect them to be able to get the free leg into the high positions shown in 76B and C. If they try to do this before they have acquired the requisite balance, they are liable to fall flat on their side, and the fall can be a nasty one. Spinning is a matter of constant practice.

Notice in figure 76C that the heel of the blade is only a very little way off the ice, just enough so that the first toe rake lightly scratches the ice —hence the name scratch spin. This spin is sometimes referred to as a *one-foot spin, fast spin,* or *toe spin,* but these terms are far too vague and could easily be applied to other spins. *Scratch spin* is used exclusively for the spin just described and the variation that follows below.

As will be seen from the illustration, the regular scratch spin is entered on a forward outside edge. Many other spins are entered in the same way, and for this reason they all form a class known as forward spins, regardless of the fact that the blade is usually traveling backward in very small circles during the spin itself. The forward version is considered the

Fig. 76. Scratch Spin
A. Skater entering spin on LFO edge.
B. Free leg continuing in circular action as spinning point is reached and skater rises onto toe.
C. Free leg pulled in above knee, thigh rotated outward; difficult for beginners.
D. Arms and free foot pressed downward for maximum speed.

Fig. 77. Back Scratch
Skater turning in same direction as in figure 76D but on opposite foot.

regular form of the spin, the word *forward* only being used when it is necessary to distinguish the regular spin from the back version.

Back scratch. If you look at figure 77 of a back scratch spin and compare it with figure 76D of the forward scratch spin, you will see that, although both skaters are spinning in the same direction (to the left), they are on different feet. It is not easy to come up with a concise definition of the difference between forward and back spins, but the most comprehensible explanation seems to be that if a skater is spinning to the left on the left foot, it is a forward spin, whereas if he is spinning to the left on the right foot, it is a back spin; the reverse is true if he is spinning to the right: if he is on the right foot, it is a forward spin; if he is on the left, it is a back spin.

When speaking of pirouettes, ballet dancers use the terms *en dedans* (inward) and *en dehors* (outward). Following this usage a forward spin would be *en dedans,* and a back spin, *en dehors.* Skaters might with advantage refer to their spins as inward and outward, but the present terminology seems too well established for a change to be worthwhile.

The term *back spin* has little to do with the entry edge, because this type of spin can be entered in a number of ways, such as a forward inside edge followed by a tiny three at the spinning point, or simply by changing feet in a forward spin.

Until quite recently, the term *reverse* was often used instead of *back,* which further confused matters because a lot of skaters thought it meant the reverse direction, when actually it meant the same direction but on the reverse foot. You still occasionally hear the phrase *reverse sit* when a *back sit* is meant, but fortunately this usage seems to be dying out.

Flat-foot spin. The term *flat-foot spin* describes a spin done on the flat of the blade rather than the toe. This is quite common in certain spins such as sit spins and camels but not mandatory. Two-foot spins, however, such as the cross-foot (described below), cannot be performed correctly other than on the flat of both blades.

Figure 78A and B shows the skater performing a one-foot upright spin on the flat of the blade. The camera was placed as low as possible in order to show this clearly. This upright version is surprisingly difficult, and few skaters other than the most accomplished can stay on this spin more than a few turns. The problem is that the center of gravity is so high that the lack of traction of the toe rake, slight though it may be, makes the preservation of balance extremely tricky. Nevertheless, the upright flat spin should be practiced, as most top-flight spinners start their scratch spins on the flat and only gradually come up onto the toe as they feel they have the spin properly centered.

Cross-foot spin. The cross-foot spin (figure 79) is an advanced spin rather out of favor at the moment. I have put it in this early position because it is essentially a flat-foot spin and is started just as shown in figure 78A and B of the regular upright flat-foot spin. After a few turns on the flat of the left blade, the skater drops the right foot behind the left and shifts the weight between the feet as shown in the illustration. Other methods of entry may also be used.

Fig. 78. Flat-foot Spin
A. Skater spinning on flat of blade instead of toe.

B. Notice skating heel is not lifted—a difficult spin for beginners.

Fig. 79. Cross-foot Spin
Skater on flat of both blades; with practice
can be a very fast spin.

The cross-foot is one of the required elements for men in the senior short program; the women are required instead to do the layback or sideways leaning spin, neither of which is considered a man's spin. This has had the unfortunate result that the cross-foot is now largely ignored by women; it is unfortunate because it was at one time very popular among female skaters, and it is a spin that can be done at very great speed. Few skaters, however, believe this, for the very compelling reason that their first attempts usually grind to an ignominious halt after the first one or two turns—neither do they often have the opportunity to see the spin done well. The problem is that it cannot be done at all unless it is precisely centered, i.e., kept exactly on one spot on the ice; the slightest hint of "traveling" throws the skater off the spin immediately.

Sit spin and back sit. In figure 80 my wife makes a brief appearance to demonstrate the regular sit spin, i.e., turning to the left on the left foot or vice versa. At one time all regular sit spins were done in as low a position as possible but for a time a higher position with the skating thigh parallel to the ice became popular. Either position is acceptable. Figure 81 shows the back sit. The skater is turning in the same direction as in 80 but on the opposite foot. For some rather obscure reason almost no skater seems able to perform the back sit in as low a position as is possible in the regular sit spin. The depth to which a skater can sink in a sit spin is strongly influenced by the strength of his leg muscles, the mobility of the skating ankle, and just where the center of gravity occurs when the skater is in the deepest sit position. Some skaters seem to find it a physical impossibility to go beyond a certain depth, while others find no problem at all.

Fig. 80. Sit Spin
Sit spin (counterclockwise)—Joan
Ogilvie demonstrates. Note
change in fashions!

Fig. 81. Back Sit
Back sit; same direction as
regular sit spin (figure 80) but
on opposite foot.

Fig. 82. Broken Leg
A form of sit spin with free leg
"broken" at knee; position of
arms optional.

Broken leg. The broken leg is another of those spins that one does not see around much at the moment. Figure 82 shows it to be a variation of the regular sit spin, with the free leg "broken" at the knee instead of stretched out in front. The arm and sideways leaning positions shown in the illustration are very effective when seen in action but not a mandatory part of the spin.

Camel. The camel spin (figure 83) is one of the most popular and effective spins and can be done with a great variety of arm positions. To the best of my knowledge the name came from the rather unfortunate body position of some of the early exponents of the spin. When the free leg and torso are not raised sufficiently, a most unsightly hump develops. In Britain this spin is known more elegantly as a *parallel* spin.

The entry to the forward camel is almost invariably on the forward outside edge, but at the spinning point most skaters come up onto the toe and then, when the balance has been stabilized, drop onto the flat of the blade; in fact, without the low first toe rake of the modern blade, camel spins are extremely difficult. Both the forward camel and the low camel (to be described next) were photographed almost immediately after the point of entry before the skater had dropped onto the flat. There is a very pretty variation to this spin in which the skater drops onto the flat and then rocks over onto a forward outside edge causing the skating blade to make small forward outside circles; roller skaters do the spin in this way, but it needs a tremendous amount of control.

Fig. 83. Camel
Regular, or forward, camel; a very
popular spin.

Fig. 84. Low Camel (Grafström Spin)
Same as regular camel but with deep
knee bend; arm position normally
as shown.

Low camel (Grafström spin). The low camel (figure 84) was originally named
for the Swedish skater Gillis Grafström, who won the world championship
three times in the 1920s. I have been told, however, by someone who saw
him skate, that he did not do it in quite the same position shown but was
at a more inclined angle to the ice surface and quite high on the toe. As
done nowadays the position is exactly as shown in the illustration, a
position that is characterized by the bent skating knee and the skating arm
(left) stretched forward in line with the free leg. The right arm also forms
part of this line but may optionally be held a little lower than shown in
the illustration. It is a surprisingly difficult but very effective spin, and well
worth the practice. A few years ago it formed one of the required elements
of the senior short program, but because it went under the undescriptive
name of a *Grafström spin,* nobody ever seemed to know exactly how it was
supposed to be done, and it was, probably for this reason, dropped from
the schedule. Nevertheless, simply because an element is dropped as a
requirement for the short program, there is no reason why such a move
should not be used in the free skating (long program).

Catch-foot camel. Another very effective variation of the forward camel is
the catch-foot, as shown in figure 85. The skater starts as for a forward
camel and then catches the blade of the free foot with the skating hand.
In Britain this also went under the name of *curly camel,* or *whiting spin.* This
last strange name came about because the whiting, a small, edible European sea fish, was always served with its tail in its mouth. I don't think any

Fig. 85. Catch-foot Camel
Also called a "curly camel" or "whiting"
spin (see text).

skater actually got as far as catching hold of the free blade in his teeth, but you get the general idea.

The skater can also catch the blade with the free hand (opposite to the one shown in the illustration) and draw it upward toward the back of the head. An extreme version of this is named after the Swiss world champion Denise Biellmann, who catches the blade with both hands, draws herself into an upright spin and, because of a very supple back, is able to pull the free blade directly over her head and into the axis of rotation.

Back camel. In the back camel (figure 86) the skater spins in the same direction as the forward camel but on the opposite foot. The entry is usually "flying" (see below) but there are other entries. The back camel lends itself to a variety of arm and body positions, but in its simplest form the arm position is very much like that of the forward camel. An attractive semi-layover position is shown in figure 87.

Fig. 86. Back Camel
Skater spinning in same
direction as for a forward camel
(figure 83) but on opposite foot.

Fig. 87. Back Camel (Semi-Layover)
Effective semi-layover position
in the back camel.

Fig. 88. Layback
One of several arm positions suitable for
the popular layback spin.

Layover. This variation of the back camel is an extension of the semi-layover (figure 87); the skater continues the rotation of the body until she is finally looking up at the ceiling. The position and balance are very difficult.

Layback. Figure 88 shows one of the several standard positions in a layback spin which, simply stated, consists of a backbend during a toe spin. The layback can also be done as a back spin, but a good position is much more difficult to attain. At the time of writing, the layback is exclusively a women's spin.

Sideways leaning spin. The sideways leaning spin is really a variation of the regular layback. Instead of leaning directly back, the skater leans much more to the side—a much easier position and one favored by skaters who do not have a good backbend. This spin is listed as an alternative to the layback in the requirements for ladies in one of the groups of the senior short program.

Slow toe spin. A slow toe spin is a general description of any one of a class of spins in which the skater rotates very slowly on the toe in a graceful position, creating an effect of great poise and control. This type of spin has a great appeal, especially when combined with other slow movements in a quiet part of a free skating program. Figure 89 shows an excellent example of one of these positions. They can be done equally well as forward or back spins.

Fig. 89. Slow Toe Spin
These slowly rotating toe spins lend themselves
to many variations of position.

The Flying Spins

Flying spins are entered on a forward outside edge from which the skater
jumps into a spin, either on the foot from which he took off or on the
opposite foot. The first of these ever to be performed in competition was
the "flying camel." The skater was the two-time American Olympic gold
medalist and five-time world champion Dick Button, and for a time this
move was known as a *Button camel.* There are several types of flying spin,
the most common of which are dealt with below, with some comments on
their names.

Flying camel. The flying camel is entered on the forward outside edge in
very much the same way as any forward spin is entered, but just as the
spinning point is reached, the skater continues the swing of the free leg,
makes the jump, and lands in a back camel, usually assuming a forty-five-
degree position in the air. Figure 90 shows the skater just before the
landing. Strictly speaking, this move should be called a *flying back camel,* but
the present name is now firmly established. After a certain number of
turns, the skater usually concludes the spin by rising into a fast back

Fig. 90. Flying Camel
Skater descending from peak of jump,
about to land in a back camel.

Fig. 91. Flying Sit
Position at the highest point in a flying sit spin.

scratch. This spin is very popular and forms one of the requirements of the USFSA Junior Free Skating Test.

Flying sit spin. To execute the flying sit spin—commonly referred to as a *flying sit*—the skater jumps from a deeply curving forward outside edge, assumes a sit spin position at the top of the jump, and lands on the same foot from which she took off, concluding the movement in a regular sit spin. Figure 91 shows the position at the peak of the jump.

Flying sit spin changing the foot of landing. The phrase *flying sit spin changing the foot of landing* is the official designation of this move, but it is a terrible mouthful and often abbreviated to *flying sit with change of feet.* The skater starts just like the flying sit described above but as he reaches the regular sit spin position at the top of the jump, he switches the position of his feet and lands in a back sit. This is a very difficult move to do exactly as described, and usually the switch of feet takes place on the descent just in time for the landing. It needs a lot of height, which makes it easier for the men.

Death drop. The death drop takes off from a forward outside edge and the landing is made in a back sit position as in the flying sit with change of feet, but the movement is quite different. In the death drop the skater starts as for a flying camel, retaining the typical flying camel position in the air (figure 90). Just before the landing toe touches the ice, the skater starts a scissoring action of the body and free leg, which continues as the skater sinks into the final back sit position. Unfortunately, the majority of skaters land as for a flying camel and continue for at least half a turn while they struggle to get into the final position, thus completely robbing the move of its effect.

Fig. 92. Spiral (Straight Line) One of the many arm positions possible; note excellent extension of free leg.

Miscellaneous Moves

There are countless combinations of jumps, spins, turns, and changes of edge and position that would qualify as miscellaneous moves, but I shall deal here with five moves that are dignified with names of their own. They are the spiral, the spread eagle, the Ina Bauer, the butterfly, and the illusion.

Spiral. For those who have a reasonably limber back the spiral closely resembles an arabesque in ballet; many positions or movements of the arms during the spiral are possible. Figure 92 shows a skater with fine extension and an excellent feeling for arm position. Spirals are named for the edge used—for example, forward outside spiral, back inside spiral. They may even be executed on the flat of the blade as in figure 92, in which case they are sometimes called a straight-line spiral. Which brings us to the peculiarity of the name. I cannot do better than to quote from my earlier book, *Basic Ice Skating Skills:*

> The word "spiral" originally referred to the pattern that was usually made on the ice when skaters assumed an arabesque position. They would start on a very large circle that covered practically the whole rink and then hold this position while the circle got smaller, thus forming a spiral pattern on the ice. Skaters today have so many jumps and spins to get into their competition programs that they cannot afford to spend all this time in one position; spirals, therefore, got shorter and shorter until the word came to mean the position itself.

To show that skating is a man's sport after all and to prevent the women having it all their own way, the author makes another appearance in figure 93, executing a deep forward inside spiral. The "open" position

Fig. 93. Spiral (Forward Inside)
To show that skating is as much for the men as for the women, the author demonstrates a deep forward inside spiral.

—that is, with the free shoulder and arm pressed back—is not an easy one and needs a lot of speed to attain an effective lean. The picture was taken in those carefree days before teaching had started to turn my hair gray.

Spread eagle. The spread eagle is a position in which both feet are fully turned out, as shown in figure 94. In this case the skater has both blades on the outside edge, but the inside edges may also be used. The term *spread eagle* is usually abbreviated to *spread,* and you will hear skaters speaking of an inside spread and an outside spread. The spread eagle is a very useful and effective move but requires a particular type of physique. The skater in the illustration is fortunate in having a very natural turnout from the hips, which makes the position very easy for her, but many find it very difficult indeed. Most skaters can make some sort of attempt at it if they choose to do the right exercises—in fact, a friend of mine acquired a spread eagle by spending hours reading on his back with his feet screwed into an old-fashioned trouser press, but his movement on the ice always look strained and awkward (the trouser press had, of course, been removed). One either is or is not a spread-eagler, and if one is not gifted in this direction, it might be as well to forget it.

Fig. 94. Spread Eagle
Skater is fortunate in having a natural turn-out from the hips.

294

Fig. 95. Ina Bauer
Skater moving toward camera—an unusual
but effective position at speed.

Ina Bauer. The Ina Bauer is named for the former West German champion, who invented the move. Figure 95, in which the skater is moving toward the camera, shows it to be an offshoot of the spread eagle. It is a strange position but can be very effective at speed. As can be seen, the feet track in roughly parallel lines, but the back foot is always on the inside edge. The front foot can be on the outside edge, the inside edge, or on the flat, which means that this move can be made on curves in either direction, or in a straight line down the rink. There is a variation in which the skater does a back bend sideways to the line of travel, looking directly upward. Skaters who have problems with a spread eagle can often perform the Ina Bauer with little difficulty.

Butterfly. In the air the butterfly looks like an exaggerated flying camel, but the entry and exit are quite different. The usual method is for the skater to make one or two two-foot turns in a rather crouched position and then, when she feels she has sufficient momentum, to jump off the left foot (presuming she is a counterclockwise jumper), throwing the right leg powerfully up and round, lifting her head and arching her back strongly as she does so. At the same time the left leg is whipped up and back, resulting in a position in the air as shown in figure 96. It can be landed as a back spin on the right foot, but more frequently the skater lands on two feet, adopts the crouched position again, makes another turn on two feet and repeats the move. Some skaters can do six or more in a circle without loss of height. This move is sometimes referred to as an Arabian, but this is a misnomer.

Illusion. I do not know how the illusion got its name, and unfortunately I do not have a photograph available, but it is done in the following

Fig. 96. Butterfly
A spectacular move. Several are often
executed in succession.

manner: Presuming the skater is a counterclockwise spinner, she (and it is usually the girls who do this move) steps onto a right forward *inside* edge as though about to go into a spin and, as she does so, swings the left leg up and around at waist level until it starts to press back behind her, at which point, in one lightning movement, she drops the left arm down to touch the skating toe and at the same time swings the left leg directly upward so that for a fraction of a second she is in a vertical split position. In a continuation of the movement she resumes her upright position and usually finishes in one turn of a back spin.

25

Parental Involvement

A significant factor affecting the success or lack of success of a skater's career centers on the degree of involvement of the parent, or parents. The psychological relationship between parent and child is so different from family to family that, apart from the cynical and often unjustified "feed them, transport them, pay the bills, and keep out of it," it is impossible to lay down hard and fast rules. The greatest dangers are overinvolvement and involvement for the wrong reasons.

Overinvolvement

By overinvolvement I mean interference that is detrimental and counter-productive to the skater's progress. To avoid this trap a parent must be constantly self-critical and conscious of the effect that he or she may be having on the child or teacher.

Many parents fail to recognize the disastrous effect their mere presence in the rink may have on their child's skating. At the beginner level this frequently shows up by diversion of attention during a lesson: The teacher is suddenly aware that the young student's eyes are constantly straying to some part of the rink where the parent is sitting; the distraction is so great that the remainder of the lesson becomes a waste of time. At the higher level, a skater practicing jumps may react to the presence of a parent by going completely to pieces and falling all over the ice, quite often simply because the extra effort and tension caused by the desire to do well is putting the skater's timing off. I particularly remember one brilliant student who would look me straight in the eye while I was instructing her, but I would suddenly see that a veil had come over her expression, and although she had apparently not moved her eyes or head, I knew she had become aware that her mother had entered the rink. It was really quite uncanny. Although the mother was a charming woman who never apparently put any pressure on her daughter, all further training was useless until she had left the building. My wife and I are in agreement that at a rough estimate, approximately 90 percent of skaters from about eleven up are, to a greater or lesser degree, adversely affected by the presence of parents at training sessions. Where the parent may be of great assistance, however, is at practice sessions for the young beginner below the age of ten or eleven. A parent's presence will often encourage the younger child to practice. Note that this does not apply to lessons but to being there and showing interest during practice sessions. From eleven on the child tends to rebel, however, and it is important, though by that time it may be difficult, for the parent to withdraw from the scene.

From time to time, provided they are not pressured, these adolescent skaters will indicate to their parents that they may be privileged to watch an occasional practice session. If you are so honored, be careful what you say: It is better to admit ignorance than to make some obviously foolish remark. If, for example, your skater pulls off an unusually good double Lutz, some cautious remark such as, "That looked fine to me—were *you* satisfied with it?" may be in order, but if you refer to it as a double Axel, you may be exiled from the rink for some time to come. If you don't know, it is far better to admit it than to make the sort of blunder that, when coming from parents, seems to drive teenagers berserk.

Overprotection of a child's interests is a frequent cause of difficulties, often where none would otherwise exist. If and when difficulties *appear* to exist, these are usually best left to the teacher to sort out. For example, most efficiently run clubs start their patch session right on time, not a few minutes after. If a patch is not claimed at the beginning of the session, it may be assigned to a skater on standby, or to a skater on an end strip. On arrival home, a skater who has lost a patch through unpunctuality may interpret the incident as, "Nancy took my patch today and wouldn't get off it"; a perfectly true statement, but the fact that Nancy was quite within her rights is left out.

Beware, too, of statements made over the phone or by letter by children away at summer skating schools. It is rare that a child will tell his parents anything good about the school or what is happening there, and the parents frequently get the impression that there is little to choose between the school and a badly run penal institution, or perhaps the local branch of the Spanish Inquisition.

Here is what I believe to be a typical conversation between skater and parent—if, indeed, it can be called a conversation. David is having a wonderful time at summer school and receives a call from his mother while he is watching his favorite television program.

"Hello, David, how are you getting along?"
"Okay."
"Getting plenty of ice time?"
"Yeah. Look, I gotta go."
"How's the dorm?"
"Cold."
"Do you have enough blankets?"
"Look, Mom, I gotta go."
"David, are you all right?"
"Yeah—fell off my bike yesterday."
"What happened?"
"Oh, they took me over to the hospital."
"But David, what *happened*?"
"I'm okay I tell you. They're going to take a couple of X rays."
"David. . . ."
"Gotta go—goo'bye." (*click*)

If the frantic parent does manage to get a little more information out of David, it is to the effect that he is being bullied by his pro, the housemother is a monster, the dorm's obviously a menace to public health, the food's awful, and he has decided he probably won't take his Third Test this summer after all. But he is happy to return to the school next year.

It would be unwise for the parent to interfere with the close and delicately balanced relationship existing between skater and trainer. Competitive skating needs tremendous physical effort and willpower—qualities which, if they flag, must be stimulated in the student by the trainer.

As I mentioned earlier, one of the hardest things a trainer has to do is to make a skater go through his program with everything in it. It is one thing for a skater to do a difficult jump in his own good time, in a favorite part of the rink, and under no particular pressure. It is quite a different matter to put that jump into a program in a totally different context, while trying to interpret the music, and in all probability at quite a different speed from that at which he normally practices it. In addition, the execution of a total program in which nothing is left out takes infinitely more out of a skater physically than just slopping through it with little rests here and there— he must train for the program by doing the program, not a travesty of it.

With most students this stimulation to extra effort is a battle the pro is constantly fighting, drawing on his own personal reserve of will power and sometimes having to feign anger he does not necessarily feel. Until the student sees the need for it—and all those who get to the top do so eventually—he may resent the pressure. Until he reaches a measure of understanding, however, it is highly likely that he will try to work out his resentment on the trainer or parents. But the experienced trainer who wishes to avoid an early demise will not allow himself to be drawn into deep emotional enmeshments, and thus will be able to resist any attempt by his student to vent his displeasure on him personally. So the student turns on the parents, who will have to show extreme restraint and understanding. If the parents intervene between skater and trainer when such a situation arises, they will in all probability not only alienate the trainer, but nullify his attempts to bring out the best in their child.

Leaving It to the Trainer

And now we come to the parent who, equipped with a bare superficial knowledge of the sport, is afraid that the pro is missing the obvious and would like to get into the act. There are, thank heaven, not too many of these around—a fact that contributes immensely to the improvement of American skating. "A little learning is a dangerous thing" must have been written with skating in mind.

Many parents (and others) who have taken part in serious athletic activities develop into accurate observers of skating movements and can frequently make some very astute and helpful observations on a skater's style, musical interpretation, and general impressions. It is when they venture into the technical field that the majority tend to come to grief. Although their perception of an obviously faulty movement may be correct, their conclusions and remedies are rarely so, and their well-meant comments and interference in the skater's training can cause irritation, not just to the pro, but to the child, who is probably working on the often unjust assumption that her parents do not, and never will, understand anything about skating. (Generally speaking, boys seem to take less notice of outside comments than girls do.) The problem is that an incorrect movement that is clearly apparent to the eye of the layman is, nine times out of ten, not in itself the cause of the failure of the total movement but a symptom of some other and far less obvious error. For example, a skater does a jump at the top of which he quite clearly has one hand above his head. "Look!" says the father standing at the barrier—his mind suddenly illuminated by the brilliant light of genius—"He's got one arm too high!" The pro, with the restraint expected of all good PSGA members, gives a polite nod accompanied by a watery smile and, keeping his thoughts to himself, continues his analysis of the true cause of his student's difficulties, which may be related to excessive lean in the air, mistiming, wrong direction of impetus, incorrect hip position, or half a dozen other things. The skater's high arm may simply have been an attempt to keep his balance in an otherwise untenable position, and if the pro just tells him to keep his arm down, the skater may well fall flat on his face.

The skill of the experienced professional lies not merely in the ability to recognize faulty movements but in understanding the relationship between them, thus enabling him to trace an error back to its true source, the origin of which may lie in the action of a muscle group that, to the layman, may seem completely unrelated to the failure of the total movement. In other words, the expert pro knows where to look for trouble; he knows which movements he can for the moment disregard as being symptoms of something deeper, or as purely matters of individual style having little or no technical significance. Having ascertained the errors, he must know in which order to correct them; a skater cannot think of everything at once, so the most fundamental mistakes, i.e., those which, if not corrected, may make any attempt at the correct total movement completely hopeless, must be corrected first. A collection of errors often forms a typical syndrome related to a particular skating movement; thus the expert can often look at a jump just once and recognize half a dozen things that are wrong with it. Over the years he has seen and analyzed the syndrome so often in that particular form that little further analysis is necessary. If the skater is lucky, a trainer may just be able to put his finger on the one basic error which, if removed, may automatically remove other secondary errors, or at least make their correction possible.

Methods of teaching new movements, exercises for the correction of faults, the variation of techniques to suit the needs of different students, and a host of other aspects of the teaching (as opposed to the learning) process could be expanded into a whole book, but I think I have said enough to make the point. This might be summed up as: Too many cooks spoil the broth, particularly if one of the cooks has only got to the stage of learning to boil an egg.

Involvement for the Wrong Reasons

The following paragraphs contain a rather strong indictment of certain persons the skating world could well do without, i.e., those who are in it not for the good of their child but for the good of themselves, at the child's expense. The vast majority of parents are well-balanced, kind and thoughtful people who take legitimate pride in their children's achievements. But in rare instances a child's achievement becomes a vehicle for the fulfillment of the parent's self-gratification or unachieved ambition. This creates a painful situation. Under the guise of improving his work habits and spurring him on to better things, the parent hounds and bullies the child, who is deprived of praise even when justly earned, since he can rarely do anything right in the parent's eyes. Anyone in the vicinity who has the slightest connection with the child is made to suffer. Fortunately there are a few young skaters with noble souls who seem to be able to withstand such treatment, but many respond by becoming balky and uncooperative. The parent is shunned by all, and this in turn tends to isolate the child from his colleagues.

By now it must be evident that I am speaking of the creature known as the Skating Mother. The Skating Father is comparatively rare (though common in other sports), but when roused can be more aggressive and dangerous than the female. While the Skating Mother tends to snarl and scratch when brought to bay (I still bear the scars of numerous encounters), the Skating Father, like the rogue elephant, tends to go on real rampages of devastation. It's all very well to say, "Nice guys don't win," but that is only partially true in figure skating. In any highly competitive sport aggressiveness plays a large part, but in figure skating I suggest that it should be channeled toward the achievement of higher goals, not misdirected in aggressive behavior toward others, such as hogging the ice of a skater on the opposite patch, or deliberately getting in a competitor's way during a freestyle session. (Let us hope that figure skating never degenerates into a contact sport.)

The truly unpleasant skater and parent rarely make it to the top—they usually alienate so many people on the way up that few are left to root for them. At that stage there is little in the way of useful advice to give—and they probably wouldn't listen to it anyway. What should be said here is that all parents must be alert to the possible stirrings of the emotions I have described, and at the first glimmer must pull themselves up short before irreparable damage is done. Fortunately for all of us the breed known as the Skating Mother (or Father) is relatively rare, and if these words help to reduce their numbers and make it a little easier for some young skater, they will not have been written in vain.

26
Talent and
the Learning Process

This chapter is not intended to be a deep discussion of the psychology of learning but a collection of observations gathered over many years, which may help the parent and skater to understand the spasmodic, transient, and apparently ephemeral character of the learning process when applied to ice skating. Maddening though these characteristics may be, some realization that they are universal and do not occur in your child alone will help you to attain the patience and tranquillity of mind that we as trainers like to believe are the attributes of all skating parents.

We must start by assuming that the trainer is competent for the job at hand. The qualifications of a trainer have been dealt with at some length in a previous chapter, but the talent of the student, and what that talent consists of, has not yet been touched upon.

What Is Talent?

It is my experience that 95 percent of all students brought to me are, according to their parents, of outstanding talent and get straight A's at school. In some cases there is a strong implication that it is rather unreasonable on the part of the authorities to require them to wait another four years before taking part in the Olympics. Very occasionally apologetic parents will admit that their child is not doing too well academically and has no apparent physical aptitudes other than falling over his own feet or colliding with open doors. Nevertheless, it is surprising how often this apparently untalented child will make good progress in skating, often surpassing his more brilliant colleagues. So what is talent? It is not just physical ability, but an ability to harness and make best use of whatever gifts, physical or otherwise, the skater may be fortunate enough to possess. Such an ability is the most important talent of all.

Determination and self-discipline are two of the greatest gifts a skater can have. If these two qualities are lacking, no matter how talented a skater may be in other respects, his chances of getting to the top are minimal. Such a skater may be so confident of his own physical prowess that he finds it difficult to put his full effort into practice now, believing that he will only need to put in a burst of concentrated training at the last moment in order to pass the test or win the competition. These skaters do not, or will not, realize that the acquisition or refinement of physical movements requires regular practice over a long period for the correct patterns in the nervous system to become automatic or "second nature," and that this cannot be achieved by cramming. These so-called talented skaters are often beaten by the persistent plodders—it is the old story of the tortoise and the hare all over again.

The Learning Plateau

One of the greatest causes of concern to parents and skaters alike is the apparent irregularity of progress. It is a common phenomenon in academic studies for a student to progress well for a time and then hit a plateau, where no progress appears to be made at all—he has become stale. Then, after a period of frustration, and for no apparent reason, off he goes again and his learning curve resumes its former climb. In skating, the learning curve often shows more violent fluctuations, the plateau sometimes being replaced by a sudden dip, with the result that the curve begins to look like the Dow Jones industrial average (with the trend generally upward, or so we hope). During such a dip the skater may not only appear to make no progress but may temporarily lose a portion of what he has already gained. At such times nothing seems to help, and the skater has the option of continuing doggedly on until he comes out of his slump, or—possibly less frustrating—taking a short break away from the ice to do something entirely different. This latter course is not such a waste of time as it may at first appear. Provided the correct information has been fed by the trainer into the student's mind, the phenomenon of latent learning will be taking place. The deeper levels of the mind are organizing the separate basic constituents of a desired movement into a larger and more comprehensive whole; and then, quite suddenly, the total movement becomes functional, the skater comes out of his slump and, to everyone's surprise, lands his Axel on one foot, or succeeds in some other hitherto seemingly impossible movement. Unfortunately for everybody's peace of mind, this sudden success is not usually permanent. The coherence of all the bits and pieces that make up the total movement, and which the lower levels of the mind have so carefully organized, tends to break down, particularly if the skater becomes too aware of what he is doing.

In the normal course of events the skater's consistency of performing a movement improves only gradually, so that at first he may land, let us say, a double Salchow twice out of ten tries, then five out of ten, and eventually ninety-nine out of a hundred. The pattern of the individual movements that make up the whole jump has, by constant practice, become so ingrained that the skater can perform the movement automatically and with no more thought than that he wants to do a double Salchow. Regrettably, many parents believe that once a skater has finally succeeded in landing a jump, it is there for all time. The truth is that for a long period it will appear and disappear quite alarmingly. Provided the techniques are sound, however, the skater will eventually perform the movement without conscious thought, and it will become resistant to outside pressures such as competitions and parental expectations. I remember a student of mine who, just a week before competition, was lucky (or unlucky) enough to land several very nice double loop jumps on one foot, with the result that the parents pressured him to put the jump into his program. They were quite upset when he missed it in the competition itself, and blamed him for not trying, or not thinking of what he was doing. That was just the trouble: He *was* trying and *was* thinking of what he was doing—the movement had not yet become anywhere near sufficiently automatic to take the chance of presenting it in public. He was not, however, a boy who allowed his parents to worry him unduly, and eventually I managed to make them understand some of the facts explained in this chapter.

A stale period for an individual movement can even occur during the relatively short period of a lesson. The skater receives the required technical input from his trainer and at the end of five minutes may suddenly manage to put it all together and perform the movement excellently two or three times. But then, after perhaps ten minutes, the whole ability to perform anything approaching the correct movement will abruptly disappear—the skater has suffered an attack of mental indigestion. Trainers have different methods of dealing with this situation, but the realization that this can happen helps both skater and trainer to avoid frustration.

There appear to be several causes of plateaus and recessions, the commonest of which seem to be boredom, discouragement, and perhaps most important, the "incubation" time required to digest new information and instruction. This latent learning period seems to be the cause of the true plateau, whereas boredom and discouragement, unless the underlying causes are removed, can produce a permanent, rather than temporary, slowing down. Latent learning plateaus are natural and inevitable, but boredom is often the result of local conditions. Apart from periodic tests away from the ice, a skater should occasionally be exposed to the stimulus of visiting other rinks and being among other, and possibly better, skaters —particularly if he is the best skater on his home rink.

Determination: Talent's Vital Ingredient

We come now to what is probably the most important quality influencing a skater's career, namely, determination. The determined skater rarely yields to discouragement, and it is he who can make the maximum use of minimum training or barely adequate facilities. He is the one who concentrates during patch and who lands his jumps even when his technique and timing are a little off. Indeed, it is in jumping that the absence of determination works its most insidious wiles. I say this because many skaters who are not apparently afraid of what they are doing show a surprisingly low level of consistency in landing their jumps. They are not themselves aware that their failures are due to lack of determination.

This reluctance to "go for the jump" is often mistaken by the trainer, and even the skater, for a fault in technique. And in a sense it is, because when a skater holds back, he cannot carry through with the correct movement. It so often happens that at the moment of entry, just at the crucial point of takeoff, the skater experiences a barely conscious instant of self-doubt or fear that prevents him from following through with the movement—the body does not lift, the head does not turn, he does not go for the jump. Then again, the takeoff may be good, but the jump may feel a little different in the air from how the skater normally experiences it, with the result that—particularly if he is a perfectionist—he may be afraid he is not going to make it, and give up just before or at the landing. The experienced trainer should be able to tell whether the error is a genuine mistake or an unconscious holding back; but he may have to watch the skater for a considerable time before drawing a definite conclusion. I have even seen this lack of confidence manifest itself in skaters of world-class caliber, especially when they are going for triples. It also frequently occurs with lesser skaters attempting the doubles, particularly the double Lutz.

If you have a child who is naturally determined, you are several steps ahead of the game. But many skaters possess abundant determination if they are sufficiently stimulated to produce it. It is amazing how, by the offer of a small reward, or by making a bet, some skaters can be spurred on to land a jump when on previous occasions they seem to have found it almost impossible. Of course, a little bullying by the trainer can some-times help the determination process enormously, but it is usually only effective with certain skaters, some of whom positively enjoy and expect it. Nevertheless, it is a bad principle for a skater to be too dependent on the will of his trainer. And with certain skaters, bullying is completely inappropriate and may destroy any rapport existing between them and the pro.

In the early days of free skating, when the knowledge of sound tech-niques was in its infancy, it was determination alone that enabled the early "primitives" to land their jumps. Although many skaters in those days achieved a certain elegance even with the poor techniques then in exis-tence, there were an amazing number of skaters who would spring into the air in a tangle of arms and legs out of which they would suddenly produce a foot and land on it—the result of sheer determination and athletic ability. Essential though these last two qualities are, they must now be accompanied by good technique—brute force and pure courage are no longer sufficient.

Getting the Most out of Training

You will now have seen that talent, as the term applies to skating, is a conglomerate of sub-talents, the mixture differing so much between one skater and another that they inevitably progress at different rates, a situation that some enthusiastic parents may find difficult to accept. To complicate matters further, many parents simply are not able to afford to pay for the same number of lessons and ice time as others. Nevertheless an intelligent and dedicated skater will maximize what little he may have not just by the exercise of good working habits on the ice, but also by devoting time and thought to the subject at home. Provided it is not made too much of a chore, the main points of a lesson should be jotted down, and if there is anything at all that the skater does not understand, he should ask about it at the next opportunity. A few films or videotapes of top-rank skaters can be of immense value. They should be watched again and again so that as much information is extracted from them as possible. If you are not fortunate enough to own a video cassette recorder, it is quite practical to shoot movies from the TV screen. In the past I have used color film with a speed of ASA 160 at an aperture of f 2.8, but the illumination of the screen differs from set to set, so you will need a few experiments to get the exposure just right.

Many years ago imitation played a large part in a skater's learning process, and so it should today. By this I do not mean that a skater should pirate his competitor's unique moves as soon as he has invented them (eventually they will come into the public domain and become fair game for all), but a skater can watch how the best performers stroke, how they move over the ice, the way they use their arms, how they use their heads in jumping, what the most common spin and jump combinations are, and what types of footwork are used. These methods should all be used as a supplement to the training of a skater irrespective of how many lessons he can afford to take. Other things being equal, the skater who can think for himself has a considerable edge over the competitor who relies entirely on his pro.

27

How to Save Time and Money

The following advice is written for the family who has made a definite commitment to the goal of giving their child the opportunity to reach as high a standard in the sport as time, energy, and purse will allow. The sections below discuss the most common causes of wasted time and money, with some practical advice as to what you may be able to do about them. Most of the information has already been given or implied earlier in this book, but a summary here may prove useful.

Find the Right Path Early On

Many parents are so bewildered by the complexity of the sport and the seeming multitude of systems, tests, and badges that they waste a couple of seasons before becoming fully oriented and setting their child on the right path. This can only be avoided by a thorough understanding of the sport and by searching inquiries into the aims of any instructional and training programs offered. It was the plight of these puzzled parents that inspired the writing of this book in the first place.

Be Sure the Equipment Is Suitable

Inadequate equipment can be a menace at the very early stage and, for different reasons, at a later stage. The beginner burdened with equipment that will not enable or help him to keep his ankles erect is not going to get past the second badge of the USFSA Basic Tests. At a later stage the lack of a second pair of skates designed or adapted specifically for figures may cause unnecessary delay in passing figure tests. What may have to be paid out in extra lessons and patch time might better have been invested in suitable equipment.

Obtain Adequate Instruction

Lack of supervision or inadequate instruction is bad at any time, but particularly so in the formative stage. Bad habits, once formed, are notoriously hard and very expensive to cure. You do not have to go to the top trainer in the world to get excellent instruction. There are many trainers with impeccable qualifications all over the country who are quite capable of teaching your child through the Gold Test level and further. There are also many pros who are only qualified to teach up to a certain level, but up to that level they are highly competent. They will usually be the first to tell you if they feel they cannot take your child further, and will probably be able to recommend someone who can. And in fairness to all pros, remember that their results are always dependent on the talent of the student they have to work with.

Allow Sufficient Time for Technical Training

Sometimes in the early stages the development of a skater's program is allowed to crowd out crucial technical training. A family may set too much store on seeing their child perform in public. The child, who cannot see the whole picture, may also be putting pressure on parents and pro to be given a program. So the available money and time are directed almost entirely to the program, and the techniques are neglected. By the time the error is realized, the child has either fallen behind in contents or developed habits that are expensive to put right. You should also bear in mind that if a child is given a program too early, he may not have sufficient contents to fill out the time. The program may have to be constantly revised to accommodate the addition of new material as it is learned, and as the skater rapidly matures the original music may become so childishly inappropriate that completely new music must be chosen.

Understand the Importance of Figures

Very few children like to do figures, although at a later stage, when their early scratchings have developed into visible and symmetrical designs, a surprising number of the more successful skaters derive considerable satisfaction from them. It must be made clear to the would-be world champion that the figures are a necessary exercise and an unavoidable requirement for any serious competitive skating. The sooner they get down to them the better.

Insist on Discipline During Practice Sessions

Much as liberal-minded educators may deplore the fact, there is no time for permissiveness in any serious competitive training program. It is surprising how many skaters appreciate and expect clear-cut guidelines (the modern euphemism for *rules*). A little time ago, just before my wife and I started the season at a club where we had not previously taught, a group of teenage girls came to us and told us quite frankly that what they really needed and wanted was discipline during patch sessions. Until then they had been accustomed to talking together, going on and off patch when they liked, arriving late, and generally horsing around. They knew they were getting nowhere, but were quite unable to do anything about it—not one of them would take the risk of appearing overly virtuous in her colleagues' eyes by getting down to work. But as soon as rules were established, and they had no option but to follow them, they were perfectly happy and the standard of skating rose rapidly.

If you have problems in this area, make your feelings known to other parents, the pros, and club officers. Firm patch and freestyle rules can best be enforced by the pros; all they need is backing from the parents, club, or rink management. If the pros cannot do it, or they cannot get together on the matter, there is something badly wrong with the setup and the best thing to do is to find another rink or club.

Understand and Obtain Good Sharpening

The effect of improper sharpening does most damage in the figures. For this branch of skating the hollow is rarely too flat; in the majority of cases it is far too deep (see the section on sharpening in "Equipment for the Advanced Skater"). The edge of a blade with the ultra-flat hollow dulls very quickly, so it must be treated with care. If allowed to get too blunt, the skater quite unconsciously tends to drop the ankle excessively to get a grip. Should this become a habit, the skater has to readjust when the blades are resharpened. A dull blade with an ultra-flat hollow tends to run much more slowly than a sharpened blade with the same hollow. It is amazing what a properly sharpened figure blade can do for novice skaters learning the back serpentine, a figure in which it is particularly difficult to maintain a fast run of edge.

Too deep a hollow for the freestyle blade (and I have seen some hollows so ridiculously deep that you could fit a pencil into them) waste the skater's time because the blades need a long breaking-in period before the skater can comfortably spin and jump on them again. These really deep hollows can also have a disastrous effect on the Axel takeoff, particularly if the skater is used to a slight skid just before leaving the ice. On the other hand, too blunt a freestyle blade can cause unnerving and totally unexpected falls on the entrance to certain jumps and spins, particularly the double loop, the flying camel, and even the regular camel. This kind of fall very understandably takes away the skater's confidence and he may hold back from the move until he feels a sharp blade under him again.

Allow Sufficient Practice Time

You may well say that more practice time is going to cost you more time and money rather than save it. But if you take the long view that you want your skater to achieve a certain test or competitive level within a certain number of seasons, inadequate practice time can make that goal impossible to attain—you may be put into the position of having to decide whether you are going to abandon the goal entirely or put out more money to give the skater a fair, but possibly remote, chance of catching up. I can best illustrate this point by the following example.

We had a student at one time who did well in her early tests despite the fact that she was never allowed to use early morning ice (6:00 A.M.) and therefore did not get as much practice time as her colleagues. Her goal was to pass her USFSA Eighth Figure Test. She did a reasonable Seventh Test but when she came to the Eighth the amount of ice time logged up over the years was not sufficient to have given her the power and control so necessary for the Gold Medal. By then it was too late to do anything about it. A burst of concentrated practice at the end of one's career does not have anywhere near so beneficial an effect as spreading it out over the whole period.

Encourage Good Ice Conditions

One of the most serious hindrances to learning the compulsory figures is posed by white hockey ice in combination with lighting from the wrong angle. These two conditions make the skater's tracings on the ice almost impossible to see unless viewed from a considerable distance. The inability to see the tracing adequately while skating the figure (a particular problem with young, light skaters) quite naturally makes the skater untidy and unaware of obvious errors. Unfortunately, there is not a lot one can do about the ice itself, but it does sometimes help to turn off all the lights except those down the sides of the rink. Figures seem to be most visible to the skater when a very directional type of lighting hits the ice surface at an angle of forty-five degrees or less—which is why they are usually much more visible from the barrier. Rinks with daylight from side windows seem to provide the best lighting conditions.

Rough ice, often resulting from an insufficient cut by the Zamboni, tends to jump the blade out of the ice, destroying the skater's feel for what the edge is doing, as well as making the quality of the turns almost impossible to assess. After hockey a better surface is usually obtained if the ice-man makes a dry cut before the regular cut with water; but this will take a minimum of twenty minutes, probably twenty-three or twenty-four. It must be understood that the ice maker's job is a difficult one, and one in which many Zamboni operators take great pride. So when he makes a good surface, tell him so. He will appreciate it.

Make Use of Off-ice Facilities

Dance training (ballet, modern, jazz), running (sprinting, middle distance), and gymnastics are all of tremendous help and less expensive than on-ice training. Dance training is, in fact, now quite indispensable. Even so it should be realized that there are certain movements in ballet that are not applicable to ice skating, particularly the timing of the knee action. If you can find some dance teacher—especially one used to appearing professionally in front of the public—who has devised methods to adapt his, or her, knowledge of dance to the ice, you will have the best of both worlds. Former ice-show skaters, even those who have not studied dance formally, are usually very good in this field and can be very helpful in teaching a skater how to present himself in a program. There is an ever-increasing number of professionals specializing in this type of dance training as it applies to ice. The fees will be about the same as regular on-ice training.

Get an Early Start

A start by the age of six or seven is advisable, but there are many skaters who have started considerably later and still made it to the top. We have always had reservations about introducing two- and three-year-old children to the ice, but it does seem to have the advantage that, at an age when the skills of balance in walking, running, jumping, and other motor activities are developing, the totally different sense of balance and the reactions appropriate to skating seem to be most easily learned. Balance acquired at a very early age seems to be more refined than that learned later in life.

During my teaching career I have often been struck by a remarkable phenomenon. During a class of adult beginners in the category of "never been on ice before," some large man in his forties will to my horror suddenly take off across the ice, arms waving, body weaving to and fro, feet scrabbling, but just as he seems to have completely lost his balance he twists like a cat, gets a foot underneath him and continues triumphantly to the other side of the rink. His reactions are quite different from those of other skaters in the class. I ask him casually if this is really his first time on the ice, and he replies proudly that it is. When I press the point and ask, "Were you never on the ice as a tiny child?" he replies, "Well, yes, I remember I did skate on a pond for two or three months when I was about three years old. But that's forty years ago!" In a similar way, skaters who have started at a very early age and have taken the sport seriously seem to be able to land jumps and pull off other difficult maneuvers even when they have made serious mistakes that would have caused other skaters to fall. The skater who starts at a later age can still reach championship standard, but he does not seem to have quite so much margin for error. At a guess I should say that this ability to acquire what might be termed "super balance" on the ice probably decreases gradually as the child approaches the age of seven or eight.

It appears, therefore, that there is one very definite reason to put a child on the ice at a very early age, and that is to acquire this refined and sophisticated sense of balance, but that may be the only advantage. As I wrote in *Basic Ice Skating Skills,* there is the danger that by the time the parents think the child is ready for lessons he will be so familiar with the ice that there is no novelty in the action of skating, and therefore little enthusiasm left to progress further. I feel strongly that girls below the age of five and boys below six should most certainly be supervised when on the ice, but that no serious attempt should be made to teach them anything. They are, after all, learning without effort something that is unteachable—super balance. In fact, I think it might be a wise move to put a child on the ice at the age of two or three (if he really wants to do it) and, when he has learned to skate forward and backward quite happily, take him off for a couple of seasons; then, at about five or six, put him back on the ice in a class situation. But at no time should a tiny tot be pressured, not even when he's as old as five or six.

If, with a view to later development, you do decide to put the child on early, you must be sure that the equipment is reasonably good (no double runners, please!), or else the whole purpose of the operation is defeated.

Begin USFSA Tests as Soon as Practical

I am not now talking about the USFSA Basic Tests, but the official USFSA test structure starting at the Preliminary Test level. When I specify USFSA tests, this in no way implies any disparagement of the ISIA test structure —it is simply that the USFSA tests form the only available path to the U.S. National Championships and, therefore, a place on the U.S. World Team. By all means continue to take ISIA tests and compete in ISIA events—they offer a wonderful opportunity to build up experience in performing before the public—but the skater must get started on the USFSA tests without delay. If the start is left too long, the skater may waste valuable time, perhaps a season or more, in adjusting to the discipline and requirements of serious competitive skating. Just as important, however, is the fact that an early start gives the skater time to space out the taking of tests (particularly the figures) so that the movements at each test level can be sufficiently mastered to enable the skater to make a good job of the following test. Scrambling through several tests in one season with barely minimal passing marks (perhaps awarded by an unusually lenient panel) never pays off and will cost you time and money in the long run. This occurs with unfortunate frequency in the early years of training, with the result that the skater gets stuck at about the Fourth Test, which he cannot pass until his skill catches up with his, or his parents', ambitions. In the meantime the skater, if he has taken and failed the test several times, may get frustrated and obsessed with a sense of failure—feelings that may make the new test even more difficult to pass.

Stick to Your Schedule

Having set up a training schedule for your child, it is essential that you see it is carried out. It is your responsibility to get your skater to the rink on the right day at the right time. Certainly the pro can exert pressure but he can't go round at 5:30 in the morning, or any other time for that matter, collecting everybody. There is usually no great difficulty as far as the freestyle is concerned, but problems frequently arise when it comes to patch. After taking on a new student (it doesn't usually happen with the old ones), I often become aware that I haven't seen her on patch for a few days. When I corner her and ask how many patches she has during the week, she may look me in the eye and say, "Eight a week—two on Monday, one on Tuesday . . ." and so on. So I alert my wife and we watch. It turns out that she is never actually present on more than three of them. When faced with this, she actually looks a little surprised and says something like, "Well, my aunt was here last week," or, "We couldn't get the car started yesterday," or the classic, "My ride couldn't make it." She genuinely believes she is taking eight patches a week but that just sometimes, by an unfortunate stroke of luck, she occasionally misses one—and I shouldn't be unreasonable. But the fact remains that she never actually succeeds in arriving at more than three of them. And those patches are being paid for —the family is not getting a refund. The remarkable thing is she rarely misses the freestyle sessions. Need I say more?

28
How the Ice Is Resurfaced

We take the fact that a new ice surface can be provided within the space of ten to fifteen minutes very much for granted nowadays. But it was not always so. When I was a boy learning to skate on the London rinks, we were lucky if the job was completed in an hour and a half. Then as now, the first thing that had to be done was to shave a very thin layer (approximately $1/32$ inch) off the ice surface. This was accomplished by pulling a steel blade set in a low metal frame across the ice by means of a small tractor (figure 97), or, in later years, a jeep. Very often the frame (or plow, as it was called) had handles so that it could be directed and controlled by a man following on skates. The resulting shavings, in the form of snow, had then to be removed with snow shovels, dumped into a deep pit at the side of the rink, the ice surface swept with brooms and, finally, sprayed with water. I remember once counting nine men involved in the whole operation: the driver of the tractor, a man on skates guiding the plow, three men with snow shovels, three men with brooms, and one man spraying with a hose. It also seemed to take much longer for the ice to freeze in those days, possibly because more water was applied. Some of the more efficient rinks eventually got the operation down to forty-five minutes, but the method was still very uneconomical.

Then Frank Zamboni, owner and operator of the Iceland Skating Rink in Paramount, California, entered the picture. He, too, was struggling with the same problems as the British operators and decided it was time that somebody came up with a practical solution. Was it possible, he asked himself, to devise a machine that would cut the ice, remove the snow, wash

317

Fig. 97. An early plow and tractor ice planer.

and squeegee the surface and, finally, deposit a thin film of water, all in one operation and controlled by one man only? This would mean a saving of many hours of labor during the day and at the same time allow the rink operator to sell more ice time. By 1947 he had built a prototype, one of the main principles of which was to be a snow tank attached to the machine so that the ice shavings could be picked up cleanly and carried off the ice surface. With the first experimental machine there were great difficulties in elevating the snow and distributing it evenly in the snow tank; but Frank Zamboni persevered. In 1949 he produced a model (figure 98) which, though primitive, seemed to solve all the problems. It gave control of the blade to the driver, conveyed and stored an ample amount of snow, and washed, squeegeed and watered the ice surface.

One problem still remained and that was what to do with the snow once it was in the machine; it had to be disposed of before the next resurfacing was due. For some years the only solution was to wait for it to melt, to run warm water over it, or to laboriously shovel it out. Many

Fig. 98. Model A, 1949. The problem of what to do with the snow is nearly solved.

more models were constructed, each more efficient than the last, until in 1969 the model HDB was produced (figure 99). Now, by the simple operation of a lever, the snow tank could be opened, tilted, and the load of snow dumped wherever the operator wished. One of the great advantages to skaters of the dumping feature was that the ice-man was much more willing to make an extra resurfacing when necessary now that he did not have to shovel out the snow. This model is now popular all over the world.

That is a very brief summary of the history and methods of modern ice resurfacing. For further details I suggest that you ask the ice-man at your rink to let you look at his machine. I am sure that he will be happy to give you any information that may interest you provided you do not ask him just as he is rushing out to resurface the ice. He may have a bare ten minutes to do the job and he will get nasty looks from the skaters waiting to go onto patch if he is late.

It is really quite surprising how little ice resurfacing is understood.

Fig. 99. Model HDB, 1969. The final solution: at the touch of a lever the operator can now dump the snow wherever he wishes.

Some people believe that the machine actually makes the ice, a belief doubtless fostered by the fact that resurfacing the ice is commonly referred to as "making the ice." I remember some years ago wandering round the site of a new rink under construction and getting into a conversation with some young men who were going to take over the ice duties. When I asked when they were going to put the ice on, they told me that the new Zamboni machine had not yet been delivered. On further questioning I found they believed that all you had to do was to run the machine out over the raw concrete and it would lay down an ice surface, rather like rolling out a carpet. Well, Mr. Zamboni, if you really want a challenge, there it is.

The presidency of the Frank J. Zamboni Company has now been taken over by Frank Zamboni's son Richard, and the elder Zamboni has become chairman of the board. Their machines are sold all over the world and the company is now expanding into the field of related products. Let us all give thanks to this inventive genius for having lifted us out of the dark ages of scrape, sweep, and spray.

29
Where to Go for
Further Information

Important Addresses

United States Figure Skating Association
    20 First Street, Colorado Springs, CO 80906
    Telephone: (303) 635-5200
International Skating Union
    Promenade 73, Postfach, CH-7270 Davos Platz, Switzerland
Canadian Figure Skating Association
    333 River Road, Ottawa, Ontario K1L 8B9, Canada
    Telephone: (613) 746-5955
Professional Skaters Guild of America
    P.O. Box 5904, Rochester, MN 55903
    Telephone: (507) 281-5122
Ice Skating Skating Institute of America
    1000 Skokie Boulevard, Wilmette, IL 60091
    Telephone: (312) 256-5060
American Society of Composers, Authors and Publishers (ASCAP)
    1 Lincoln Plaza, New York, NY 10023
    Telephone: (212) 595-3050
Broadcast Music Incorporated (BMI)
    320 West 57th Street, New York, NY 10019
    Telephone: (212) 586-2000

Skating Magazines

Skating
    An official publication of the United States Figure Skating Association.
    Reaches over 30,000 readers. Articles on all aspects of figure skating;

reports on national and international championships; personal interviews, etc. Plentifully illustrated with photographs in color and black-and-white. Ten issues per year. One year $12; Canadian and foreign $27. Order from:

Skating, 20 First Street, Colorado Springs, CO 80906

American Skating World

Nonaligned, newspaper format, normally 32 pages. Features technical articles, profiles on well-known skating personalities, and reports on major skating events. Photography in color and black-and-white. Published twelve times per year. One year $14.95; Canada $26.95; overseas $52. Order from:

American Skating World, 1216 Grandview Avenue, Pittsburgh, PA 15211, or call toll-free 1 (800) 245-6280

Professional Skaters Guild of America Newsletter

An official publication of the PSGA. Guild activities and technical articles, many on training-related subjects. Lists pros seeking clubs and clubs seeking pros under "Job Placement Service." Published every two months. $10 per year. Order from:

PSGA Newsletter, P.O. Box 5904, Rochester, MN 55903

Recreational Ice Skating

An official publication of the Ice Skating Institute of America. Articles cover ISIA activities including hockey and precision skating, also certain USFSA events. Photographs in color and black-and-white. Four issues per year: fall, winter, midwinter, and spring. One year $8. Order from:

Recreational Ice Skating, 1000 Skokie Boulevard, Wilmette, IL 60091

Ice and Roller Skate

Nonaligned British magazine dealing predominantly with ice skating. In addition to British news, features extensive and refreshingly outspoken coverage of international ice figure skating events. Nine issues per year. Annual subscription: U.S. and Canada, $17 surface mail; $34 airmail. Order from:

Ice and Roller Skate, 1 Strathmore Close, Caterham, Surrey CR3 5EQ, England

Books

USFSA Rulebook

Exhaustive coverage (over 300 pages long) of all rules relating to figure skating in the U.S. Diagrams of figures, jumps, and compulsory dances. Names and addresses of member clubs, judges, and officials of USFSA committees. Revised annually. $5.50 per copy. Order from the USFSA.

Evaluation of Errors in Figures

Primarily written for judges, but should be studied by all serious skaters of figures. Details of what to look for in the tracing and how the errors should be assessed in the marking. Section on free skating. $3.50 per copy. Order from the USFSA.

ISU Regulations

An official ISU publication giving rules for speed and figure skating in international and Olympic events; also rules for ISU tests. $10.50 per copy plus 63¢ shipping and handling. Order from the USFSA.

Basic Ice Skating Skills

By Robert S. Ogilvie. Published by J. B. Lippincott Company and distributed by Harper & Row, New York. Sponsored by the USFSA, this is an official how-to-do-it handbook for the USFSA Basic Tests. Over 300 photographs of skaters in action. Softcover may be ordered from the USFSA at $6.95 per copy. Hardcover available through booksellers and many skate shops.

The above prices of magazines and books were valid at the time of publication of this book but may have increased by the time this book gets into your hands. Your pro, skate shop, or local USFSA officials may be able to help you find current prices.

There are dozens of books on skating—far too many to be listed here—but many are handled by the USFSA and advertised periodically in *Skating* magazine; the USFSA will supply a list. The USFSA itself publishes many other booklets dealing with such subjects as how to run practice sessions, timing of music for ice dancing, and how to run Basic Test competitions. They also put out the *Basic Tests Manual,* which not only gives the contents of the tests but, under the "Notes and Standards" section, gives some very good advice on how they should be judged. Several other aspects of the Basic Tests are also covered.

Index